THE DREAM AND THE PLAY
Ionesco's Theatrical Quest

INTERPLAY 1
*Proceedings of Colloquia
in Comparative Literature and the Arts*

Editors:
  Moshe Lazar
  Ron Gottesman

Published under the auspices of
THE COMPARATIVE LITERATURE PROGRAM
and THE CENTER FOR THE HUMANITIES
University of Southern California

THE DREAM AND THE PLAY
Ionesco's Theatrical Quest

edited by
Moshe Lazar

UNDENA PUBLICATIONS
Malibu 1982

The photographs in this volume
are reprinted from *Domenico Tiepolo's Punchinello Drawings,*
Indiana University Art Museum, 1979

Library of Congress Card Number: 81-71734
ISBN: 0-89003-109-6 (cloth)
0-89003-108-8 (paper)
© 1982 by Undena Publications

All rights reserved. No part of this publication may be reproduced or transmitted in any form or by any means, electronic or mechanical, including photo-copy, recording, or any information storage and retrieval system, without permission in writing from the author or the publisher.

Undena Publications, P. O. Box 97, Malibu, CA 90265

TABLE OF CONTENTS

Preface vii

On Being Very, *Very* Surprised:
Eugène Ionesco and the Vision of Childhood 1
   Richard N. Coe

Ionesco and the Fairytale Tradition 21
   Martin Esslin

Beyond Realism:
Ionesco's Theory of the Drama 33
   George E. Wellwarth

The Theatre of Ionesco:
The Ghost and Primal Dialogue 49
   Robert W. Corrigan

Ionesco's Political Interplay 63
   Emmanuel Jacquart

Ionesco: Symptom and Victim 81
   David I. Grossvogel

Journey to the Kingdom of the Dead:
Ionesco's Gnostic Dream Play 93
   Rosette C. Lamont

Ionesco, or a Pregnant Death 121
   Jan Kott

The Psychodramatic Stage:
Ionesco and His Doubles 135
   Moshe Lazar

Culture and Politics 161
   Eugène Ionesco

Dreams to be Staged Eventually:
Three Unpublished Dream Scenes 169
   Eugène Ionesco

PREFACE

After serving as Artist in Residence at the University of Southern California in the Spring of 1980 and having participated actively in the Symposium dedicated to his works, Eugène Ionesco sent the following remarks to be published as a foreword to the first volume of the *Interplay* series:

> Why should we make art and literature: to help better understand the world in its real depths or to help people discriminate between existential problems and those unimportant, non-metaphysical worries. Literature should tear people away from their mediocrity. Art and literature should give back to people a certain taste for the ultimate knowledge, the absolute and total one, which the sciences—being analytical in nature—are able to present only in a fragmented way, therefore insufficient, in their lack of synthesis. Only art has the power to bring back to the world a spirit of synthesis which has been lost. Art and literature, alas, are becoming strongly fought polemic battles in order to grant glory to this or another disputable genius. They themselves become instruments of glory, i.e. personal instruments of power. In politics, as in literature, human vanity is overwhelming. Forty years ago someone proposed that artworks should not be signed anymore. In fact, any work of art, especially any masterpiece, should belong to a sort of anonymous community. It is not the signing of his books which enables the social person to mature; only his creations help him to grow up. For us to know in what period, to what country the works belong, dates, numbers and pseudonyms would be sufficient.
>
> To what should music lead? To silence, which is the most beautiful music once the speaking music has been absorbed. To what should the philosophical discourse lead? To what should the anguished dialogue of characters lead? From question to question up to the ultimate question which is the question without answer. It might seem strange, coming from a playwright in this case, that he should hope to succeed in formulating the most fundamental

questions, the metaphysical inquiries, for which answers are found only in mystical ecstasy, whether it exists or not.

In reality, no one ever knows "why?" One never knows why "really"? Literature, going beyond itself, should lead us to the brink of tragic anxiety, where all the questions are put to question again, where we descend into the most authentic mystery which routinely we hide from ourselves; it should lead us to the confines of our Self, where all the identities are separated, driven apart, where everything has to be redone or, better, nothing has to be done anymore. This quest of literature should lead us beyond all the worn-down paths, where we finally realize that all that we thought to have understood is no more than a total misunderstanding. Answers? Yes, if we consider wonder and contemplation as possible answers, the only ones which our mind can grasp and the only ones able to annihilate pride, self-love, and vanity.

We may observe, incidentally, that history is progressively bringing us to it: no intelligent person can believe anymore in any of the new societies, all over the planet, for even empirically his needs were better answered once by rituals, symbols, and archaic myths.

Let literature and science make us understand, ontologically, the falsity of all our methods.

Let the human being only be the silent question mark, the only possible counterpoint and counterweight to night, to nothingness.

Samuel Beckett is already, perhaps, the modern writer, the only one to have reached the summit.

From Shakespeare, in his *Macbeth,* we learned that the world "is a tale/ Told by an idiot, full of sound and fury/ Signifying nothing," and in his *Tempest* he made us also understand that life is not something natural, something "normal."

We have added to the Proceedings of the Ionesco Symposium three hitherto unpublished "dream scenes" which Ionesco had not included in the final version of his latest play "Voyages chez les morts" (*Journeys to the Land of the Dead*). We are very grateful to Eugène Ionesco for sending these scenes for the present publication. I wish also to thank John Ramsay Bickers for his editorial assistance.

M.L.

ON BEING VERY, *VERY* SURPRISED...
Eugène Ionesco and the Vision of Childhood

Richard N. Coe

> Le génie n'est que l'enfance
> retrouvée à volonté.
> Baudelaire

In the plays of Eugène Ionesco, the theme of "being suprised" is present from the outset. The bemused wonderment of the Smiths, as Mme Martin tells the tale of the gentleman down on one knee on the pavement beside a café, engaged in retying his shoelace ("Incredible! Fantastic!"), is echoed over and over again in innumerable different contexts: by Jacques, in the enthralment of his discovery of the seemingly infinite possibilites of the word *chat* in the French language; by the Bérenger of *Tueur sans gages,* in his disbelieving dazzlement upon first beholding the Radiant City, and again later, albeit in a different and more sombre way following the death of Dany, in his stupefied amazement at the nightmare events that can occur "here... just near here... in our own town... terrible things... unimaginable!" In the later Bérenger of *Rhinocéros,* this characteristic is more apparent still, as he alone retains the ability to be surprised—to be, in fact, "very, *very* surprised"[1]—at the transformation of human beings into pachyderms, while all those around him come progressively to accept the fact as commonplace and absolutely normal; nor indeed does this sense of *émerveillement* weaken

---

[1] This is still more emphatic in the original French text: "On est trop violemment surpris pour garder son sang-froid. Moi, je suis surpris, je suis surpris, je suis surpris! Je n'en reviens pas!" (Ionesco, *Théâtre,* Gallimard/N.R.F. edition, III, p. 88. All references, where possible, will be made to this edition; note, however, that the pagination of Vol. I in the earlier impressions—which are those used—differs slightly from that of impressions issued after 1960.)

even in the more recent plays, for the same note will be heard again from Jean in *La soif et la faim,* while even the Anonymous Individual whose silence so dramatically dominates *Ce formidable bordel* is moved to a kind of dazed incredulity, not so much at anything *in* the world, but at the very marvellous, miraculous, inexplicable fact of the existence of that world in the first place: "All that! . . . All that! . . . All that!"

If we take the earlier plays in isolationn it is tempting to explain this obsessive element of "surprise" in the face of the most commonplace, as well as the most outlandish, of occurrences, simply as the negative polarity of "acceptance." In other words, in a world whence all normal sequences of logic and causality have been removed—the world, in fact, of "the Absurd"— anything, quite literally *anything,* can happen, and therefore everything is surprising simply because nothing is surprising. To be surprised implies a previous expectation or anticipation of something occurring *different* from what has actually taken place; and this anticipation itself assumes that events will follow each other in a comprehensible sequence, enabling them to be predicted with reasonable certainty. But where "Aristotelian" logic gives way to the "principle of dynamic contradiction," then to predict anything whatsoever, whether in the material or in the psychological field, is in itself "absurd"; and the words "surprised"/"unsurprised" themselves become meaningless. The difference between them is no more than one of sound, similar to the sounds that the King of Hearts once juggled with in *Alice in Wonderland:* "'Important—unimportant—important—unimportant' he went on to himself in an undertone, as if he were trying which word sounded best."

In the light of the later plays, however, and also in that of many of the essays and autobiographical writings, this is clearly an inadequate explanation.[2] As the comparatively rigid structures of "anti-logic" recede more and more into the background of Ionesco's preoccupations, to be replaced by a much more fluid structure of dream and nightmare, at once more "real" and more profoundly disconcerting, these reiterated expressions of *émerveillement* begin to assume a new significance. Far from representing a mere negative polarity opposed to that of the platitudinous (the platitude being in this case, the ultimate embodiment of unsurprised, unthinking acceptance), they reveal themselves as something very much more positive. If the amazed gasps of the company listening to the narrative of Mme Martin express the absolute meaninglessness and emptiness of themselves and of the world they inhabit—the Void at the Centre of Things—the wonderment, whether in delight or horror, but more often in delight, expressed by Bérenger and his

---

[2] If I can appear categorical about this, it is because it was the explanation I offered myself when writing about Ionesco in 1960, and now feel obliged to reconsider.

successors seems to have its roots deep in Ionesco's own personal experience of a mode of being-in-the-world, and to allow us intimations of whole unsuspected vistas and landscapes of Otherness, which are a far cry from the intellectual word-games of *Le tableau* or *Le nouveau locataire*, of *La nièce-épouse* or *Le salon de l'automobile*. This wonder, at times, seems to be nothing less than the symbolic, poetic or dramatic expression of a mystic's vision of the universe, a vision in some ways closer to that of John Bunyan or of Saint Teresa of Avila than to that of Alphonse Allais or Alfred Jarry. The amazed astonishment is not just baffled incomprehension inspired by the stupidity of the human race and the obstinate unpredictability of Things, but rather an expression of ecstasy and exaltation as, just for one fleeting instant, the poet encounters, here and now in the world of everydayness, some echo of experience retained from another dimension altogether. And this "other" dimension is at once transcendental, yet at the same time unquestionably *real*. In this interpretation, the plays would appear as the reflections of an interior landscape: not that of some surrealistic Magritte or Chirico, but of Ionesco's own lived and remembered experience. They are echoes of the Paradise-Lost of his own childhood.

Ionesco's contribution to that unexplored yet fascinating genre, the "Souvenirs d'enfance et de jeunesse" still remains to be appreciated and evaluated. The "Autobiography of Childhood" is something very much more than a "standard" autobiography which, for some reason or another, has been allowed to remain incomplete; it is a clearly-distinguished sub-genre in its own right, which began to emerge in Europe during the decade 1830–40 (Stendhal's *Vie de Henry Brulard*, of 1835–36, is one of the earliest "pure" examples), and which, since the 1950s especially, has proliferated as irrepressibly as the eggs in *l'Avenir*, the coffee-cups in *Victimes du devoir*, or the mushrooms in *Amédée*. It has, as a literary form, its own specific structures, it obeys laws imposed by its own inner necessity, it produces its own archetypes, both of character and of experience.[3] This is not the place to enter into the detail of these unique laws and structures which govern the literary patterns of the child-Self re-created. It is enough to observe here that Ionesco is by no means exceptional among his generation in this quasi-obsessive fascination with the recall of his own childhood; and that writings such as *Au moulin*,[4] *Printemps 1939*,[5] and above all *Découvertes* (1969), are not only

---

[3] This essay draws on a study, recently completed, covering some 500 specimens of the genre, drawn from a variety of different cultures.

[4] Originally published in *Biblio*, XXXI, 8 Oct. 1963; reprinted in *Journal en miettes* (1967), pp. 7–22.

[5] Originally published in the *Cahiers de la Compagnie Madeleine Renaud—Jean-Louis*

minor masterpieces in the genre, but are essential for any true understanding of the "inner landscape" of the plays.

In these excursions into the experience of the past-Self, Ionesco contrives to be at once archetypal and unique. He is archetypal (that is, certain of the experiences and situations which he recounts are common to roughly 75% of all those writers who have been attracted to this form of literary expression), firstly in his relationship with his parents—the failed or absent, or else brutal and detested Father ("pauvre Papa —pauvre con!"), and, set against him, the deeply-beloved but weak and ineffective Mother. He is archetypal, or almost so, in his early encounters with the major experiences of adolescence: the discoveries of Evil and of Death, of Love ("I am in love with Ribot's little sister. Beauplet's little sister, unquestionably, is much prettier, but . . .")[6]. . . and of Theatre. Only in the absence of any account of the discovery of his own sexuality does he differ from the norm, and this may simply be due to that most subtle form of "pudeur" which is also discernible in the plays, where eroticism appears as a kind of secret, sub- or supra-linguistic form of communication, rather than as a significant experience in its own right. He is archetypal in his use of the Garden as a symbol of the intimate *paradis-perdu* of early childhood, although strangely the garden-symbol appears more effectively in the plays (*Les chaises, Victimes, Amédée*) than in the autobiographical writings themselves. And finally, he is almost more-than-archetypal in his wondering recall of those three related experiences of childhood-as-Paradise—the experiences of "magic," of "luminescence," and of "abundance" (or *plénitude*)—which seem, over and over again, to link the child-that-was with the Poet he is to become.[7]

This last group of experiences is so ubiquitously, and so powerfully, present, especially in the *Journal en miettes*,[8] that it may serve to link that which is archetypal in Ionesco's experience with that which is exceptional or, indeed, unique. For if his childhood was both "magical" and "abundant" (setting aside for the moment the third attribute, that of being "luminous"), it was because of his acute awareness that, in his previous existence as a child, he

---

Barrault, No. 29, Feb. 1960, pp. 220–33. Reprinted in *La Photo du Colonel* (1962), pp. 169–238.

[6]Ionesco, *Journal en miettes*, p. 10.

[7]It is a significant fact that the majority of *Souvenirs d'enfance* are written by authors who have *also* written poetry (this applies to Ionesco, of course). It would appear to be primarily a *poet's* form of expression.

[8]Ionesco, *Journal en miettes*, pp. 83–189. This section was originally published under the title "Journal" in *Preuves*, XV, No. 175, Sept. 1965, pp. 3–18 and No. 176, Oct. 1965, pp. 29–41.

stood "outside time." He had lived, as it were, a Beckettian "instantaneous-infinite," a Self immobile at the centre of all Being, observing itself, observing itself observing a moving panorama of events circling that sentient point of immobility, *not in time but in space*. At the age of nine, he recalls,

> ... when I lived at Le Moulin, everything was joy and everything was *presence*. The seasons seemed to unroll *in space*. The world was a stage-set, now dark-hued, now light, with its flowers and grass appearing and vanishing, coming towards us, going away, unfolding beneath our eyes, while we ourselves remained ever in the same place, watching time go by, yet ourselves aside from its movement.[9]

A curious feature of this passage is the transition from "I" to "we." The sense of immobility and of timelessness, it would seem, is so intense, that it extends outwards from the child-Self to include all those within its immediate vicinity, forming a tiny but densely-inhabited island of extra-temporality, shut off by absolute and impenetrable barriers from the remainder of creation. But the second major theme here, the awareness that "everything was *presence*," is, in the light of the poet's later development, perhaps even more noteworthy. That it is a purely mystic concept, appertaining to the realm of transcendental-irrational experience, is possibly best brought out by setting it beside the parallel recollections of another writer who was unquestionably a mystic, and indeed an intensely religious thinker, for whom the experience of childhood was a *direct* exposure of the Self to the Divine Presence: the seventeenth-century English "Metaphysical" poet, Thomas Traherne.

The parallels between Ionesco's recall and that of Traherne (both in the *Divine Reflections on the Native Objects of an Enfant-Ey* and in the *Centuries of Meditations*) are striking indeed, and we shall see more of them later on. But already in this first matter of the child-Self immobile at the centre, *observing* a universe which is at once a total-presence (a *plénitude*) and a source of intense luminosity, the correspondence in the experience is well-nigh absolute:

> Then was my Soul my only All to me,
>   A living, endless Ey,
>   Scarce bounded with the Sky,
> Whose power, and Act, and Essence was to see . . .

writes Traherne in one poem ("The Praeparative"); and in another ("Felicity"),

---

[9] Ionesco, *Journal en miettes*, p. 14.

> No empty Space; it is all full of Sight,
>   All Soul and Life, an Ey most bright,
>   All Light and Love . . .

"To see is to understand, after another fashion,"[10] echoes Ionesco; and the essential "découvertes" of his childhood were precisely those of light and fullness: the fullness of the very *essence* of Light.

It is in the context of this ecstatic-mystic vision of childhood that we can situate another of the more exceptional features of Ionesco's auto-biographical writings. One of the very basic characteristics of the *Souvenirs d'enfance*, considered as a genre, is that the end of childhood and the completion of the literary form coincide. In other words, the narrative (be it 20 or 2,000 pages) finishes at that point of maturity, when the child-that-was realises its full and final identity as a conscious Self: the Self of the writer-who-is-to-be. Most of Ionesco's essays in this field are too fragmentary fully to reveal this pattern; none the less, the sense that "something ended" is all-pervasive: the dramatist who created *La Cantatrice* and *Le Piéton,* the polemics and the reminiscences, *is not* the child who once he was. This transformation seems to have come early—early, at least, compared with many others. But in the unusual feature about it (again as with Traherne) is that it would appear to have been a metaphysical, rather than a sensual, sexual, social, emotional or intellectual turning-point, as happens in the vast majority of cases. "Suddenly I felt old," he recalls:

> Ever since I was fifteen, I believe it is since I was fifteen, that is to say, ever since the moment when all that remained to me of childhood slipped away from me, that is to say, ever since the instant when there was no more a present, nothing but a past rushing forward into a future, that is to say, into the abyss, ever since the minute when the present died and was replaced by time, ever since I became fully aware of time, I have felt old, and I started to want to catch up with life.[11]

On the other hand, and rather unexpectedly, the chasm that divides the two Selves is not wholly unbridgeable. Many writers and poets, beginning with St. Augustine, have had the feeling that their past-Selves—themselves as they were as children—are gone for ever. Whatever they may be now, one thing is certain: they are Other than what they were. "Je" (very definitely) "est un autre." Whether this be a matter for regret or for self-congratulation

---
[10] Ionesco, *Découvertes* (Geneva: Skira, 1969), p. 73.
[11] Ionesco, *Journal en miettes*, p. 32.

depends on individual temperament—André Gide, for instance, has nothing but the most unspeakable contempt for that "état larvaire" which incarnated himself-as-he-was. Moreover, the fact that this "other" Self belongs irremediably to the past raises a further question: namely, if the only tool for re-creating the past is memory, how far can the evidence of memory be accepted as reliable?—even allowing that it does not fail altogether, leaving gaps, as Stendhal remarks, "like a fresco, of which large sections have flaked away with time, and are lost forever."

Ionesco solves the frustrating memory-problem of childhood-autobiography in a way which is virtually unique:[12] a direct continuity of past-existence into present-experience through the medium of dream. Even though, in the profounder Sartrian sense, the past can have no real-existence at all, save in so far as it is refashioned in the present, none the less, for Ionesco, the "reality" of a past relived in dream is more immediate, and ultimately both more accurate and more meaningful, than a past recalled haphazardly and fragmentarily, through memory. Admittedly, neither solves the ultimate riddle: "Memory, as much as dream, makes me realise in the depths of my being, the unreality, the evanescence of the world."[13] For all that, dream is the more vivid experience. Dream can supply the gaps that conscious memory leaves empty, dream can engender a Proustian continuum in the reliving of the past which conscious memory, by the very fact of its consciousness, destroys. And dreams can build up on past experience, not merely in itself, but as already re-lived through other dreams. "I recognize this house. I had not been back there for many years. But I have revisited it several times in my dreams."[14] The uncertain and problematic reality of the child-Self is assimilated into the immediate dream-reality of the Self in the present.

The importance of this opposition, which is at the same time an intermittent continuity, between past child-Self and present adult-Self, is that, when analysed in detail, it affords us a new and more satisfying explanation of that dynamic contrast between polarities of experience which, in its turn, dictates the substantial form of Ionesco's theatre. In earlier analyses—based primarily on interpretations offered by Ionesco himself in a series of notable articles, such as the famous "Point de départ" of 1955—it was virtually inevitable that this polarity should be discerned as an opposition (or alternation) between

---

[12] It could be argued that Ionesco's dream-memory technique for recalling the past Self is at bottom a variant of the Proustian technique of "total-recall" (also used, incidentally, by W. H. Hudson in *Far Away and Long Ago*, 1918; and by John Raynor, in *A Westminster Childhood*, 1973); there are, however, significant differences.

[13] Ionesco, *Présent passé, passé présent* (1968), p. 272.

[14] Ionesco, *Journal en miettes*, p. 197.

"heaviness" on the one hand and "evanescence" on the other, between "delving down" and "flying up" (*Victimes du devoir*), between "shadow" and "light," between "the unreal transparency of the world and its opaqueness."[15] However, in the light of the autobiographical writings which we have been examining, this original comparatively primitive opposition of contrasting "poles of awareness" seems likely to prove inadequate. Not, of course, that it can be wholly superseded. But, to begin with, it left from the first a number of questions unanswered (for instance, is "evanescence" an intimation of euphoria, of trancendental ecstasy and of the pure poetry of Being? Or is it simply a foreboding of the Void of absurdity and un-meaning which constitute the essence of the world?); and further, it can now be supplemented, through Ionesco's revelations of his own childhood, by a number of more specific, and more readily analysable oppositions. There is the opposition between colour and non-colour (and specifically, between "blue" and "grey"); that between luminescence and the absence, or dimming, of light; and in particular, that between "fulness" (*la plénitude*) and emptiness (*le vide*). This last contrast is the most revealing, since, from the evidence of the *Souvenirs d'enfance*, it would seem that *la plénitude*, which hitherto it had been impossible not to equate with the concepts of "heaviness" and of "opaqueness," none the less represents the glory, and not the damnation, of the human condition.

The experience of childhood—as re-told or re-created by those poets who have felt impelled to set it down on paper—is more rarely than one might suppose a Paradise-Lost. In point of fact, among major writers at least, those for whom childhood was the realm of boredom, frustration or, more impressively, of sheer and unadulterated Hell, perhaps marginally outnumber those for whom it came enveloped in trailing clouds of glory.[16] Ionesco, then, belongs already to a minority. But in this context, as in the one discussed earlier, it is even rarer to find a poet whose recollection of childhood as a *paradis perdu* is spiritual and metaphysical, rather than primarily sensual and emotional.[17]

To recapitulate: the essential components of this earlier state-of-being, as they appear in recollection (or in present dream-reality) include, firstly, a sensation of "euphoria." This was not simply an experience of comfort, security and well-being, but rather one of "magic"—of Otherness, of a kind

---

[15] Ionesco, *"Point de départ,"* originally published in *Cahiers des Saisons*, No. 1, Aug. 1955. See esp. p. 17.

[16] Cf. Juliette Adam, Hervé Bazin, Jean-Jacques Bouchard, Maxim Gorky, Edmund Gosse, Claire Martin, Jules Vallès . . . to name only the most obvious.

[17] As an example of the non-metaphysical *paradis perdu*, cf. Laurie Lee's *Cider with Rosie* (1959).

of mystic or transcendental exaltation, later recapturable only for fleeting instants, before it is swamped once more by the greyness (*la grisaille*) of adult existence. Secondly, a permanent and overwhelming sense of *surprise*. The entirety of the world was new-fashioned and new-created—as everything may appear new-fashioned and new-created when it is apprehended for the first time. Once-upon-a-time there was, ever-present, the freshness that Agnès recaptures for so fleeting an instant in *Ce formidable bordel:*

> There will be a new sky, newly-washed, newly-cleaned, as blue as blue can be. As we begin to head towards the coast, first we shall see white boats filled with black men, fishermen, and then we shall see gulls, and then we shall see the land itself, the *new* land. We shall make our landfall on an unknown continent, no-one will have ever beheld it before, no-one will have discovered it, not even Christopher Columbus. There will be trees laden with fruit which no-one will ever have tasted. . . . [18]

Thirdly, an awareness of the world, in relation to the Self, as an "absolute-presence," both in the temporal sense of being "outside time" and therefore established rock-like in the permanence of an immutable and essential reality, and also in that of being apprehended directly in the immanence of its essential being. To use Gabriel Marcel's phrase, the child knew constantly and intuitively the feeling of "being-with" (*être-avec*) the world, that the adult has lost for ever. And finally—the key to all the rest—the consciousness of an all-pervading, all-embracing "plenitude," of the total fullness and one-ness of all creation, devoid of gaps or spaces—of the Self and the cosmos as a *unity,* present, positive and as exalting to the Western mind as is the parallel unity-in-non-being, or Nirvana, to the Eastern:

> As adults, we keep the memory of a *present,* of a *presence,* of a *plenitude* which, by whatever means, we strive to recapture. [19]

Unquestionably, this is a mystic experience of the highest order; and, in the last analysis, it is the transmitting of this experience, through the paradoxical medium of *comedy* (that is the genius of the thing!), which has given Ionesco the status of one of the most influential dramatists of the present century. It is, in the fullest (religious) sense, the description of a "state of Grace," both in its notion of *plénitude,* and in its experience of wonder, surprise and *émerveillement.* It is an experience which leads us straight back,

---

[18] Ionesco, *Ce formidable bordel,* p. 105.
[19] Ionesco, *Journal en miettes,* pp. 64–5 (my italics).

once again, to Thomas Traherne. In the miraculous, dawning awareness of the child, wrote the English poet in one of his most famous passages,

> The corn was orient and immortal wheat, which never should be reaped nor was ever sown. I thought it had stood from everlasting to everlasting. The dust and stones of the street were as precious as gold; the gates were at first the end of the world. The green trees when I saw them first through one of the gates transported and ravished me, their sweetness and unusual beauty made my heart to leap, and almost mad with ecstasy, they were such strange and wonderful things. . . .[20]

"Such strange and wonderful things. . . ." This leads us directly into an alternative interpretation of Ionesco's theatre, not, certainly, *replacing* the traditional definition of a "Theatre of the Absurd" as being a profoundly pessimistic, even nihilistic, exposition of the utter meaninglessness of human existence seen *sub specie aeternitatis,* or, more scientifically, in terms of the second law of thermodynamics, but running parallel to it, hidden in the background: a clue to the meaning behind the most evident un-meaning. For that which is "absurd" to the adult is by no means so to the child; and the child is wiser in its own generation. To the adult, the (dream-) phenomenon of levitation is "absurd"—but to the earlier Self, the Self in the state-of-Grace. . . ? "Walking on air is *childish,"* remarks Bérenger significantly to Marthe; and then again, later on, "It's child's-play."[21] The child, in the state-of-Grace, *can* levitate. One has only to consult another English poet, Richard Church, for confirmation:

> I exercised [my] will, visualising my hands and feet pressing downwards upon the centre of the earth. It was no surprise to me that I left the ground and glided about the room (which was empty) some twelve or eighteen inches above the parquet floor. At first I was afraid of collapsing [. . .] I soared higher, half-way up to the ceiling. This thoroughly frightened me, and I allowed myself to subside. . . .[22]

So, if the adult is to recapture intimations of the state-of-Grace, it can be by way only of childish things: a return, however ephemeral, to the physical

---

[20] Traherne, *Centuries of Meditations,* III, 3. The question, whether Ionesco actually *knew* the writings of Traherne is irrelevant. In answer to a question asked him by the present writer, he replied that he did not; but that he had encountered the identical experiences recounted in virtually identical language in the writings of certain Eastern mystics.

[21] *Théâtre* III, pp. 166 and 171.

[22] Richard Church, *Over the Bridge* (London: Heinemann, 1955), pp. 160–61.

dimension of childhood. It may be through landscape—through the "miniature" houses, cottages, castles and railways of *Le piéton de l'air*—or it may be through a reconstruction of thought-patterns: the simplified, lucid and relentlessly logical thought-patterns of the six-year-old:

> It's usually on Thursdays that the sky starts to grow blue. And since we are much nearer the equator than is the centre of the town or the northern suburbs, the sun is much bigger and much closer. The days are longer, too, and the night holds far more stars.[23]

This, characteristically, is taken from *Ce formidable bordel* (1973), one of Ionesco's later plays. It is fascinating to observe how, progressively, the sophisticated anti-logic of *La cantatrice* and of *La Leçon* yields to the inspired anti-logic of the child. The greatest of all students of the poetic inspiration of childhood, the Russian Kornei Chukovsky, observed once that "every child is a linguistic genius . . . up to the age of six." What, then, kills the "poetry" (or destroys the "state-of-Grace") in childhood? What is it that occasions the *angoisse* of Ionesco's later plays? Simply, the loss of the child-dimension, the "becoming-transparent" of remembered bliss. It is the Dante-theme,

> Nessun maggior dolore
> che ricordarsi del tempo felice
> nella miseria. . .

For Samuel Beckett, the ultimate indictment of God-the-creator lies in the decay of the body—the break-down of the bicycle which symbolises the potential eternal-perfection of the being whom God *could* have created. For Ionesco, it is the fading of the state-of-Grace in the child. If the child is aware of the ecstatic, inexpressible miracle of Being, then why should the adult be condemned to lose this awareness? Part of the answer lies (as with Traherne) in *language*—in the contamination of the unique-inspired originality of the poet-Self by the infinitely crude commonplaceness of Others;[24] part of it has to do with politics (Ionesco's own personal, not-always-convincing obsession); but the most important part relates to the dulling of the capacity for surprise. For the adult, the world is no longer as new as it was. Everything is *déjà-vu;* and only a Bérenger can reiterate "Je suis surpris, je suis surpris, je suis surpris! Je n'en reviens pas!" . . . with the inspired obstinacy of the child.

---

[23] Ionesco, *Ce formidable bordel*, p. 77.
[24] See esp. *Découvertes*, pp. 32–6.

In relation to this remembered state-of-Grace which inspires part at least of every one of his later plays, Ionesco's creative imagination is predominantly *visual*. If this were not evident from the dramas themselves, we have in addition his own word for it. In the quasi-self-portrait which he draws, if not of himself as an individual, at least of his more intimate inner preoccupations, in *Le roi se meurt*, the dying Bérenger utters the words: "Blue . . . blue." Upon which, Queen Marguerite proceeds to comment:

> He can still distinguish colours. Coloured memories. His is not a nature attuned to language. His imagination is purely visual. . . . He's a painter . . . but rather over-fond of monochrome. Give up this Empire too! And give up your colours![25]

This is a remarkably revealing comment. In the first place, because it suggests that Ionesco's inspired juggling with the absurdities of language in plays such as *Jacques* or *La cantatrice* arises, in part at least, from the fact that language, *as such*, is not of supreme concern to him, consequently, that he can afford to treat it with the contempt it deserves. And in the second place, because it prompts one to reconsider Ionesco's dramatic output as a whole from scratch, and to attempt to classify and interpret the plays in a totally new way: as simple *visual* structures rather than as intricate intellectual *tours de force*.

As soon as we apply this visual criterion,[26] we find that the plays separate roughly into two groups: (i) a group whose tonality is primarily black/white/grey—a tonality which is sometimes expressed more simply still as opposition or alternation between light and dark; and (ii) a group in which colour predominates. Between these two groups there is remarkably little overlapping. Exceptionally, here and there, the colour red will intrude into a black/white play; but this would seem to be quite conscious and deliberate, and to carry a symbolic significance of its own.

And if, as the next step, we examine the visual tonalities of these plays in the context of those recollections of childhood which we have been analysing, we discover immediately that each group is directly related to one particular sublime or ecstatic instant of childhood experience.

---

[25] *Theatre* IV, p. 72. The bulk of the passage quoted, for some reason, is omitted in the Donald Watson translation. See Eugène Ionesco, *Plays,* V, pp. 90–1.

[26] It will be evident that I am referring here exclusively to the visual elements indicated by Ionesco himself in his own text and stage-directions; not to whatever visual factors may be added by the *metteur-en-scène*.

(I) *The Black-and-White group:* most typically, *La cantatrice, Les chaises, Délire à deux;* also *Jeux de massacre* (after the first 3 pages) and *Ce formidable bordel*.

Here, the polarities lie between pure light—white, brilliant, incandescent—and non-light. The inner dramatic action of the play is a process of *fading;* the original incandescence weakens, grows dim, edges towards grey (la *grisaille*); and the shades of grey themselves shift and lose even their characteristic greyness, being extinguished eventually, either into black, or else into a negative and lightless transparency. "Switch out the light," orders the New Tenant as the curtain falls . . . and all light is for ever extinguished. Nor, in the plays of this group, is there a suggestion of colour.

The dream-vision underlying this particular form of dramatic inspiration would appear to be found in an experience—one of the "moments sublimes" which later were to shape his whole life and art—which came to Ionesco not exactly as a child, but rather as an adolescent. Details and places are not revealed, but from the context it could be deduced that he was perhaps sixteen or seventeen years old at the time, and was living in Rumania:

> A day in June, at the beginning of June [. . .] the low, white houses of the little town [. . . and then, the "vision" . . .] The houses grew whiter. Something absolutely new in the light [. . .] A world dissolved by light, reconstituted by light. Joy surged up, overflowed from the depths of my being, warm and itself seemingly luminous, an absolute presence, a presence. . . .[27]

The description of this occurrence takes up a full two pages of the *Journal en miettes;* nor is there, from beginning to end, one single hint of colour. It is a vision of pure-light, unmodified by the accidental texture of what it may chance to fall upon. Light from the source . . . "God said, Let there be Light. And there was Light." "It was a *sartori,*" explains Ionesco, "an illumination. An illumination, that is to say, something which happens *truly in the light*." A direct manifestation of a super-human presence—which is the ultimate reality that lies behind Amédée II's almost inexpressible vision of a "house of glass, house of light . . . the Milky Way . . . thick milk . . . incandescent." But it is "Amédée II"—the rediscovered, younger Amédée of "Amédée I's" dream—who has this immediacy of contact with the source of all Being. For "Amédée I," the light has decayed and faded. *His* realm is that of *la grisaille*.

In slightly different terms, it could be argued that this vision of "pure-light" is a direct experience of Essence. For Ionesco, categorically, Essence

---

[27] Ionesco, *Journal en miettes*, pp. 112–14.

precedes Existence: not all of his fear and hatred of the late Jean-Paul Sartre was rooted in politics. In *Découvertes,* he argues the origins of language from the same premise, the opponent in this case being not so much Sartre as Wittgenstein. And in this sense, it is perhaps not entirely accidental that the original experience, the "Vision of Pure Light," occurred not to the child, but to the adolescent. For the child, all experience is immediate and timeless: an absolute presence. But to the adolescent, the child is already a past-Self, and time exists. And being *in* time (perhaps the only consolation), he is able to go back *beyond* the child, beyond any being-in-time, to the "memory of a memory,"[28] when he himself participated in that Essence, before Existence had even started.

> (II) *The Colour-group:* most typically, *Le Piéton de l'air;* also *Tueur sans gages, Le roi se meurt, La soif et la faim, Voyages chez les morts.*

Here, the polarities lie between the brilliance of pure colour—colours of a very limited range, and virtually all contained within the spectrum—and the fading of those colours, first into pastel-shades, eventually into nondescript greys or browns; more rarely, between the colours themselves, and the non-colours' black, white, transparency or . . . "the frightening colour of the water in the Seine."

Again, behind the visual structure of the plays there lies a childhood "Vision"—or perhaps, in this case, a double one, since the virtually identical experience seems to have been vouchsafed on two separate occasions, once at the age of three[29] (place unknown, probably close to Paris), and a second time at the age of nine or ten, at La Chapelle-Anthenaise. The second is the Vision that he describes in the greater detail; but in both passages, the parallels with Traherne's field of "orient and immortal wheat" are striking. One Sunday after lunch, recalls Ionesco,

> I cross a deep lane filled with shadow. I emerge into bright light: red poppies amid yellow wheat, a sky so blue so blue. Never since have I seen so resplendent a red, so yellow a yellow, so intense a blue, a light so young, so fresh, so new. It could not have been other than the first day of the birth of the world. The world had scarce yet been created, and all was virgin. Since that day everything has wilted, and the colours have grown blurred.[30]

---

[28]The phrase is taken from the Russian poet, Andrei Bely, who, in *Kotik Letaev* (1918), recounts a similar experience.

[29]Ionesco, *Découvertes,* p. 55.

[30]Ionesco, *Présent passé,* pp. 35–36.

This theme of emerging from a dark lane suddenly, over a ridge, into a brilliantly-coloured Garden-of-Paradise recurs in various contexts, and is obviously one of the very deepest of all Ionesco's childhood memories. In this instance, moreover, it does belong truly to childhood, rather than to adolescence, and as such it is subtly different, and rather more complex, than Vision No. I. It contains in fact two sets of phenomena, which can be separated, although it might be wiser not to do so. Firstly, there is the element of *luminosity* which, as in Vision No. I, incarnates a pure Essence, a power and a presence outside the Self, by which the Self is overwhelmed. But, secondly, there are the colours, and these are not of Essence, but of Existence; they are the miracle-vision, or dream, of the past child-Self, but that Self is already very much in the world, and of it. They embody the whole new-made world of childhood; and, thanks to that state-of-Grace which enables the child to "be-with" all that encompasses it, for an instant at least it *becomes* the colours which dazzle its wondering eyes. "I am," exclaims the adult re-kindled in the flame of childhood by the Dream, "I am—oh—my colours, the colours of the world."[31]

If we care to take this analysis a step further, we have three sets of evidential data at our disposal. Firstly, the plays themselves. Secondly, the illustrations (in various media, but all in the quasi-primitive manner of child-art) to *Découvetes*. And thirdly, the various *Souvenirs d'enfance*—the autobiographical writings about childhood. From a comparative study of these sources, the following patterns emerge:

    A.   *Primary (spectrum) colours* (absolutely dominant):
        Plays: Red, green, blue (almost exclusively).
        Illustrations: Red, orange, yellow, green, violet (very little blue).
        Souvenirs: Red, yellow, green, blue.
    B.   *Compound colours:*
        Plays: Pink—but only from *Le tueur* (1959) to *Le piéton* (1963).
            Brown (only 2 examples, both of doubtful significance, since they refer in conventional terms to the colour of the hair).
        Illustrations: Brown; and a sort of pale amethyst.
        Souvenirs: Gold (usually symbolic).
    C.   *Non-colours (I):*
        Plays
        Illustrations   } Black, white, grey, transparency. (Silver occurs in the plays only, and chiefly as a means to symbolise luminosity.)
        Souvenirs
    D.   *Non-colours (II):*
        Total absence: almost anything which is not a clear, primary colour

---

[31] Ionesco, *Présent passé*, p. 43.

(except as under *B* above) is left totally unidentified. Marthe, for instance, in *Le piéton*, describing a handbag which she and her mother had seen in Piccadilly, refers to it as "pale-coloured, I can't describe exactly the shade." This neglect of, and contempt for, nuances of shading is absolutely characteristic in all three categories.

Set out thus in tabulated form, the distribution of colour throughout the range of works we have been discussing emerges clearly, and something of the patterns of Ionesco's own (visual) creative imagination becomes discernible.

To begin with, the pattern is simple almost to the point of starkness. Nearly all the earlier plays are in black-and-white; and when colour begins to intrude, as it does in 1959 with *Tueur sans gages* (and, significantly, it was in 1960 that Ionesco began to publish his fragmentary *Souvenirs d'enfance*), it goes no further than a basic scattering of child's finger-paints in primary colours—nor does it use all of these. The over-all impression left by virtually *all* the plays, with the solitary exception of *Le piéton*, is still that of a bold design in black and white (like the Massin photomontage of *La cantatrice*), picked out here and there with blobs of brilliant colour stuck on with a palette-knife; colour, however, which makes its own, independent pattern, related only indirectly to the principal design and, in the end, subservient to it. For, in the last resort, the colours of the child's vision of the Self-in-the-world are powerless against the ultimate, pure luminosity of Essence, and of its enemy, *la grisaille*, forerunner of the transparency of Nothingness, or the black of eternal night.

Working from the same evidence, it is also tempting to reinterpret Ionesco's early rejection of Surrealism and his denial of any affiliation with the neo-Surrealist movements which flourished after 1945. In two important statements, "Expérience du théâtre" (1958) and "Le Rire? L'aboutissement d'un drame!" (interview with Edith Mora, 1959), Ionesco argued that the Surrealists were insufficiently *lucid* in the handling of the material which their techniques had liberated from the subconscious. "The waters must be allowed to come flooding out," he asserted. "But *afterwards* comes the sorting, the controlling, the understanding, the collecting."[32] This lucidity the Surrealists did not possess; therefore he could not be counted as one of them.

But we can see now that Ionesco's primarily *visual* sensibility, clearly in evidence from his childhood onwards, must have biased him against the Surrealists from the beginning. For Surrealism was first and foremost a move-

---

[32] Interview with Edith Mora, reprinted in *Notes et Contre-Notes*, p. 100.

ment in the visual arts; and Surrealist painting, whatever its subconscious inspiration, was technically a highly-sophisticated art-form. For all that Guillaume Apollinaire, who first coined the word "surréaliste," was also one of the pioneer investigators in the field of child-art, there is nothing childish in any sense about the work of Arp or Dali, Max Ernst or Giorgio di Chirico. On the other hand, perhaps it is the same affinity with the child-vision which goes some way to explaining the kinship which Ionesco felt at this same period (1950–60) towards the 'Pataphysicians. For the painters associated with the celebrated Collège de 'Pataphysique were precisely those who—like Jean Dubuffet[33]—had followed in the footsteps of Alfred Jarry, and who *did* cultivate a specifically child-like neo-primitivism. The painters he truly admired—the Douanier Rousseau, Utrillo, Chagall, Dufy, above all Juan Miró[34]—all possessed something of this child-vision, Dufy and Miró in particular employing much the same range of primary colours as Ionesco himself. "Give a dream-atmosphere," exhorts Ionesco in the stage-directions to *Le piéton,*

> None-the-less, this dream-world should be conveyed by the techniques of a primitivist, pseudo-clumsy artist, rather than by the means of a surrealist painter. . . .

Behind the apparently straightforward stage-direction there lies a whole programme of informed preferences in modern art, and more than a hint of Ionesco's own *art poétique*.

Finally, it is worth observing that, for all the apparent spontaneity evident in the selection of colours, there is also, in the plays at least, a background of expressionistic symbolism, almost as strictly codified as that which we find in the writings of Jean Genet. This, too, is "primitive"; but it is effective none the less:

Blue: colour of the sky, the Empyrean, the ultimate, the Essence; colour of Paradise and love; colour also of the transcendental and the mystic, of that which lies before and after life. "Bleu, bleu," whispers the dying King Bérenger; while, on a homelier level, Joséphine of *Le piéton* is dressed in blue throughout the play—first of all in a "dark-blue housecoat with white patterns," later in "a sky-blue coat and skirt." The latter, alas, has a dark-red rose pinned to the lapel.

---

[33] See *Cahiers du Collège de 'Pataphysique,* Dossiers 10 and 11, "8 Clinamen LXXXVII" (= 1960).

[34] Cf. the collection of lithographs by Juan Miró, *Quelques fleurs pour des amis . . . avec un coup d'oeil sur le jardin par Eugène Ionesco.* Paris, 1964.

Green: spring, joy, childhood, the birth-of-the-world, the wonder, not of Essence, but of reality newly-fashioned. The colour of hope—and of surprise.

Red: colour of death, of danger and menace, of evil and of the end of the world. The colour of the judge's robes in *Le piéton*, his sentence foreshadowed by the red rose on Joséphine's costume. Red is the only colour which appears with black, making the black more positively dire; red-and-black as the symbols of political hatred (*La soif et la faim*); red-and-black in the Swastika-emblem of the Nazis, which appears on the Professor's armband at the end of *La leçon*, and again inside the head of the Fascist in *Voyages chez les morts:* "Your brain is black and red."

Pink: the only compound colour with a symbolic value, and the most rarely-used. A compromise: hope, perhaps, not for the Self, but for others. Marthe, in *Le piéton,* wears pink as she dreams of the future. But pink is a fragile colour, as fragile and as nebulous as a mirage, as hope itself, or as the "little pink, flower-bedecked pillar" which comes and vanishes in the same play. It is a promise, but unwise is he (or she) who trusts it too far.

Perhaps this is too categoric. Most examples fit in well enough—Lady Duncan, for instance, appears at first clad in a "long, green, floral-patterned dress"; but its augury of life-renewed, as we learn, is a delusion, and later on she reveals herself in her true colours, in a "glittering bikini, with a red-and-black cloak over her shoulders"—but one or two others are more puzzling. How, for instance, should we interpret the symbolic banner of La Mère Pipe's jack-booted storm-troopers in *Le tueur:* "white goose on green background"? Again, as a delusion, a lie, a cynical promise destined never to be fulfilled? It would be incautious to exercise *too* much ingenuity in interpretation. Or at least, not until we have solved a puzzle more curious still than the presence of certain colours in the plays, and that is the absence of others. It is as though violet, orange, yellow had never existed . . . why? Even the sun, when it appears (*Le tueur*), is red. There was yellow enough in the cornfields of Ionesco's childhood, beneath the amazing blue of the sky; there is violet, there is orange enough in the child-drawings in *Découvertes;* but in the plays, while the blue remains, the yellow, the violet and the orange have vanished, seemingly for ever.

From this study it will be clear, I think, that at the root of Ionesco's dramatic vision there lies a dream-reminiscence of certain unforgettable experiences of childhood: not in the Freudian sense (far from it!), but rather in the sense that the child-Self retains vivid impressions of "one-ness with the Totality,"[35] of which the adult-Self only exceptionally is aware.

This mystical Vision formerly vouchsafed was of a Self transcendentally irradiated with pure Light, which light was destined subsequently to deteriorate into murkiness and *grisaille*. It was one of a world steeped in brilliant and primitive colour, which colour was doomed gradually to grow dull and tarnished, eventually to fade away altogether. And it was one finally which, like a painting, existed timeless and out-of-time; and as such, as soon as time assumed its sway, it was fated to disintegrate and leave no place for anything save the *angoisse* of eventual annihilation.

And, in the last analysis, it is in this Vision of childhood that the all-pervasive *émerveillement* of Ionesco's theatre has its origins: a child's wonder at the newness and freshness of the blue-green-yellow-red of the sudden, sunlit world; a child's wonder at the simple, yet miraculous, undeserved and inexplicable fact of "being-there" and "being-with." An adolescent's wonder, maybe, at finding itself without warning in the presence of the pure white light of Essence, which existed before the Self was in the world at all. Later still, the adult's wonder—or anguish—at the fact that this wonder itself exists no more, save only in dream, and that the dream itself is condemned, by the fact of mortality, to irretrievable extinction. And last of all, the Poet's reduplicated wonder—a wonder at the wonder of his own child-Self's former amazement at the luminous, primary-coloured marvel of existence:

> All Time was an Eternity, and a perpetual Sabbath. Is it not strange, that an Infant should be Heir of the whole World, and see those Mysteries, which the Books of the Learned never unfold?[36]

Perhaps, in the last analysis, every *true* poet shares this gift of being very, *very* surprised.

University of California at Davis.

---

[35] Bernard Berenson, in *Sketch for a Self-Portrait* (1949), describes an identical experience, which he refers to as "the sensation of being immersed in *It*ness."

[36] Traherne, *Centuries of Meditations*, III, 2.

IONESCO AND THE FAIRYTALE TRADITION

Martin Esslin

> Ich weiss nicht, was soll es bedeuten,
> Dass ich so traurig bin.
> Ein Märchen aus uralten Zeiten,
> Das kommt mir nicht aus dem Sinn . . .
> Heine
>
> Das Mährchen ist gleichsam der *Canon* der Poesie—
> alles poetische muss mährchenhaft seyn. . . .
> Novalis[1]

Ionesco, I know, does not want critics to chase after influences for his work. And nothing could be further from my intention. What I should like to do is to try and draw attention to an area of literature which seems to me to exude an atmosphere, a spirit very closely akin to much of Ionesco's *oeuvre* and to situate him if not within its confines so at least within the penumbra, the outer sphere of radiation of that world: the world of the fairytale.

I dislike the term fairytale. I think it has slightly pejorative connotations in English; there is an element of condescension inherent in the word. Nor do I think that the French equivalent *conte de fées* is a particularly felicitous one. There are not always fairies in fairytales. That is why I much prefer the word *Märchen*, which is merely a diminuitive of a word meaning story, just as the Russian word *skazka*, or the Italian *fiaba* or *storiella*, or the Danish *Eventyr*—which H. C. Andersen used—with its connotation of adventure, the wonderful event.

The fairytale, to stick to the word, the only one we have in English, has, I feel, been neglected as a genre by literary critics. That is a pity: for in many

---

[1] "Novalis," *Dichter über ihre Dichtungen*, ed. Hans-Joachim Mahl, Vol. 15 (Heimeran, 1976), p. 194, hereafter cited as *Dichter*.

ways this seems to me one of the most important and influential of all literary genres: after all, most children, and therefore also most writers, receive their first and decisive impulses to the future workings of their imaginations from the tales they are told as children. Moreover: Not only is the fairytale a highly relevant constituent of all popular and folk literature, it is also a form practised by some of the greatest literary figures of all time.

Why has the fairytale received such relatively scanty treatment by serious literary critics? Partly I believe this is due to its having been regarded as a minor form, intended for children and thus not to be taken too seriously; but mainly because somehow, this being so basic and "primitive" a form of literature, the folk fairytale has been largely abandoned to the folklorists and ethnologists who have done brilliant work on the subject, unearthed important facts, but who, quite naturally, have been using the folk-tale largely as an instrument for other purposes than literary: to trace the lines of cultural and racial interaction between different areas of the world, to catalogue the *motifs* and archetypes that recur in fairytales throughout the world as indicators of the workings of the popular psyche, as repositories of the remnants of old religions, tribal customs, kinship relations, etc.

Where does the genre of the fairytale situate itself among the many types of popular narrative literature? The exact boundary lines between myth and Märchen on the one hand, and Märchen and saga, legend, fable, anecdote, *facetie* (Schwank—joke) on the other, are difficult to trace.

I should say that the fairytale (Märchen) shares with myth the occurrence of miraculous and dreamlike events. But while myth is on a lofty scale and deals with Gods and heroes that are the embodiment of tribal or national ideals and aspirations, while myth concerns itself with events on a cosmic scale, the fairytale or Märchen remains on a domestic, family level. One might say that in the sphere of myth the individual or the tribe or the nation dream of enlarging themselves to a cosmic plane; that the myth transfers individual problems and aspirations to a cosmic level, while the fairytale, although still using such elements as kings, queens, and princesses, brings them *down,* reduces them to a domestic, family scale. We tell our child a story about a king and a queen and a beautiful little princess, but the child knows that we are only talking about father, mother, and herself. Also: myth is on the whole tragic; the narratives of myth often have unhappy endings. The fairytale tends to end on a happier note. Myths are there to accustom us to the harsh ultimate realities of the human condition. Fairytales, on the whole, serve the purpose of reassurance. At the other end of the spectrum the fairytale does merge into the animal fable (there are talking animals in both the saga or legend and even the *facetie,* but these more earthy forms of folk narrative do not rise too high above the ground of everyday, non-miraculous events.

There is, of course, also a significant connection between the fairytale, the Märchen and the dream: "Ein Märchen ist eigentlich wie ein Traumbild" says that great poet and purest of the German Romantics, Novalis, "Ohne Zusammenhang—ein *Ensemble* wunderbarer Dinge und Begebenheiten — z.B. eine *musicalische Fantasie*—die Harmonischen Folgen einer Aeolsharfe, *die* Natur selbst," which is to say: "A fairytale is at bottom like a dream image—without internal logical connection, an ensemble of miraculous things and events, for example a musical improvisation—the harmonic sequence on a aeol's harp—*nature itself.*"[2] Here we are, I feel, very close to what we know of Ionesco's own method of composition, the dreamlike trancelike yielding to the images that come flooding in and which play on the writer (whose skills, linguistic and intellectual, are like the strings of the aeol's harp) as the wind itself plays on that instrument.

But, if Ionesco's method of composition has points of contact with the very nature of the fairytale, is not his vision, unlike that of the fairytale, ultimately a tragic one?

I should, on reflection, dispute that view. Ionesco's vision is, above all, a comic vision, even though a tragicomic one. But are his *endings* really tragic? Does not Amédée float up into the air, freed from his domestic entanglement? *Le piéton de l'air*, admittedly, has seen a terrifying vision of ultimate destruction and the void, which the bystanders do not believe in. But that play also ends on a note of acceptance, however ironic:

> peut-être que que les abîmes se rempliront . . . peut-être que les jardins . . . les jardins . . . les jardins . . .

Bérenger *has* seen the abyss and the void, but perhaps what matters even more is that he has accepted that vision. And similarly, the old man in *Les Chaises* dies happily, believing in the transmission of his message to future generations. Does it matter that his optimism has been unfounded? He too has accepted his situation and come to terms with it. What, then of Bérenger in *Rhinocéros*? I also feel that the ending of that play is ultimately a good ending. Bérenger is refusing to become a pachyderm, we leave him in the hour of his triumph, his victorious, if perhaps futile, defiance. And the Bérenger of *Tueur sans gages*? Does he not submit to the knife? Yes, but does he not do so willlingly, having accepted the ultimate absurdity of death and of the *condition humaine*?

There is thus in these plays of Ionesco's—and one could give other examples—a point at which the inherently terrible and tragic ending is, at the last

---

[2]*Dichter*, p. 173.

moment, reversed, by the very act of the acceptance of the tragic situation. It is like the point of reversal in those fairytales when the hero or heroine accepts the necessity of doing something deeply repugnant, like that of kissing a horrible beast, or going to bed with a frog, and by that very acceptance reverses the situation into its opposite. Here too it might seem apposite to quote Novalis, probably the only one among major writers who devoted much thought to the fairytale:

> Bedeutender Zug in vielen Märchen, dass wenn ein Unmögliches möglich—zugleich ein anderes Unmögliches unerwartet möglich wird—dass wenn der Mensch sich selbst überwindet er auch die Natur zugleich überwindet—und ein Wunder vorgeht, das ihm das Entgegengesetzte Angenehme gewärt, in dem Augenblicke als ihm das entgegengesetzte Unangenehme angenehm ward. . . . . Vielleicht geschähe eine ähnliche Verwandlung, wenn der Mensch das *Übel* in der Welt liebgewänne—in dem Augenblicke, als ein Mensch die Kranckheit oder den Schmerz zu lieben anfienge, läge die reizendste Wollust in seinen Armen—die höchste positive Lust durchdränge ihn. Könnte *Kranckheit* nicht ein Mittel höherer Synthesis seyn—je fürchterlicher der Schmerz desto höher die darinn verborgene Lust. *(Harmonie)* Jede Kranckheit ist vielleicht notwendiger *Anfang* der inneren Verbindung zweier Wesen—der nothwendige Anfang der Liebe. Enthusiasmus für Kranckheiten und Schmerzen. Tod—eine nähere Verbindung liebender Wesen. *(Poëtik des Übels)*[3]

> It is a significant feature of many fairytales that when something impossible becomes possible—at the same time some other impossible event suddenly becomes possible unexpectedly—that when man overcomes himself he simultaneously overcomes nature too—and a miracle happens which awards him the opposite, pleasant thing at the very moment when he finds the opposite unpleasant pleasant. . . . . . . Perhaps a similar transformation would occur if man began to love the evil of the world—at the very moment when someone would begin to love sickness or pain, the most charming joy would lie in his arms, the highest poetic voluptuousness would pervade him. Might not sickness be a means for a higher synthesis, the more terrible the pain the greater the joy, concealed within it. *(Harmony)* Every sickness is perhaps the necessary start of the inner union of two beings—the necessary beginning of love. Enthusiasm for sickness and pain. Death—a closer union of two loving beings. *(A Poetics of Evil.)*

These are profound thoughts about the nature of transformations and metamorphoses in the world of the Märchen—the fairy tale. And there is one play

[3]*Dichter*, p. 172.

of Ionesco—a highly significant and important one, though also much neglected—namely *Le Tableau,* in which such a transformation actually occurs rather than being merely potentially possible and hinted at.

In that play the fat gentleman transforms his ugly sister Alice into a beautiful princess by shooting her with his pistol, and he does likewise with the ugly old neighbour woman, and finally transforms the painter, also by shooting him, into a Prince Charming. Only the fat gentleman himself remains as ugly as he was before. And so he begs the audience:

> Aah, et moi? Et moi? *(désolé)* Oh . . . je suis toujours pas beau! *(Au public, tendant le pistolet)* Voulez-vous tirer sur moi? Qui veut tirer sur moi? Qui veut tirer sur moi![4]

Which also sheds some light on the intended, but abandonded, first ending to *La Cantatrice Chauve* in which the author was to appear on the stage threatening to shoot the audience, and thus provoking them to attack him.

In *Le Tableau* Ionesco probably comes closer to the actual world of the fairytale than in any of his other plays, the world, that is, of the folk fairytale, which is the outcome of the collective subconscious of a whole nation, a whole culture. Many of the stories in the Bible, in Homer's *Odyssey,* and in Ovid's *Metamorphoses* fall into that category, as do many of the stories collected by Perrault, the Brothers Grimm, and other collectors of genuine folk fairytales. But parallel to the folk fairytale there is the Kunstmärchen, the consciously artistic fairytale written by known and often highly admired authors. How far back should we go to the earliest examples of this kind of consciously composed fairytale? Probably as far as Hellenistic times. Lucian's stories are *Kunstmärchen* and so is a work like *The Golden Ass* of Apuleius. I feel also that Rabelais' work is a prime example of a very early highly artistic use of the fairytale form. His Gargantua, and his Pantagruel, are, after all, modelled on the giants of the folk tale, and so is the story of a voyage or quest. Moreover, there is a quality of dreamlike fluidity and improvisation in Rabelais that I, for one, find very closely akin to much in Ionesco. And are there not affinities between the fragments of speech that float through the arctic region, which are frozen particles of language now melting in the sun, and the dead fragments of speech floating around in *La Cantatrice Chauve;* are not Rabelais' orgies of language, his long lists and accumulations of synonyms somehow reminiscent of the verbal gymnastics in plays like *Salutations*?

---

[4]Ionesco, *Théâtre III*, p. 273.

Another great early practitioner of the Kunstmärchen is Jonathan Swift. *Gulliver's Travels* is a fairytale as well as a sharp satire. And indeed, from Rabelais and Swift onwards the element of satire is one of the outstanding characteristics of the *Kunstmärchen* as against the *Volksmärchen*. In the age of the enlightenment to which Swift belonged, as well as the German writers J.K.A. Musäus and Christoph Martin Wieland, the telling of fairytales aquired ironic and satirical overtones because the writers felt themselves in some way superior to the folk tale's childish narrative technique and subject matter. The same is surely true of Voltaire, whose *Candide* clearly belongs to the same genre. And this ironic, satirical tone persisted in most of the great Kunstmärchen of the Romantic period, when the fairytale really came into its own, in France with Nodier, but above all in Germany with writers like Ernst Theodor Amadeus Hoffman, the master of the *Contes d'Hoffman*, whose great tale of *The Golden Pot* was translated into English by Carlyle, and whose story of the *Nutcracker and the King of the Mice* became Tchaikovsky's famous and oft-performed ballet. Many of Hoffman's tales are satirical as well as romantic. I particularly like *Klein Zaches*, the story of a dwarf who is awarded the miraculous gift that anything good or worthy that happens in his presence is attributed to having been *his* work—the classical satirical portrait of the sterile person who somehow gets the credit for things he has not done. That, as a subject, seems to me very close to some of Ionesco's work, the Bartholomeuses in *L'Impromptu de l'Alma*, Brechtoll in *La Soif et la Faim* have something of Klein Zaches. And then among the masters of the satirically ironic *Kunstmärchen* there is Clemens Brentano, whose *Gockel, Hinkel and Gackeleia* seems to me an immortal masterpiece. There is Brentano's partner in the collection of German folk songs, Achim von Arnim, and Wilhelm Hauff, that genius who died at the age of twenty-five and who left some of the most wonderful satiric fairytales, notably *Zwerg Nase* and *Das kalte Herz*. The greatest of the German poets, Goethe, wrote a number of fairytales; his masterpiece is simply called *Das Märchen:* it is a marvellous story of a broken culture which will be made whole by the sacrifice of a heroic creature, a snake which, when it throws itself across the river which divides the world, turns into a bridge of jade over which the traffic of peace and harmony will henceforth be able to pass. This is a great cosmic allegory full of deep and solemn meanings, but even here Goethe has used the ironic satire of the eighteenth century *Kunstmärchen* to good effect. There is a pair of *Irrlichter* (will-o'-the-wisps, ignes fatui) in this tale who need only to shake themselves to make pieces of gold rain from them, but those who touch that gold notice to their horror that the hand that has touched it disappears. And the *Irrlichter* have to devour more gold to fill up again, for when they have lost some of its glitter they get dangerously thin.

Ludwig Tieck, the translator of Shakespeare, wrote many fairytales, more pessimistic and dark than the other German romantics. But he also was a pioneer of the fairytale in drama. His *Der Gestiefelte Kater* (1797) is not only a dramatisation of the famous tale of *Le Chat Botté* from Perrault, it is also one of the first plays to break the boundaries of the stage convention, involving the spectators and the author himself, who comes out to defend himself against the spectators' attacks and even tries to re-write the play while it is in progress to meet the audiences' demands. There is much of the spirit of Ionesco in that play.

In England authors like Dickens and Thackeray wrote fairytales as Christmas Books. Everyone knows Dicken's *A Christmas Carol,* which is far too moralistic and sentimental to be mentioned in one breath with Ionesco, but Thackeray's *The Rose and the Ring,* with its petty bourgeois royal court, is much closer to him in spirit. And so, of course, is the greatest of the English tellers of fairytales, Lewis Carroll, whose *Alice in Wonderland* and *Alice through the Looking Glass* have played an important part in French surrealism. There is something also of the true fairytale spirit in Oscar Wilde's fairytales, which are a little sentimental but have much of the sharp satirical spirit as well.

But the practitioner of the *Kunstmärchen* closest perhaps in spirit to Ionesco is Hans Christian Andersen, that truly childlike fantasist from Odense on the isle of Fyn. I feel that a play like *Le Roi se meurt* with its transposition of a bourgeois family situation into the milieu of a bedraggled and decaying royal household is very close indeed in spirit to many of Andersen's tales, which incidentally, have repeatedly been dramatised and have thus played a noticeable part in the literature of fairytale drama. Ostrovsky's *Snyegoruchka* ("The Little Snowflake") is a fairytale play very much in the spirit of Andersen as well as that of the Russian *skazka*. Another Russian playwright of great talent and a very dissident turn of mind in the Stalinist period, Yevgeni Schwartz, dramatized *The Emperor' New Clothes,* among others of Andersen's fairytales. His very original fairytale play, *The Dragon,* is perhaps the best satire on Stalinism—and revolutionary politics in general— to have come out of Soviet Russia. For the fairytale is an excellent vehicle for satire of a dangerous political kind in totalitarian societies; after all, its idiom is what George Lukacs used to call *Aesopian* language.

Here, then, we have entered the sphere of *Märchendramen* or "fairytale plays." The fairytale has always had a great affinity with drama and lent itself to dramatic treatment. Shakespeare's *Midsummernight's Dream, Winter's Tale, Cymbeline,* and above all, *The Tempest* are fairytale plays, and so are other Elizabethan dramas, like Dekker's *Old Fortunatus.* The Romantics also loved the fairytale form—I have already mentioned Tieck's *Der gestiefelte*

Kater; one might also quote Grillparzer's *Der Traum ein Leben* with its oriental setting. And of course the Viennese folk theatre of the late eighteenth and early twentieth century developed the fairytale play, *Zaubermärchen,* to a fully fledged dramatic genre. The best known example of that genre, on the international plane is, of course, Mozart's *Magic Flute,* with its libretto by Emmanuel Schikaneder based on a fairytale by Wieland. There, just as in Ionesco's *Le Tableau* we have an old hag who turns into a beautiful young girl and the whole panoply of fairytale magic. The greatest of the Viennese Zaubermärchen, however, have never found international recognition because their idiom is Viennese dialect and their verbal virtuosity is untranslatable: Ferdinand Raimund's *Der Alpenkoenig und der Menschenfeind* is one of the masterpieces of this genre, as is Johann Nestroy's *Lumpazivagabundus.* These plays are full of magic but also of satire. They show a cosmos ruled by inefficient and lazy spirits, cosmic bureaucrats, bungling demons.... It would be idle to speculate on direct connections between this kind of theatre and Ionesco's world. But it might be pertinent to say that these plays did dominate the stages of the Austro-Hungarian Empire right to the days of its collapse and thereafter as well—and influences from there might well have reached into Rumania via Hungary—there is something of Nestroy, for example, in Caragiale, whom Ionesco does acknowledge as an influence.

The fairytale on the stage: much could be said on the subject. From Gozzi's combinations of the fairytale and the *commedia dell'arte* tradition (*Il Re Cervo, L'amore delle tre melarance, Turandot*) which was, in Scandinavia, continued by Adam Gottlieb Oehlenschlaeger, the great Danish poet, in his play *Alladin* and, through his influence, by Strindberg, who acknowledged that he had written his early fairytale play, *Lucky Peter* (1881) under the direct influence of Oehlenschlaeger. Strindberg's case is interesting: there the dark, pessimistic poet, who is mainly famous for his bitterly naturalistic and equally bitter expressionist dramas, shows a connecting link between these two periods in his practise of fairytale plays (*Abu Casem's Slippers, Kronbruden—The Virgin Bride, Swanwhite*) which directly link up with his most profound dream visions (*Dreamplay, To Damascus, Life's Highway,* and *The Ghost Sonata*). As Novalis recognized, there is an intimate relationship between the fairytale and the dream. In his prefatory remarks to his *Dreamplay,* Strindberg says:

> The author has in this dreamplay tried to imitate . . . the disconnected but seemingly logical form of the dream. Everything can happen, everything is possible and probable. Time and space do not exist: on an insignificant basis of reality the imagination spins on and weaves new patterns; a mixture of memories, experiences, free inspiration, inconsistencies, and improvisations. The characters divide, double up, recapitulate themselves, evaporate, con-

dense, melt away and recombine. But one consciousness stands above it all, the consciousness of the dreamer; for in it there are no secrets, no inconsistencies, no scruples, no law. He does not judge or acquit, he merely reports; and as the dream is mostly painful, less frequently joyous, there is a tone of wistfulness and pity with all living things that pervades the dizzy story. Sleep, that liberator, often appears as a tormentor, but when the pain is at its strongest, there is an awakening and it reconciles the sufferer with reality, which, however painful, at this moment is a pleasure, compared to the tormenting dream.

There is a close parallel here to the passage about fairytales from Novalis that I have quoted earlier. And from Strindberg's *Dreamplay*—and *To Damascus* or *The Great Highway*—very close parallels can be drawn to Ionesco's later plays, *La Soif et la Faim* and *L'Homme aux valises*.

For Strindberg, the transition from naturalism to the late visionary expressionism of his mature plays was facilitated and prepared by his love of the fairytale element in the plays he had written for children. The liberation of the imagination which the fluidity and infinite potentiality of the fairytale brings, where everything can happen, the more unexpected or illogical the better, is also the basis for the visionary art which derives from the recognition that dreams, in mirroring our inner world, represent a reality more profound and significant than the photographically reproduced reality of a sterile naturalism.

The area of the children's theatre, the puppet theatre, and other forms that are usually regarded as marginal, is thus, in many ways, a storehouse of new impulses. The *Punch and Judy* show, in Ionesco's case, clearly played an important part in his developement. He himself has described how fascinated he was by the *guignol* in the Jardin de Luxembourg of his early childhood. The literature of puppet theatre is scanty in its written-down form. But, for example, the Kasperl plays of Count Franz Pocci,the Munich painter and graphic artist (1807–76) are well worth studying. They are charming fairytale plays very much in a spirit of satire mixed with wonder.

The English *pantomime*, the fairytale theatre which still flourishes in England at Christmastime is another case in point. It is perhaps the most ancient form of folk theatre still alive in the Western world: it originated in the *Harlequinade* and is thus a direct descendant of the *commedia dell'arte* but nowadays always has the plot of a fairytale (*Alladin, Puss in Boots, Cinderella*) as the very loose framework for much grotesque fooling, bawdy *double-entendre* (which will delight the grown-ups and remain incomprehensible to the children), transformations scenes, improvised topical political satire as well as variety acts (jugglers, magicians, etc.) of the most varied kind. This is genuine folk theatre, in terribly bad taste, but of a fantastic vitality, total theatre at its most vulgar—and at its best.

Well, perhaps all this may seem to have very little direct bearing to our reading and understanding Ionesco. But I for one believe that we can gain a better insight into the nature of all that fairytale literature itself and of Ionesco's *oeuvre* if we set them side by side, without wanting to construct too many direct connections (although I have pointed, tentatively and humbly to one or two) and try to find the common ground from which they spring.

There is first of all, Ionesco's insistence —most eloquently and memorably expressed in *Découvertes*—which I regard as a masterpiece of critical insight into his own creativeness, one of his least-known but most important works— that to him the state of mind of the child, the freshness of his vision even as a child of two is the very basis of his creativeness. *Retrouver l'enfance* is the motto under which, at the end of that great book, he establishes his hope for the future. It is the world of the fairytale, the *Märchen,* which, in all literature is the closest to the spirit of that freshness of vision, that total lack of preconceptions which such a freshness entails.

The fairytale, like Ionesco's oeuvre, above all manifests an immense capacity for wonder. Ionesco has stressed, over and over again, that the essence of his *oeuvre* is that sense of wonder before the world's infinite capacity to surprise us. *L'insolite* is the *primum movens* that informs all of Ionesco's plays and narrative prose. No wonder, then, that it has its affinities with the world of the fairytale. The fairytale is the most *fluid* of all literary genres, the one in which the imagination is at its freest. The slightest impulses of the subconscious can freely make its aeol's harp resound (to borrow Novalis' metaphor.)

But if the fairytale contains a maximum of *l'insolite* it can also accommodate a maximum of another of Ionesco's favourite ingredients, *le cocasse:* in no other literary genre can the poetic and the grotesque live in such happy symbiosis side by side, can the transitions from the avowedly sentimental to the most grotesquely comic, or indeed horrible or obscene, be so easily accommodated and accomplished, without a break in style, atmosphere and consistency. And similarly in this genre there is no breach of any etiquette or convention, if the profoundest and deepest matters of life and death and the last things, the cosmic problems of the universe are mixed and intertwined with social satire, topical comment, or simple nonsensical fooling. Where everything is possible, where the imagination can move without let or hindrance, there are no disharmonies, no inconsistencies or illogicalities, provided, of course, that the tone of the narration, the tone of voice of the playwright, remains within that mysteriously delimited area which marks the boundaries of the fairytale style; that is: a directness and simplicity, a genuine naiveté of vision, without pretention, without affectation, without obvious attempts at cleverness or profundity. For this is the ultimate criterion here: we intuitively *know* whether a narration has that fairytale tone or not. Attempts have been made to define it. The fairytale has been categorised as being the *simple*, as distinct from the complex, forms of literature; it has been said that it is uni- or two-dimensional, flat, linear; and there is a good deal of truth in that too, but it is not a weakness here: The characters in the fairytale *need* no great introduction or exposition. They are simply there and we instinctively know their motivations and their natures. In this, Ionesco's work really harmonises with the fairytale tradition: do we need to know who *le nouveau locataire* is? or Jacques? or Amedée? or indeed the Bérenger of the plays in which he appears? They are immediately accessible and defined, characterised and intuitively understood, simply because they are *the given*, the basis of a whole world; they are the consciousness of the dreamer and as such immediately identified with by the audience who is taken into the dream, in exactly the same way in which the child does not need to be told what kind of psychology the youngest son of three has, who is going out into the world to see his fortune, because he or she immediately knows that the youngest and most vulnerable child is him- or herself. And the other characters then, being seen through the eyes of the self, have the simplicity and clarity of "the others" that are seen from the outside and thus appear simple and well defined.

Ionesco has achieved the immensely difficult feat of retaining the freshness and clarity of his childlike vision; hence his direct appeal to the child—which is to say our basic being, or archetypal self, before it has become encrusted and polluted with all the accidentals of the outside world. That is why we can intuitively and immediately identify with Ionesco's archetypal dreamer, his basic character, whether it is Choubert, the victim of duty; or the Professor of *The Lesson,* who, also basically, is only a naughty boy, or indeed, the girl pupil in *The Lesson* who is the archetypal schoolgirl; or Jean or *l'homme aux valises* or any of the other leading characters in Ionesco's plays and stories. In the sense that these characters are all ourselves, that they are Everyman—or rather the Everychild that hides in every man or woman—Ionesco's *oeuvre* is very close to the world of the fairytale.

And that, at least in my scale of literary values, is very high praise indeed. Let me quote Novalis once more and conclude: "Das Mährchen ist gleichsam der *Canon* der Poesie—alles poetische muss märchenhaft seyn." Which, in English, might be rendered as: "The fairytale is, as it were, the hallmark of poetry—all poetry must be *märchenhaft,* all poetry must have something of the quality of fairytales."

Stanford University

BEYOND REALISM:
IONESCO'S THEORY OF THE DRAMA

George E. Wellwarth

Few authors take the trouble to elucidate their works for the benefit of their readers or viewers; even fewer think deeply and write about the technique of their craft and the structure of their works. Eugène Ionesco is a notable exception. Among prominent modern playwrights Shaw and Brecht were other notable exceptions, but they make such an ill-assorted triad that it would perhaps be best not to pursue this rather tenuous analogy any further. In any case, the motivations were entirely different with each writer. Shaw suffered from an obsession for homiletics, his original contribution to that activity being an unique ability to practise it without instantly welling over everyone's boredom threshold. Brecht left the actual preaching to the official theorists for the most part, and concentrated principally on devising a technique that would convert the theatrical experience into a purely hortatory one. Ionesco, on the other hand, is mercifully devoid of any proselytizing intention in his writings about the theatre and about his own plays. His attempts at elucidation seem to have their origin entirely in his dissatisfaction with the writings of his critics, who, he feels, have for the most part misunderstood him and have failed to transmit to their readers any cogent appreciation of what he has tried to do. Among these misinterpreting and unappreciative critics I find to my considerable consternation I am obliged to number myself.

It is a tremendously sobering experience to read an essay by an author in which he states that one's published interpretation of his works is wrong, that one has misunderstood him completely, and, in short, that one has made an utter fool of oneself. In print. Such was my own experience recently on reading through some of Ionesco's remarks on his own plays. *The Bald Soprano,* it seems, was *not* concerned with the impossibility of communication. Communication is easy, Ionesco informs us: "It's the fact that we do understand one another that I don't understand."[1] Our problem, in fact, is an excess of communication: "Man is never really alone."[2] In another commentary, however, Ionesco, availing himself of the privilege of inconsistency—a quality for which critics rightly face condemnation—asserts that the impossibility of communication has always been one of his principal themes.[3]

What are we to make of this? Does this mean that authors in general and Ionesco in particular don't know what their own works mean? Certainly not. What it means is that while a play such as *The Bald Soprano* is obviously about the impossibility of communication—or at least about one particular aspect of that all-inclusive problem—Ionesco is rightly incensed by the *pronunciamentos* of critics who would confine his meaning so narrowly. In retrospect, taking into account the later development of his ideas, *The Bald Soprano* is about the misuse of communication, the reduction of communication to meaningless but fatally comforting slogans—a sort of deadly lullaby that perverts the function of language. But it is also about the restriction of communication to a protective encirclement of the human being with a barrier of pointless verbiage to shelter him from the isolation in chaos that he instinctively fears. Language, Ionesco affirms, is both powerless *in se* and irresistible when misused and perverted. In *The Bald Soprano* he shows language to be a device for keeping the primal fear of ultimate isolation at bay at the same time that those who use it for that purpose unconsciously affirm that isolation by extirpating meaning from language and using it as decorative verbiage to cover over the subconsciously felt fear of being in a reasonless void, of being an effect without a cause. Since everyday life, whether meaningless or not, depends for its coherence entirely on the coherence of speech patterns, it follows that if our speech patterns are meaningless, everyday life in general is meaningless *as far as we are concerned* (it is possible that to an individual the world does not appear meaningless, but since he has no means of communication with other people except through intrinsically senseless speech patterns, it follows that his view is actually nonexistent in practice). Even if the world appears ordered and coherent to *everyone,* Ionesco is saying, it is still meaningless because each person is trapped inside his own individual cell by the inadequacies of his means of communication. The play thus becomes an attack on, or a lamentation about, the state of mind that characterizes that part of mankind—the great majority—that Ionesco has variously excoriated

---

[1] Claude Bonnefoy, *Conversations with Eugène Ionesco,* trans. Jan Dawson (New York: Holt, Rinehart and Winston, 1971), p. 61.

[2] Bonnefoy, p. 61.

[3] Eugène Ionesco, *Notes and Counter Notes,* trans. Donald Watson (New York: Grove Press, 1964), p. 227.

as the *petite bourgeoisie* (interestingly, Brecht's *bête noire* too, though for different reasons) or as the world's sheep, the mindless automata programmed by cynical political opportunists, self-styled Messiahs, and deluded revolutionaries into becoming rhinoceri, still ovine in mind but physically transformed into power figures by donning armor-plate and horn (i.e., uniforms) and parroting the tag-ends of morally vicious and intellectually nugatory rhetoric. The proliferation of this linguistic scourge of platitude, rodomontade, and tautology, so characteristic of the present century and so masterfully portrayed by Ionesco in *The Lesson,* is to a considerable extent the result of the decline in intellectual respectability of religious thought, which could no longer credibly promulgate the ideational validity of a universal morality. For most people only the ritual of religion survives while its underlying myths have degenerated into fairy tales. In modern times new myths have sprung up: the myth of the all-enveloping social megamachine and the myth of the Utopia to be created by the ultimate triumph of Science over Nature. The first myth has replaced the religious moral code, the second embodies the hopes formerly placed in the Second Coming. The new religion has its rites as well, one of which is the systematic corruption of language. The slogan has replaced prayer. While prayer may have been senseless, objectively speaking, since it was a supplication of the void, it was at least a direct and specific supplication. The slogan, on the other hand, may be defined as a phrase that reassures and inspires through the removal of meaning. Man becomes united to the human machine through the ritualistic utterance of catchword phrases that have a soothing subjective meaning while relentlesssly destroying objective meaning—or, in other words, the possibility of the perception of reality.

I return, finally, after a long digression into the kind of criticism Ionesco disapproves of, to Ionesco's view of what a critic should be. Ionesco feels, rightly, that the critic is inferior to the author, that he is a parasite feasting on the author's creation. No one who is capable or feels himself capable of creating criticizes by preference. The critic is always a creator *manqué*. Unless the author creates, the critic is as helpless as a pilot fish without his whale. Ionesco objects to the kind of critic who takes it upon himself to tell the author what he should have written or how he should have written it as well as to the critic who indulges himself in flights of fancy on the subject of the author's work instead of confining himself to a sedulous application to the work itself. Ionesco conceives the ideal critic to be a sort of abecedarian New Critic and criticism to be *explication de texte* raised to the nth degree. "The bad critic," Ionesco asserts, "is the arrogant one, who wants to foist himself upon the work, and who assumes a superior attitude towards it. Instead of adopting a school-masterish approach, the critic should be the pupil of the work . . . the critic who describes the work, who follows the work . . . step by step throws light on it."[4] There is clearly no question that the critic can learn from the work with which he is dealing, but he must assimilate it and criticize it from his own point of view—which, of course, may itself have undergone change as the result of reading the work under discussion. The critic, according to Ionesco, should be "the representative of total objectivity," as the author is "the representative of total subjectivity." Both these formulations seem to me profoundly wrong, but even if we accept them it should be clear that the critic as the "representative of total objectivity" is able to view the work from the perspective of external reality, including history, while the author as the "representative of total subjectivity" attempts to *create,* to produce that which is new, to build that which can realign the perspective of reality. It is not the critic's task to diffuse light upon obscurity, to follow the work "step by step" and elucidate it. That is the crib writer's task. It is, indeed, arguably the author's task, for a work that requires a step by step exposition, that requires light to be thrown on it in order to be understood can legitimately be said to be badly written, particularly if it is a dramatic work. Ionesco, however, steadfastly insists that the critic's function is solely to explicate: "The critic must repeat the itinerary of the poet. Often the poet has moved forward in a kind of darkness or twilight. The critic covers the same ground with a lamp in his hand and illuminates the path. . . . The work must be solidly constructed. It is the critic's business to notice if the roof is leaking or the staircase likely to collapse, or whether doors are locked, thus preventing access to certain rooms, or if there are any other snags."[5] It would be simple to say that this is a description of the functions of an editor or play doctor rather than of a critic, but the implications are more serious. Ionesco is saying here, like the most extreme of the New Critics, that the work of art is an entity *in se* and that its attributes are to be referred only to itself. The criticism of a play does not, in other words, involve a consideration of its functions, intentions, ideas, or putative effect; only of its structure. Ionesco illustrates this by comparing plays to symphonies and buildings. What matters about a symphony is the way in which it is composed; the feelings that may have inspired the composer are irrelevant—and always were except to the composer himself. What matters about a building is the way in which it is built; the functional intentions of the architect are irrelevant—and always were, no matter to what use the building was put. What matters about a play is its dramatic structure and its uniqueness *qua* play. "The building and the symphony reveal nothing but the laws of architecture or the principles that govern the moving architecture of music. . . . A play too is a construction of the

---

[4] Eugène Ionesco, "The Writer and His Problems," *Encounter,* Sept. 1964, p. 9.
[5] Ionesco, "The Writer and His Problems," p. 9.

imagination which should also stand entirely in its own right; its essential nature should be such that it cannot be confused with a novel written in dialogue, or with a sermon, a lesson, a speech or an ode. . . . A play can only be precisely this and no more: different from all those other things, which are *not* plays."[6] There is a certain degree of confusion here, due partly to false analogy and partly to a faulty definition of critical function. A symphony is far too abstract to be compared to a building or a play. It is a written scenario for performance, as is a play, but it is written in a radically different form of language. The language of music is non-verbal and therefore without meaning. No one can write *about* music, as witness the witless maunderings of those so-called music critics who natter on and on about the programmatic quality of music. One can only *describe* how the work of music has been written in much the same way one can describe how a soup is made; but such descriptions can only be of interest to the music student or the culinary apprentice. A piece of music can no more *mean* than a bowl of soup can. The case is quite different with a play. A play is not a polonaise nor is it a bowl of soup. A play is written in a verbal language the concrete referents of which are inescapable, no matter how much one might like to avoid them. One *can* confine oneself to an examination of the structure of a play, but only if one is a student of playwriting or a Broadway play doctor. For all others, no matter how interested in the structure they might be, the meaning transmitted explicitly or implicitly by the words of the play is primary. When one considers a building the case is the same, although no language is involved here. The building *qua* building, the way in which it is put together—the stresses and strains, the joists and jointures, the archivolts and architraves—is of interest only to the professional student of architecture. For all others a perception of the function of the building is unavoidable. Taking a temple as an example, Ionesco tells us that he does not "need to know that this building is a place of prayer; its intended use matters little, is irrelevant, neither subtracts nor adds anything. . . . The essential characteristic of a building is simply that it is something built."[7] This way of looking at a building—and, by analogy, at a play—is unquestionably valid, if rather austere and bloodless. It is, however, calculated to attract the interest only of the abovementioned student of architecture—and then only while he is thoroughly absorbed in his slide rule, blueprint, and plumb line. For everyone else the function of a building, although admittedly not connected with its structure and having nothing to do with the building *qua* building, is obviously the principal area of interest. The temple, as Ionesco says, could be used as a Christian church, a barracks,

---

[6] Ionesco, *Notes and Counter Notes*, pp. 146–47.
[7] Ionesco, *Notes*, p. 146.

a garage, a hospital, an insane asylum or a hall for political meetings, but no matter what its current or former function, the consciousness of that function will have an effect on the visitor. An atheist may admire the structure and design of a catherdral as sincerely and extravagantly as a devout person, but the admiration will be unavoidably accompanied by repulsion and contempt as the devotee's will be by exaltation and respect. The same remark might be applied equally to T. S. Eliot's *The Cocktail Party*.

Ionesco's ideal critic would be essentially an explicator. He would be the ultimate incarnation of the New Critic, with a *soupçon* of Structuralism and a dash of Semiotics thrown into the pot. In his entirely understandable and justified reaction against critics who usurp the author's prerogative and, instead of writing about the play itself or about its subject matter, fatuously lecture on what they think the author *should* have written or against critics, equally fatuous in their self-conceit, who have developed a critical "system" and "criticize" a play by pronouncing judgement on it according to the extent to which it conforms to their standards or by sticking it into one of their classifying pigeonholes, Ionesco has gone to the other extreme of demanding that the critic refrain from criticizing. What we would get from Ionesco's ideal critic, "the representative of total objectivity," is a sedulous line by line, sentence by sentence, and even phrase by phrase commentary. A good example of this sort of thing would be Roland Barthes' widely—and incredibly—acclaimed dissection of Balzac in *S/Z*, a work that paradoxically manages to shroud Balzac's crystalline clarity in clouds of obfuscation while purportedly undertaking the entirely supererogatory task of explicating it. Heavy-handedness and pretentiousness can all too easily turn critical dissection into butchery. Indeed, the Barthian method, like the novelistic method of Butor or Robbe-Grillet, is not objective in the true sense but self-consciously and ostentatiously objective—and that is to be genuinely uninvolved, non-caring, emotionless, and, finally, hopelessly solipsistic. The true artist does not need objective explication because his identifying mark is the instinctive congruence of his vision with his audience's subconsciously apprehended truths. His function is to scrape away the dross and mildew with which social influences and linguistic perversions have encumbered the human mind so that the essential apprehensions immanent in it may effloresce.

The critic's task is to interpret, not to explicate. Interpretation is the broadening of the vistas of new thought opened up by the artist. This is a radically different process from pointing out whether a work's roof is leaking or its staircases wobbly. The true critic embodies the paradox of the unoriginal artist. He cannot initiate new metaphoric forms to transmit his thoughts. As H. L. Mencken put it, he needs the stimulus of the already created work to set him off on what should ideally be a creative commentary. He neither describes nor prescribes: he *adds*. The artist inspires and stimulates him to expand on his (the artist's) thought. The ideal criticism is a set of variations stylishly counterpointed on the artist's theme. Another way of putting it would be to say that the critic verbalizes the audience's instinctive response to the artist's creation. The critic who remains totally objective and does nothing but annotate, who writes a gloss on the body of the work and not on its soul, fails in his responsibility to the artist, to the audience, and to the craft of criticism itself.

Eugène Ionesco's contributions to the art of the drama are both thematic and structural. Thematically, as we shall see, he has attempted to write drama that portrays a reality that lies beyond our immediate consciousness, that brings to the surface a deeply buried and instinctively suppressed inner awareness. Structurally, he has devised a theatrical method that uses the artistic resources peculiar to the theatre in order more clearly and cogently to encapsulate his thematic intentions. The structural innovation characteristic of Ionesco's drama is the use of a dramatic symbol as a linchpin holding all the elements of the play, both theatrical and philosophical, together, This innovation consists of a fine distinction that involves some radical changes in the basic structure of dramatic writing. Historically, a play has been defined by its plot; that is to say, a play has always been an animated story told in theatrical terms. Theatrical terms may be defined as the physical appurtenances of the stage—scenery, costumes, lighting, special effects—and the contribution of the actor, which consists in his incorporating a set of mannerisms supposedly typifying the psychological essence of a character other than himself. By a curious coincidence, probably traceable to Aristotle's unfortunate use of the term *mimesis* and the uncritical acceptance of "imitation" as its translation, actors throughout the ages have consistently preened themselve on the "realism" of their approach to a role. This seemingly endless intensification of realism, with each successive generation of actors congratulating itself on producing a closer approximation of life off the stage as if the climactic moment toward which all art was moving would be attained with the invention of the newsreel camera, the tape recorder, and the "feelie" movies that Aldous Huxley imagined in one of his more blackly prophetic moments in *Brave New World,* climaxed in the staging methods of André Antoine at the Théâtre Libre and the acting methods of Constantin Stanislavski at the Moscow Art Theatre. These methods still constitute the controlling ground drone on which variations of dubious originality are embroidered by the actors and directors of the popular theatre today. Similarly, the popular theatre is still dominated by the writing methods appropriate to the theatrical methods of "realism," to wit, a story presumably credible in real life terms told in a linear manner. Aristotle's sententious remark that a story must have a beginning, a middle, and an end is still looked upon as a profundity by the present generation of professional theatre people. This is not to say that stories in linear progression animated for the stage are necessarily bad. It is to say that such stories are in the profoundest sense untheatrical. They are adaptations into theatrical terms of narratives. For narratives—stories, novels, epic poems—linear progressive structure is essentially suitable; but it has nothing to do with the theatre. Adaptations are compromises—sidesteppings of the true issue, which is the finding of the structure adequate to the form. To retell a story in theatrical terms using the linear progressive structure that is so suitable to the narrative form is to ignore the nature of the theatre and to force it on to the Procrustean bed of another and totally unrelated form. What differentiates the theatre from other forms is that it can do what these other forms cannot. That essential characteristic of the theatre is the ability to encapsulate. The error that has always been embedded in most dramatic writing is the assumption that theatre is animated narrative when it is in fact animated poetry. Narrative language is linear and descriptive; but description needs to be animated only for those whose imagination is enfeebled to the point of semi-paralytic listlessness. Linear structure condemns the theatre to an inevitably inadequate reproduction of the temporal dimension to which reality is bound. Poetic language, on the other hand, is timeless and symbolic. A symbol is a linguistic nucleus that radiates meaning. Where the narrative is leisurely and expansive, the poem and the play are forced by their form to have a compressive structure and to rely on suggestion rather than on information. The spectator cannot pause to examine the playwright's ideas during the play. The playwright must therefore plant in his mind the seeds of ideas that will take root and flower long after the play is over. The most effective way to do this is through the use of the dramatic symbol, which is simply the poetic symbol made concrete. The structure of narrative may be compared to a long string with a series of knots in it; that of the poem or play to a molecular nucleus radiating streams of energy. The reader of the narrative can pull himself along the line knot by knot and thus gradually perceive the author's intent. The reader of the poem or spectator at the play must perceive the concentrated set of meanings contained in the nucleus instantly or lose them altogether. (The reader of the poem or play can, of course, doggedly read and re-read until he has got the meaning, but the spectator has only that one chance, no normal theatre-goer being willing to go to a play night after night until he is satisfied he has understood it.) None of this is intended to suggest that the successful spectator must be a person of inherently superior intelligence. Quite the contrary. The theatre must speak to the illiterate as easily as to the literate, and consequently it is the playwright who must have technical skills superior to those of the narrator.

It was Ibsen who devised the most trenchant dramatic symbol that the stage has seen with Peer Gynt's onion. When Ibsen used the onion to symbolize Peer Gynt's essence, he created an instantly comprehensible philosophical nucleus whose ramifications continue to permeate the theatre, prefiguring the whole concept of mechanistic man in Meyerhold's Constructivist theatre, of man as a function of socio-economic forces in much of Brecht's theatre, and of man as a helpless puppet in the cosmically deterministic theatre of Absurdism. In the modern philosophical drama man is always a function of something else, a series of façades desperately covering up a barely sensed void: all husk and no core, like Peer Gynt's onion.

Ionesco's thematic contribution to the art of the drama consists in an attempt to break away from realism and penetrate to an inner reality, to a reality that, as he puts it, lies somewhere beyond. Ever since Freud and Jung, both of whom have profoundly influenced Ionesco, it has become evident that the last and most inscrutable frontier lies within man. Within us, we have learned, repose the palisaded bastions of the unconscious mind from which the motivations that control the shadow play of surface reality leak out. The playwright's task is to make the unconscious conscious, to make the intangible concrete. A work of art, Ionesco asserts, "is above all an adventure of the mind."[8] That adventure is the search for "essential fundamental truths" and is aborted by those who confine their search to the surface, or social, reality: "they try, stupidly and desperately, to shackle and imprison us within the blind walls of the narrowest kind of realism, calling it life when it is really death, and light of day when it is really the shades of night. . . . I . . . maintain that it is not our monotonous everyday lives but our dreams and imagination . . . that contain and reveal essential and fundamental truths."[9] Art thus becomes a form of revelation showing what is beyond rational thought, which Ionesco looks upon as a barrier that man throws up—indeed, spends his whole life assiduously constructing and then ornamenting until it becomes a kind of rococo grotesque, in order to obscure the hard facts of his existence: "I believe that the social crust and discursive thought conceal man from himself and cut him off from his most repressed desires, his most

---

[8] Ionesco, *Notes*, p. 149.
[9] Ionesco, *Notes*, p. 150.

essential needs, his myths, his indisputable anguish, his most secret reality and dreams."[10] The principal preoccupation under that façade that discursive thought and the social crust desperately try to cover up is the knowledge of mortality. That knowledge is a knowledge that we both do and do not have, for while the consciousness of his finitude divides man from animal as much as the ability to reason in abstractions, it is also true that "nonexistence is inconceivable."[11] Only the theatre has the power to animate this knowledge and make it capable of being perceived since description and discussion can only give the *illusion* of even an approach to its understanding. It must be perceived instantly and instinctively, with the shock of unwelcome recognition or not at all. To subject the concept of death to the operations of discursive thought is, paradoxically, to shield ourselves from the consciousness of it. There can be no apperception of horror, only a total submersion in it and yet, as one of Ionesco's critics has put it, ". . . la mort. . . . C'est le seul problème humain sérieux . . . . nous sommes destinés à la mort et nous haïssons de mourir. . . . le roi se meurt, et ce roi, c'est nous-mêmes."[12] It is we ourselves who cry out in that marvellously poignant speech of Bérenger's in which he begs for the spurious immortality of remembrance though he knows that his own death, the death of each one of us, is the extinction of the whole universe that we carry *in petto:*

> Without me, without me. They'll laugh, they'll joke, they'll dance on my grave. I will never have existed. Ah, let them remember me. Let them weep, let them despair. Let them perpetuate my memory in all the history books. Let everyone know my life by heart. Let everyone re-live it. Let the students and the scholars have no other subject of study but me, my kingdom, my exploits. Let them burn every other book, let them destroy all the statues, let them put mine in all the public places. My image in all the ministries, all the police stations, all the internal revenue offices, all the hospitals. Let them name all the airplanes, all the ships, all the motor cars, and all the push-carts after me. Let all the other kings, warriors, poets, tenors, and philosophers be forgotten and let there be no one but me in everyone's mind. One single baptismal name, one single family name for everyone. Let them learn to read by spelling out my name: B—é—Bé, Bérenger. Let me be on the images and on all the millions of crosses in all the churches. Let them say Masses for me, let me be the Host. . . . Let them call on me for ever and ever, let them pray to me, let them implore me.[13]

[10]Ionesco, *Notes,* pp. 233–34.
[11]Leonard Pronko, *Eugène Ionesco* (New York: Columbia University Press, 1965), p. 40.
[12]Robert Abirached, "Ionesco et l'Obession de la Mort," *Etudes,* 317 (1963), p. 88.
[13]Eugène Ionesco, *Le roi se meurt* (Paris: Gallimard, 1963), pp. 79–80. Translation mine.

In this speech, and in others in the same play, Ionesco touches on one of the profound truths of our existence: that reality as we know it, the particular reality of the essential self and the general reality of universal perception—whatever it may be in each particular case—is extinguished with the death of each individual mind *as far as that individual mind is concerned*. And that, of course, is all that matters to anyone. Ionesco has perfectly captured here the artist's essential mission: to use his power of creation, which is the concretization of his free flow of thought into universally meaningful images and metaphors, in order to evoke hitherto unsuspected correspondences in the recipient minds for which he writes.

In *The Lesson*, for example, while there is a clearly marked primary sociopolitical level of meaning in the depiction of the totalitarian mind as owing its dehumanization and murderousness to the perversion of language, there is also a more generalized level on which the play is about life and death without any temporal references. The Pupil, with her naive thirst for total knowledge and her instictive proficiency in addition and multiplication, is a personification of the life impulse, as the Professor, with his hysterically obsessive emphasis on subtraction and disintegration, personifies both death as an irresistible force and the Freudian death wish. In other plays Ionesco skilfully uses the seemingly endless proliferation of matter as a death symbol. Matter represents mindlessness, which is death; and it represents inertia, which is death. That mindlessness and inertia have a powerful attraction for the human being, in whom the desire to give up, not bother, to sleep forever is always latent as he is always under the spell of the universal death wish. We can see Ionesco's adaptation of the proliferation of matter as an avatar of the universal death wish in the New Tenant's self-entombment as he retreats into a protective womb of artificial matter to lead a death-in-life, barricaded from thought and feeling. In *Amédée* the constant growth of the dead body serves the same purpose. Amédée and his wife are gradually pushed further into a more and more restricted living space by the constantly swelling body, a flaccid, spongy malignancy that mirrors the mushrooms that grow on the walls of the tomb-like apartment where Amédée drags out an existence that is more a life-in-death than anything else. The ascent of Amédée and the body, which turns into a balloon and lifts him up into the sky, is a burlesque of the traditional ascent to Paradise, an ironic *Himmelfahrt* of the damned. The burlesque and irony should not mask from us the essential despair of the play's conclusion. Amédée and the dead man float happily—and amusingly—into the celestial regions, thoughtfully scattering such earthly dross as shoes and cigarettes as they go; but what we are really witnessing is the extinction of a typical human being who has never really lived. The expanding body that Amedée rides to eternal oblivion is the death wish he has nurtured in himself all his life. As it grew it encroached ever more on his living space and on his consciousness of himself as a living essence. Like the New Tenant, like the old couple in the *The Chairs,* like Bérenger in *The Killer* who seeks out and helplessly succumbs to his subconscious death wish, Amedée blights his life by pursuing death and casting himself into its corrosive embrace. Not until we come to the Bérenger of *Rhinoceros* do we get the antidote to this attitude. This Bérenger is a dramatic rendition of the Camusian *homme révolté* who refuses instinctively —not rationally—to succumb to the most overpowering of all temptations, represented in his play by the herd-like abandonment of the self opted for by the rhinoceros-men. For Ionesco the willing submersion in a half-life, in a life that flees the consciousness of self and is thus a death-in-life, is typified by the *petit bourgeois:* "The petit bourgeois is for me a man of fixed ideas, one who turns up at every period in every society: a conformist, a man who adopts the thought patterns (or the principal ideology) of whatever society he happens to belong to and stops asking questions . . . the petit bourgeois is the person who has forgotten the archetype and is absorbed in the stereotype."[14] The discovery of forgotten archetypes, Ionesco goes on to say in the same passage, "changeless but expressed in a new way," is the function of the true creative artist. To sink from archetype to stereotype is to lose one's essence as a living being. When it is multiplied by a factor representing the majority of the population, as in *Rhinoceros,* the whole state becomes totalitarian, or, to put it in Ionesco's terms, the population succumbs to a mass death wish.

There is a complementary theme in Ionesco's work to the theme of the omnipresence of death. Throughout his work, in the non-dramatic writings as well as in the dramatic, there are poignant images and evocations of the beauty and joyousness of life. The archetype whose re-creation is the artist's function "is always young" and is the avatar of life. The characteristic sign of the archetype is the boundless and insatiable longing for life, which involves the courage to create and assert one's self. This courage is preserved only in a few, the few who have the strength to stand off from the herd and refuse to be submerged into a stereotype. The rest, worn down by hopelessness or by the blandishments of religion, whether transcendental or political, look on life as the worst imaginable horror and flee from the harshness that goes with a sense of the monadic uniqueness of the self to the safety residing in a shapeless multiplication of undifferentiated selves. For Ionesco, to be alone, an archetype "always young," is not only to be defiantly independent like the

---

[14] Ionesco, *Notes,* p. 131.

Bérenger of *Rhinoceros*. It involves a purely personal as well as a social level. It means also to have an æsthetic sense of oneself and of one's relation to life. It means to be conscious in the fullest sense, to indulge in a sensuously wondering contemplation of the physical lambency and mental complexity—a complexity that must be contemplated *in se* and cannot be unraveled—of existence; an existence apprehended as it strikes our senses as an endlessly variegated shifting pattern not necessarily imbued with an analyzable meaning.

Ionesco's preoccupation with human temporality as expressed in his emphasis on the refulgence of life and the adumbration of death is an intensely individualistic statement that evokes an empathetic response in audiences lacking the assurance that comes with a belief in a beneficent transcendency. The modern playwright, in short, can no longer partake of the cosmic complacency that his predecessors shared with their audiences. Ionesco has himself put the modern playwright-as-thinker's position succinctly enough: "My impression is that there is no reason for anything and that we are driven on by some incomprehensible force. Nothing has any reason. Everything within oneself is debatable; that which is eternal . . . is irrefutable. Irrefutable and, for me, devoid of any reason for existing or not existing."[15] The viewpoint expressed here by Ionesco may be described as being quintessentially modern. Prior to the 20th century it would have been virtually impossible, and prior to the second half of the century highly unlikely. It is not, or course, peculiar to Ionesco. Quite the contrary: contemporary dramatic and philosophical thought might arguably be said to be an elaboration, metaphoric in the former case and discursive in the latter, of the intellectual position asserted in the statement.

That Ionesco subscribes to the nihilistic way of thinking implied in his statement there can be no doubt. But his adherence to it is uneasy, for he has not entirely given up. "Reality," he has said, "lies somewhere beyond"; and his dramas attempt to pierce the map and show the impenetrable darkness of the void that lurks behind it. Tragedy for modern man is the consciousness of death, of the immanence of its possibility; it is the distillation into dramatic form of the emotionally unbearable and the intellectually insoluble. There are only questions in life, no answers: "No final solutions . . . to ask oneself a question without supplying an answer is truer than not asking oneself questions at all."[16] But he is not completely metaphysical, for he is concerned with the quality of life as it is lived as well. In his one thoroughly committed play, *Rhinoceros,* he writes passionately of the need for existential independence within the context of temporal life. The nobility of Bérenger lies in his

---

[15] Ionesco, "The Writer and His Problems," p. 7.
[16] Ionesco, "The Writer and His Problems," p. 6.

instinctive knowledge that ". . . an un-workable solution one has found for oneself is infinitely more valuable than a ready-made ideology that stops men from thinking . . . [that] a free man should pull himself out of vacuity on his own, by his own efforts and not by the efforts of other people."[17] In *Rhinoceros,* surely one of the supreme plays of the modern theatre, he foreshadows a theme that is only now in the process of becoming one of the most important in modern drama. Its importance was stated and its nature defined in an uncannily prescient and all too little known essay by Paul Valéry in 1925:

> The machine rules. Human life is rigorously controlled by it, dominated by the terribly precise will of mechanisms. . . . The most redoubtable machines, perhaps, are not those that revolve or run, to transport or transform matter or energy. There are other kinds, not built of copper or steel but of narrowly specialized individuals: I refer to organizations, those administrative machines constructed in imitation of the impersonal aspects of the mind.
>
> Civilization is measured by the increasing size and number of such structures. They may be likened to huge human beings, barely conscious, hardly able to feel at all, but endowed to excess with all the elementary and regular functions of an inordinately over-sized nervous system. . . . Each of us is a cog in one of these groups, or rather we belong to several different groups at once, surrendering to each of them a part of our self-ownership, and taking from each a part of our social definition and our license to exist. We are all citizens, soldiers, taxpayers, men of a certain trade, supporters of a certain party, adherents of a certain religion, members of a certain organization, a certain club. . . . Among living intellects, some spend themselves in serving the machine, others in building it, others in inventing or planning a more powerful type; a final category of intellects spend themselves in trying to escape its domination. These rebellious minds feel with a shudder that the once complete and autonomous *whole* that was the soul of ancient man is now becoming some inferior kind of *daemon* that wishes only to collaborate, to join the crowd, to find security in being dependent and happiness in a closed system that will be all the more closed as man makes it more closely suited to man.[18]

To live in the kind of closed system that Valéry forsaw is to live like a sheep if the system allows one to live quiescent and harmless, like a rhinoceros if it does not; but in either case it is to live life as a makeshift substitute for

---

[17] Ionesco, *Notes,* pp. 210–11.
[18] Paul Valéry, *History and Politics,* trans. Denise Folliot and Jackson Mathews (New York: Pantheon Books, 1962), pp. 77–80.

death. In his other plays Ionesco touches on this theme frequently while confronting his overriding preoccupation: the tenuousness of life and the substantiality of death. He has set himself the task of evoking a consciousness in his audiences of their relationship to the modern concept of the universe.[19]

The new aesthetics of the theatre that Ionesco has formulated postulates that theatre must ultimately be an animated distillation of the quintessence of existence, a brooding and suffering contemplation of the horror of death and a necessarily simultaneous celebration of the radiance of life.

State University of New York at Binghamton.

---

[19] A relationship to the universe is, of course, impossible since it is unknown and probably unknowable; one can only have a relationship to a *concept* of the universe.

THE THEATRE OF IONESCO:
THE GHOST AND PRIMAL DIALOGUE

Robert W. Corrigan

In the late 1960's—when, alas, Eugène Ionesco didn't figure very prominently in our minds—both the arts and the world at large were in a state of turmoil. Looking back at that period from today's equally disturbed but more placid vantage point, we see that it was a time of real revolution. This was particularly true of the theatre. It was the era of happenings, participatory performance, and group grope. Plays moved off the stage out into the streets and everyone was a performing self. In short, everything was breaking down and breaking out. All of life seemed to have been theatricalized and the riots were a ritual madness. One thinks, for instance, of the trial of the Chicago 7, which was certainly more an amalgam of Brecht, Artaud, Genet, and Ionesco than it was a court of law. The theatre, like all of the other arts, was in a state of metamorphosis. Most of us thought that—like Shakespeare's players—it was replenishing itself; although others saw it only as some kind of mad St. Vitus dance. But the point is, that at this turbulent time we felt we knew the answers. We had seen the rottenness at the core of the system and knew it for what it was. We were going to save the world by changing it, and the theatre and the other arts would be our weapons. We would stop the Vietnam war; overthrow the authorities for whom we had nothing but contempt; and we would create new communites which would provide the energizing spirit for the new "greening of America."

It turns out that Ionesco was telling us how silly we were—but we weren't listening. The aesthetic of direct experience turned out to be deaestheticizing. The arts as a political weapon proved impotent. It was, to use the title of a book describing the period, *A Time of Illusion*.[1] Looking back, Watergate was

---

[1] Jonathan Schell, *A Time of Illusion* (New York: Knopf, 1976).

the grotesque apotheosis of the Theatre of the Absurd. It revealed as much about the theatre and those of us working in it, as it did about the American people and the Nixon administration. We, too, experienced a "Watergate of the Spirit."

The politicalizing of the theatre in the 1960's may have been shortlived and of dubious aesthetic distinction, but it did have a liberating spirit. It forced the theatre to redefine itself. It brought into question—from a new and radical perspective—the always tricky relationship between art and life that exists in the theatre. And this forced us to ask some basic questions—as if for the first time: Questions about the nature of theatre. Questions, which if grappled with, will certainly enlarge our understanding of the theatrical event.

The opening lines of Shakespeare's *Hamlet* are:

> Who's there?
> Nay, answer me. Stand and unfold yourself.

Who really is up there on that and every stage? And who is it out there in the auditorium, that crowd transformed into an audience? (Could it be true, as Hamlet insists it is, that we are "guilty creatures sitting at a play"?) And what is being unfolded on the stage? We know it is unlike the world as we usually experience it, but just what kind of "world" is it that is revealed to us each time a theatrical performance takes place? Perhaps the theatre itself can provide some answers. Human beings give definition to their experience with the words they use. Therefore some of the words that have been used to define the theatrical experience will provide us with clues to some answers.

Let us begin with the word "theatre" itself. Theatre is derived from the Greek word *theatron* and it means "a seeing place where one comes to possess a new knowledge" (our words "theatre" and "theory" are derived from the same source). But what was being looked at is that the source of this new knowledge? That which took place in "the orchestra" or the "place for dancers." Knowing this would be of only slight historical significance if we were not to realize that the word "orchestra" is derived from a combination of an archaic Greek word, *ornynai*, meaning "to rise" in the sense of "to return from the dead" or "to come back to life" and the Sanskrit word, *rghayati*, meaning "the ravings, rages, and tremblings of one in a trance." This derivation is confirmed by the fact that those who danced in the orchestra in the ritual dances which eventually evolved into the Greek tragedies were referred to as *korybantes* (dancers in a state of ecstasy or divine madness) or *maenads* (madwomen who participated in the ritual mysteries). Thus it is that the earliest theatrical experience in Greece involved coming back to life from another world through some form of trance activity, and it is not just a quirk of history that in the Western world actors are often referred to as "thespians" after Thespis, the generic name of those inspired singer-dancers who "got out of themselves" in order to go the world of the gods to be possessed by them and then come back embodying them. Such was the theatre of Dionysus, the demonic god whom we associate with the theatrical muse. It was concerned with sacrifice and rebirth, limitation and transcendence; its mode was one of almost abandoned madness; it made manifest the darkest mysteries residing in the deep and tangled root of human nature.

However, the significance of this will become more apparent if we move forward into history to the time when theatre as an art form can be clearly distinguished from ritual dance. The Greek word for actor is hyprocrite, or "one who answers." The first actor was separated from the chorus in order to answer questions about the world of the gods. As the envoy from this other world he was set apart, someone different; yet he was also a member of the Chorus pretending to be someone else. Hence the connotations of dissembling and insincerity which gradually come to be associated with the word hyprocrite. But from the beginning the actor was someone who represented, spoke for, and was posessed by another realm of reality. A similar view of the actor was held by the ancient Etruscans whose word for actor was *hister*. (The original root for such words as histrionic, hysteria, and hysterectomy, and we shall see presently that it is no accident that acting, other worldness, and trance are linked etymologically to the womb.) The actor was one who journeyed to another world by getting outside of himself through some form of trance. And if we were to examine the origins of acting in every known primitive culture we would discover the same associations applied. Even today in France the word for the theatre or movie star is "vedette," a word that has its origins in possession cults and means "one who casts a spell over us." All of these meanings are confirmed when we consider the word *rehearsal*. Everyone knows that rehearsal is the essential process of preparing for almost every theatrical productionn but few people know that the word is derived from an old French word, *rehercier,* which means "to harrow again." Originally, "to harrow" meant to descend to the underworld in order to bring back the souls that reside there. Finally, not too long ago in *Time* Magazine, Elizabeth Ashley described the acting process as: "You transcend to the character, and she takes you through her journey. What you seek is to be possessed."

I don't go through these derivations of theatre words because of some kind of antiquarian preoccupation. But rather to point out that from its beginnings— and this is true of every culture—the theatre involves the making manifest of another world, what Ionesco calls an independent universe. A universe that we have a tremendous need to be in touch with; but also one which produces a compelling distrust and fear within us. And this is true every time we go to the theatre. The world that unfolds on the stage, no matter how realistic it may appear, is unlike any world we know; yet it is one which all humankind partakes in. There is something strange about the whole experience, and this uncanny strangeness and the contradictions and the ambivalent responses that it produces within us, is at the heart of the theatrical event.

The theatre is a manifestation of another world. Its concern is with mystery—those mysteries that haunt our consciousness. That mystery which Ionesco believes is ultimately beneath all of our "whys." That is what attracts us and repels us about theatre. It shows that which should not be seen—yet we must see it. It speaks the unspeakable—which we nonetheles must hear. The player plays (*ludere*) by making an illusion (*il-ludere*) which is a mockery of the playing and also a mockery of our own lives as we watch the playing. The theatre is a manifestation of mystery. This is its central concern.

This is Ioneco's central concern as well. His writings are shot full of phrases such as:

. . . "I am concererned with the fundamental mysteries which haunt human consciousness."[2]

. . . "Theatre is the revelation of something that was hidden."[3]

. . . "At the bottom of all our 'whys' is ultimately a mystery."[4]

However, it is clear that Ionesco knows that theatre is concerned with mystery in a very special way; and his plays—and especially all of those since *The Killer*—are evidence of this. Unlike myth and ritual which are similar, but finally are radically different from the theatre, it is not primarily concerned with cosmic mysteries: How did the world get here? What is the source of life? Why do the powerful forces of nature operate the way they do? Rather, theatre is concerned with the mysteries of self—the mysteries of being and identity, of loss and otherness, and why we do what we do. This explains why at the root of every lasting play there is a husband and wife, a mother and father, brothers, sisters, and sweethearts, parents and children, lovers, friends, and enemies—and their surrogates. Ioneco's plays confirm this. In Greek drama, it is the House of Atreus and the House of Laius. The genius of Shakespeare was his ability to express several levels of experience simultaneously, but at the heart of each of his plays is the family: Hamlet, Lear,

[2] Eugène Ionesco, *Present Past, Past Present*, trans. Helen Lane (New York: Grove Press, 1971), p. 90.

[3] Claude Bonnefoy, *Conversations with Eugène Ionesco*, trans. Jan Dawson (New York: Holt, Rinehart, and Winston, 1966), p. 143.

[4] Eugène Ionesco, *Fragments of a Journal*, trans. Jean Stewart (New York: Grove Press, 1968), p. 40.

Macbeth, Othello. The same thing is true of the plays of Racine, Ibsen, Chekhov, and Brecht. Even in Beckett's plays, it is the presence of the family's absence which gives the play its energizing force. The theatre's special power is to make manifest familial dead who continue to live with us. This, I believe, explains its unique and uncanny nature. And mention of the "uncanny" in this context cannot help but remind me of Freud's esay on the subject, which it might be helpful for me to introduce here since I believe it points right to the center of Ionesco's theatre.

Freud begins his essay on "The Uncanny" with an exhaustive study of the word's etymology and shows how in every language the uncanny relates to the unfamiliar. The German word is *"unheimlich."* It is the negative of absence of "belonging to the home" and hence the intimate and familiar. From this base, Freud says: "The uncanny is that class of the terrifying which leads back to something long known to us, once very familiar but now unfamiliar."[5] But it is also related to repression: "Everything is uncanny that ought to have remained hidden and secret, and yet comes to light."[6] He combines these ideas thus: "The Uncanny is in reality nothing new or foreign, but something familiar and old-established in the mind that has been estranged only by the process of repression."[7] The "uncanny" connotes the haunted and ghostly. It is related to the terrors of fairy tales, primitive animism, and especially the primitive's fear of the dead and the inanimate. But, finally, it goes back: "to that stage when the ego was not yet sharply differentiated from the external world and from other persons."[8] The source of the uncanny is the womb. It goes back to our first home where each of us dwelt "once upon a time"—in the beginning, and it manifests itself when we become conscious of our separation from the primal home. Thus Freud concludes:

> An uncanny experience occurs either when repressed infantile complexes have been revived by some impression, or when the primitive beliefs we have surmounted seem once more to be confirmed. . . . (and) these two classes of uncanny experience are not always sharply distinguishable.[9]

However, for our discussion, one of the most remarkable things about the essay is Freud's point that we experience the uncanny as animate and inanimate at the same time, Just, I might add, as we experience the mask. It is as if we

---

[5] Sigmund Freud, *Collected Papers,* trans. Joan Riviere, Vol. IV (New York: Basic Books, 1959), p. 369.
[6] Freud, p. 376.
[7] Freud, p. 394.
[8] Freud, p. 402.
[9] Freud, p. 403.

witness ourselves in a mirror, although I like Ionesco's expression (especiallly its combination of pronouns) of it better: "To recapture our past is to look at oneself as if I were someone looking at his brother."[10] In short, everything about our experience of the uncanny is related to doubleness. Freud even goes so far as to describe this experience as being able to stand outside of ourselves in order to observe ourselves in the process of acting.

Perhaps now we can see how directly Freud's observations relate to our experience of the theatre. Our experience of the uncanny in life is very similar to what we experience in theatre. I would go even further and say that the theatre's motive force has its origins in this experience, and that its chief purpose has always been to provide an occasion in which we can deal with the ghosts that haunt us in safe and creative ways. Psychologists tell us that these ghosts have their origins in our first consciousness of otherness. They go back to that moment of anguish when the infant becomes conscious of itself as a separate entity, when it becomes aware of the gulf between the self and the source of life. I believe it is significant that psychologists refer to our reaction to this condition as a "ghost reaction," and also that they note that at just this moment in our development, a reciprocal pattern of action and response must be established if life is to continue, and this reciprocity is called "primal dialogue." By primal dialogue they don't mean talking, but rather a pattern of action and response that involves all the senses. Its essential quality is reciprocity; the child must experience real interaction—first with the mother and then with others—if it is to deal with the anxieties of separateness. Indeed, if that dynamic and ongoing connection is not established and maintained, it is questionable if life can continue. It is what Ionesco meant when he wrote: "The house that's real for you is the one you had with your mother."[11] The governing impulse of all primal dialogue is to restore that state of total oneness we experienced as infants. Each of us yearns to return to a condition without tension where all of the conflicts of otherness have been removed. However, this desire to return to an eternal childhood, while understandably attractive, can only be realized in death. Nonetheless, in the meantime that sense of separation and loss which we find difficult to bear drives us to forms that will fulfill this longing. We want a world where the threat of otherness has been removed. We want a world where otherness doesn't exist. We want a world where we can experience primal dialogue without also experiencing the fear that that dialogue carries with it.

Of all human activities the theatre comes closest to meeting these con-

---

[10] Ionesco, *Present Past*, p. 25.
[11] Quoted by Rosette Lamont in her study in this volume, p. 108.

ditions. It is a place in which we are allowed to experience anxiety and aggression, conflict and fantasy without having to fear the consequences of such experiences. Moreover, the theatre not only has the capacity to make present the ghosts which haunt us without an element of threat, but also—and of equal importance—it is a place where that cycle of action and response which I've just referred to as "primal dialogue" can and must be fulfilled. It structures an opportunity for primal dialogue between the actors and the audience. My point is that every time we go to the theatre we enter into a situation where those anxieties provoked by our never-resolved childhood confrontations with both separation and loss, strangeness and inanimacy, come back to haunt us. It is a confrontation with the "doubleness" of our being.

No one is more aware of "doubleness"—both in human nature and in the theatre—than Eugène Ionesco. He says he is attracted to the theatre because in both its form *and* its means it has always celebrated the contradictions of doubleness. And I think it is no accident that this contradiction is incorporated in the emblem by which the theatre has always and everywhere been identified—the mask. The mask is the emblem of our condition of otherness. In its mysterious way it embodies and gives life to all of the ghosts that haunt us. In wearing the mask we conquer our ghost by becoming it. The guise of someone other points to the self within. We become strange to master strangeness. This face that is not a face embodies the power of the other world of mystery which the theatre makes present for us. It also evokes the excitement, awe, and fear that we feel when we experience that presence. The theatre is a masking and unmasking of another world. A world that is more and less real, more liberating and more frightening, more powerful and more vulnerable, that the realm of our ordinary experience.

One of the most eloquent explanations of the power of the mask and why it is such an appropriate emblem for the theatre was written by Ionesco's colleague, Jean-Louis Barrault in his essay "How The Drama is Born Within Us:"

> The human face reflects the human soul and the mysterious likes which might connect a human being with the supernatural world. From his earliest childhood man likes to impersonate parts, and to impersonate somebody is to change face; it is to adopt somebody else's face. The attempt to wear another man's face aims at trying to get out of oneself, and in that line of thought, the action of placing on one's face the mask of another face is something far more striking and stimulating than the act of making up to play a given part. A mask confers upon a given expression the maximum of intensity together with an impression of absence. A mask expresses at the same time the maximum of life and the maximum of death; it partakes

of the visible and the invisible, of the apparent and absolute. The mask exteriorizes a deep aspect of life, and in so doing, it helps to rediscover instinct. This kind of simultaneous exteriorization of the inner and outer aspects of life, of the relative and of the absolute, of life and death, makes it possible to reach through incantation a better contact with the audience.[12]

Barrault's description of the mask expresses the governing spirit and energy of Ionesco's theatre. And this, I believe, explains why his plays are such a powerful challenge and such a deeply satisfying experience for actors and audiences alike.

Let me conclude this section of my discussion, by saying that I believe it is precisely because the theatre's chief function is to make present mystery, that it evokes such ambivalent responses within us. Furthermore, the complexity of these responses is compounded by the very nature of the theatrical medium itself. Unlike the other arts, which communicate through inanimate or abstract means (or some combination of them), the theatre does so primarily through living human beings—human beings as actors who confront *and* present mystery at the same time. Human beings who are more and less than human. Human beings whose feelings and responses are real and not real. Just as we go to the theatre as a way of confronting and dealing with those mysteries which haunt us, so the theatre deals with them in ways that are haunting. That is why I say that at the heart of every play is a ghost. It is the real subject of every play, and that ghost must be made manifest in performance. If it doesn't appear there is no performance. The challenge to every performer: to make present an absence.

It is the absence which is at the center of Ionesco's theatre. His primal drama is one of abandonment and dispossession. He is obsessed by Freud's "*unheimlich*." Ionesco says in "Why do I write?:"

> What I am really looking for is a world that is virgin again, the paradisiacal light of childhood, that glory of the first day, a glory that is untarnished, an immaculate universe which will appear before me as though it has only just been born. It is as if I wanted to witness the creation of the world before the Fall: a happening I try to recreate by travelling back through History within myself; or by inventing characters who are variations of myself or like other people who

---

[12] Jean-Louis Barrault, *The Theatre of Jean-Louis Barrault* (New York: Hill and Wang, 1961), p. 76–77.

resemble me, all searching, consciously or not, for Absolute Light. . . . Childhood and Light come together and are identified in my mind. [13]

Or again in *Present Past-Past Present:*

Childhood is the world of miracle or magic: it is as if creation rose luminously out of the night, all new and fresh and astonishing. . . . To be driven from childhood is to be driven from paradise, it is to be adult.[14]

Or one more time—this from *Fragments of a Journal:*

Childhood is the world of miracle and wonder: as if creation rose, bathed in light, out of the darkness, utterly new and fresh and astonishing. The end of childhood is when things cease to astonish us. When the world seems familiar, when one has got used to existence, one has become adult. The brave new world, the wonderland has grown trite and commonplace. That was our true Paradise, that was how the world was on the firt day. Losing one's childhood means losing Paradise, becoming adult. You retain the memory, the longing for a present, a presentness, a plenitude that you try to recover by all possible means; to recover it, or to compensate for it.[15]

In everything he writes, Ionesco reveals an obsessed yearning to return to the lost Eden of his childhood. In fact, Martin Esslin even goes so far as to say that "Ionesco's characters are the every child that resides in Everyman." But this kind of obsession is complicated. It is filled with an acknowledged nostalgia, and it is pervaded by a sense of sadness and loss. But it is *also* driven by an overwhelming and tormented anger. The anger which each of us feels because we have been expelled from the paradise of childhood. The anger that is provoked by the recognition of our condition of otherness. This points to a dominant characteristic of Ionesco's plays. Namely, the relationship of this anger to the language of his dramas.

When we were first dealing with Ionesco's theatre twenty-five years ago, we talked of language getting out of control in *The Lesson.* We noted the inanimacy of the language of cliché in *The Bald Soprano.* We made a big thing of saying that the apparent dislocations of language in his plays was Ionesco's way of expressing our central human disasters. While all of this was true, it was also too simple. It did not take into account the creative/

---

[13] Eugène Ionesco, "Why do I write?" in *Antidotes* (Paris: Gallimard, 1977), p. 316.
[14] Ionesco, *Present Past*, p. 174.
[15] Ionesco, *Fragments of a Journal*, p. 40.

destructive nature of theatrical language, nor that inseparable relationship between language and violence which has become so apparent in Ionesco's more recent plays. On the one hand, language is the life of his drama; it is also, as Jan Kott observed, his ultimate weapon against death. Words may lie, hide, and mask, but the artist's unique power resides in his ability to transform them so as to express the inexpressible. Through language the dramatist gives form to mystery. Through language he discovers mystery, preserves it, celebrates it, makes it present. In short, gives it life; or as Ionesco puts it: "In drama life becomes a word."

But this life carries with it its own death. Beckett might say, "I search for the voice of my silence." Ionesco might say, "I search for the voice of my anguish." Certainly, his plays are eloquent testimony that man's powers of speech fall drastically short of the depth of his anguish. With the result, to use Shakespeare's phrase, that "the words ache at us." The language of Ionesco's plays has a murderous energy. It is full of uncontrollable meanings. It is laden with powerful aggresions. We say with child-like innocence, "Sticks and stones can break your bones, but words can never hurt you." But they can! They can kill!!

No one has developed this idea more fully and more imaginatively than René Girard in his book *Violence and the Sacred*.[16] I cannot do justice to Girard's work in this essay, but briefly his central thesis is: The impulse towards violence is to break down distinctions—to destroy familial, social, and communal order. And the function of sacrifice is to suppress the internal violence within the community. That is, to protect the community from its own violence by choosing a surrogate victim outside itelf, and thereby restore harmony and reinforce the social fabric. Thus, he believes that "violence is the heart and secret soul of the sacred," and therefore the root force of all mystery. The function of ritual—especially ritual sacrifice—is to keep violence outside the commmunity. In ritual sacrifice, as later in tragedy, the victim is killed by words. Tragedy is a verbal extension of physical combat. "In tragic dialogue," Girard writes, "hot words are substituted for cold steel." In the theatre the words commit the violence.

Girard's other key idea (and he develops it in his brilliant essay on *Oedipus The King*) is that drama making present, as it does, familial mysteries is primarily concerned with presenting that violence (and its related sacrifice) which would destroy familial distinctions and family order. Hence its preoccupation—both manifest and disguised—with patricide and other forms of familial murder, incest, and an overpowering yearning to return to a condition

---

[16] René Girard, *Violence and the Sacred*, trans. Patrick Gregory (Baltimore: Johns Hopkins Univ. Press, 1977), p. 44.

where all distinctions are obliterated—namely, the tomb of the womb. Mention of Oedipus prompts me to make one final observation in this regard. Namely, that Ioneco's theatre has a pronounced Oedipal character. I won't pursue the ideas of incest and patricide, although I think they are there in a violently repressed form—especiallly in such later plays as *Man With Bags* and *Journey to the Land of the Dead* (which I think, by the way, are the finest dream plays written since Strindberg's Chamber Plays). But I do want to say a word about Ionesco's yearnings to return to the paradise of his childhood.

You will recall that near the close of *Oedipus The King,* as Oedipus returns to the stage afer tearing out his eyes, he cries out against his fate, shouting: "Cithæron, why did you let me live?" He calls up the image of Cithæron— the mountain on which he had been abandoned as an infant—once again just before he leaves the stage for the last time.

> Let me have no home but the mountains, where the hill
> They call Cithaeron, my Cithaeron, stands.
> There my mother and father, while
> They lived, decreed I would have my grave.
> My death will be a gift from them, for they
> Have destroyed me. . . .

What is involved in this return to the mountain, the mountain of Oedipus' infancy? And is it an accident that Ionesco's journal reveals that one of his recurring dream images is a steep mountainside cliff which he must climb to freedom? The central ambiguity of *Oedipus The King* consists of the fact that our doomed need to die is the only means of regaining the spontaneity that life loses under the alienating and repressive systems created by the intelligence. This is the curse of Adam. He paid the price of death for an increase in intelligence, and his curse dramatizes the connection between death and culture. It is from this fate that each of us would rebel.

The "Foundling Story"—and psychologically I guess each of us is, to a degree, lost, abandoned, dispossessed—is one of the archetypal expressions of this conflict. As Jung and Kerenyi have shown, the Oedipus menace exists in the form of the "eternal child" within every one of us. Imbedded in the psychic structure of each individual, it expresses itself as a fundamental urge to become ourselves through the process of losing ourselves—in a return to the Cithæron of our childhood. It is thus potentiality for self-realization. It is the act of returning to the primordial condition where lies the secret power capable of unburdening the fetters of a coercive world, and of releasing the self into full freedom. Of course, such freedom can only be found in the arms of death. Thus it is that I believe Ionesco's search for the lost mother, his desire to revisit his ancestors, his haunted concern for death, and his almost obsessive desire to return to the paradise of his childhood are inseparably related. The inter-relatedness of these powerful forces accounts for the tremendous energy of violence which characterizes his theatre.

In *Present Past-Past Present* Ionesco describes Paradise as a magnificent theatre where the whole world was full of meaning. I believe in writing for the theatre, Ionesco is seeking to recapture that Great World Theatre. It is an understandable quest, and an appropriate one too. For the theatre is:

—The realm of the eternal present moment.

—A realm of magic and bright light.

—A place where destiny has meaning.

—A place where the invisible becomes visible.

—A place where mystery is made presence.

—A place where forgotten archetypes, which are forever young—can be discovered.

—A place where language can reveal what lies outside history.

—A place where the world can be experienced with a wholeness of vision. Earlier I said the theatre was a place where that cycle of action and response referred to by psychologists as primal dialogue can and must be fulfillled. In creating his own theatre, Ionesco is discovering a personal primal dialogue with which to confront the ghosts that haunt him. He was certainly implying this when he wrote in *Notes and Counter Notes:*

> "For me the theatre—my own drama—is usually a confession; . . . I try to project onto the stage an inner drama (incomprehensible to myself) and tell myself that in any case, the microcosm being a small-scale reproduction of the macrocosm, it may happen that this tattered and disjointed inner world is in some way a reflection or a symbol of universal disruption. So there is no plot, no architectural construction, no puzzles to be solved, only the inscrutable enigma of the unknown; no real character, just people without identity (at any moment they may contradict their own nature or perhaps one will change places with another), simply a sequence of events without sequence, a series of fortuitous incidents unlinked by cause and effect, inexplicable adventures, emotional states, an indescribable tangle, but alive with intentions, impulses and discordant passions, steeped in contradiction. This may appear tragic or comic or both at the same time, but I am incapable of distinguishing one from the other. I want only to render my own strange and improbable universe."[17]

---

[17] Eugène Ionesco, *Notes and Counter Notes,* trans. Donald Watson (New York: Grove Press, 1964), p. 158–159.

In rendering his own strange and improbable universe, Ionesco reveals to us our own.

University of Wisconsin, Milwaukee

IONESCO'S POLITICAL ITINERARY

Emmanuel Jacquart

"Je me suis toujours méfié
des vérités collectives"[1]

Selecting politics as a topic may seem surprising since this is *par excellence* the area where no consensus can be found. It is all the more surprising if one remembers how Ionesco used to oppose strongly anything remotely connected with politics. Politics was poison. Yet, in a recent article pointedly entitled "A bas les politiciens"[2] he wrote: "Comment peut-on donner la direction du monde aux politiciens?" "Les trois quarts du monde sont dirigés par des fous. . . . Mais il faut que la situation change." And in his latest book of essays, *Un Homme en question* (1979), he remarked to a Roumanian critic and friend:

> J'aurais aimé cependant que tu parles, au moins une fois, de mes articles politiques, qui sont nombreux et constituent une partie importante de mon activité (. . .). J'y tiens beaucoup, car ils étaient tout de même assez insolites dans les années où ils ont commencé à paraître.[3]

How did Ionesco come to make this astounding turn-about? Was this the result of a logical and thought-out development, or the reflection of his spontaneous reactions to world politics? These are some of the questions to which I should like to address myself.

The prickly term "politics" is a convenient one, but like all abstract notions which have been bandied about, it needs to be defined. I will take

---

[1] Claude Bonnefoy, *Entretiens avec Eugène Ionesco*, Paris, Pierre Belfond, 1966, p. 26.
[2] L'Express, Jan. 9, 1978.
[3] Eugène Ionesco, *Un Homme en question* (Paris: Gallimard, 1979), p. 177.

it to mean not only Ionesco's support of a party or a political platform, but more importantly, a *prise de position,* a "philosophical" view of social life with ideological connotations. Despite Ionesco's propensity to exaggerate, his case is neither clear-cut nor static. If we take a look at his political stands over the years, the first one was his ruling out the use of politics in art. As early as 1958, when the Algerian war was raging, he stated unequivocally in "Expérience du théâtre":

> Today the theatre is blamed by some for not belonging to its own times. In my view it belongs only too well. This is what makes it so weak and ephemeral. . . . Any moment in history is valid when it transcends history; in the particular lies the universal.
>
> The themes chosen by many authors merely spring from a certain ideological fashion, which is something less than the period it belongs to. Or else these themes are the expression of some particular political attitude, and the plays that illustrate them will die with the ideology that has inspired them, for ideologies go out of fashion. . . . It is true that all authors have tried to make propaganda. The great ones are those who failed, who have gained access, consciously or not, to a deeper and more universal reality.[4]

The statement of this "apolitical animal" as he was once dubbed—discredits political themes as temporary, superficial and sectarian, and expresses a profound belief in transhistoricism, in a Montaigne-like approach to individuality, and in the view that the depths of man's nature and condition are universal. And Ionesco adds:

> Problem plays, *pièces à thèse,* are rough-hewn pieces of approximation. Drama is not the idiom for ideas. When it tries to become a vehicle for ideologies, all it can do is vulgarize them. It dangerously over-simplifies. It makes them too elementary and depreciates them. It is "naive," but in the bad sense. All ideological drama runs the risk of being parochial. . . . Ideological drama is not philosophical enough.[5]

The reasons he lists here deal with the relationship between ideology and theatre. Theatre, he contends, is not an adequate medium to convey ideological systems. Owing to its intrinsic nature and formal laws, art can only simplify or mutilate systemic thinking: here simplicity becomes simplistic.

However, the best example of Ionesco's initial stand against ideology is

---

[4] Eugène Ionesco, *Notes and Counter Notes,* trans. Donald Watson (New York: Grove Press, 1964), pp. 21–22.

[5] Ionesco, *Notes,* p. 24.

reflected in the so-called "Londonian controversy" which began on June 22, 1958. It is merely by accident that Ionesco got embroiled with politics. He was then known as an avant-garde dramatist, a representative of the antitheatre, a man of talent and originality who liked to shock and caricature and who could succesfully blend tragedy, comedy and imagination. He had already written *The Bald Soprano, The Lesson, Jack or Obedience, The Chairs, Amédée, The Shepherd's Chameleon, The New Tenant,* and several burlesque sketches; he had expressed his views in *La Nouvelle Revue française, Arts,* and *Les Cahiers Renaud-Barrault.* He had been performed abroad and was quickly becoming an international success. At that particular point, a noted critic, Kenneth Tynan, who battled to introduce him to the English public, had a change of heart which he expressed in *The Observer*. The occasion was the tremendous success of *The Chairs* at the Royal Court Theatre and the frenetic applause which, he surmised, were symptomatic of a new and dangerous cult. Ionesco had become the new prophet of the ostriches of the theatrical intelligentsia, simply because he represented an escape from the so-called "shackles of realism" illustrated by such playwrights as Osborne, Tchekhov, Brecht and Arthur Miller. Although Ionesco's world was a faulty one peopled with "isolated robots" whose dialogue was tedious, said Tynan, the ostriches "hailed him a messiah."[6] To top it all, this man who spoke like a prophet was now regarded "as the gateway to the theatre of the future, that bleak new world from which the humanist heresies of faith in logic and belief in man will forever be banished."[7] In his view, Ionesco's flight from realism negated man's faith in man, in reason, progress and civilization, and was thus opening up on to a deadend. To understand the situation correctly, one should recall, however, that both in England and in France this was a time when critics were battling for or against Brecht. Tynan, who was Brechtian, thus hastily concluded that although Ionesco's theatre was exciting, it was off the main road. Being a man of quick temper, Ionesco did not take this lying down. He felt criticized and slighted.

What had all this to do with politics? Strictly speaking, nothing. The mere mention of Arthur Miller, Brecht and Sartre, however, meant more to Ionesco than realism: they embodied propaganda and *théâtre à thèse*. The dramatist counterattacked and accused the critic of looking for messages, messiahs, for founders of religions or political philosophies. As a playwright, he could not support didacticism and social realism. "A work of art," he wrote, "has nothing to do with doctrine."[8] The supporters of art for art's sake would have applauded.

[6]Ionesco, *Notes*, p. 88.
[7]Ionesco, *Notes*, p. 89.
[8]Ionesco, *Notes*, p. 90.

Another bone of contention was predicated upon the concept of reality, a notion which varies almost as often as weather conditions. Reality for Ionesco was basically metaphysical and could not be reduced to its social dimension. Furthermore, Sartre, Osborne and Miller, he felt, exemplified leftist conformity, which he considered as pitiful as rightist conformity. And he added this baffling statement: "I believe that what separates us all from one another is simply society itself, or, if you like, politics. This is what raises barriers between men, this is what creates misunderstanding."[9] Needless to say, this smacked of a long French tradition which envisions politics in purely negative terms, as a source of bitter conflicts, as the battleground where egos and interests clash, where selfishness and ambition are rampant. Far from being restricted to man's social condition, his own concept of reality, he felt, tackled the human condition as a whole. What Tynan should demystify are ideologies because they offer ready-made solutions "(qui sont les alibis provisoires des partis parvenus au pouvoir) et que, en plus, le langage cristallise, fige."[10] Reality then transcends the social, thrusts its roots into man's anguish and dreams, and encompasses man's psychological and emotional make-up. It is above and beyond politics that what all men have in common is to be found. Thus, ideologies cannot be the essence of art because they do not express the essence of man.

The controversy did not stop here. Reasonable enough, Tynan pointed out that he had not assigned a political *mission* to the theatre, but that theatre necessarily had "social and political repercussions."[11] Art, in his opinion, was not a world closed unto itself, an autonomous activity: "Art is parasitic on life, just as criticism is parasitic on art," art and ideology "are brothers, not child and parent."[12]

Others joined in this "dialogue de sourds." Philip Toynbee dismissed Ionesco's assertions as frivolous and reflecting a lack of familiarity with Arthur Miller's works. To charge Miller with "left-wing conformism"[13] was absurd. He suspected that Sartre was the only one Ionesco knew well.

Orson Welles, who was already famous, also volunteered his opinion. In a witty editorial, which tackled several issues besides politics, he remarked that Ionesco's position seemed rather paradoxical: "To denounce leadership as incompetent, and, having done so, then insist that the 'direction' of world affairs be left strictly in these incompetent hands, is to acknowledge an

---

[9] Ionesco, *Notes*, p. 91.
[10] Ionesco, *Notes et Contre Notes* (Paris: Gallimard, 1966, p. 143). Here the English version is inaccurate and incomplete. Whenever this occurs the French text is given.
[11] Ionesco, *Notes*, p. 94.
[12] Ionesco, *Notes*, p. 95.
[13] Ionesco, *Notes*, p. 97.

extraordinary despair."[14] Everyone had had his say, and the controversy seemed to be over. Much later, however, during the winter of 1959, a relentless Ionesco gave his final reply which *The Observer* bought but never published. This lengthy profession of faith spiced with irony expresses his views on society and art, whose purpose is not equated with improving man's lot. He felt that those who try to improve man's lot always turn into tyrants or warriors. So, please, Mr. Tynan, "don't improve man's lot if you really wish him well."[15] Leaving aside his talent as a polemicist and his partiality to paradoxes, Ionesco must have disconcerted his opponent when he categorically asserted that there is, in human nature, something which "doit échapper au social ou être aliéné par le social"; [là] "où il y a fonction sociale, il y a aliénation."[16] This would be heresy for a cultural anthropologist. For example, in a famous article, Peter Berger offers the opposite view, that ". . . in a sociological perspective, identity is socially bestowed, socially sustained and socially transformed."[17] Earlier, George Herbert Mead had stated in another renowned article:

> The self, as that which can be an object to itself, is essentially a social structure, and it arises in social experience. After a self has arisen, it in a certain sense provides for itself its social experiences, and so we can conceive of an absolutely solitary self. But it is impossible to conceive of a self arising outside of social experience.[18]

Ionesco's belief subsumes a negative view of the socialization process and of society, and it presupposes that part of personality remains unaffected by the socializing process. This view of personality as a separate and superior entity is probably a romantic notion. Also surprising, although clever, is the fact that in his last bout with Tynan, Ionesco parrots his *bête noire,* Jean-Paul Sartre, to prove his point: "C'est un enfer le social, un enfer, les autres."[19] Well, Ionesco's last reply to Tynan remained unanswered and "le combat cessa faute de combattants."

In retrospect, the situation becomes all the more puzzling as about the same time (1958), Ionesco wrote *Rhinoceros,* a play with a definite social content, and a message delivered by Bérenger, the author's spokesman. The

---

[14] Ionesco, *Notes,* p. 100.

[15] Ionesco, *Notes,* p. 94.

[16] Ionesco, *Notes et Contre Notes,* pp. 162, 163.

[17] Peter Berger, in *Readings in Introductory Sociology,* ed. Dennis Wrong and Harry Gracey (New York: Macmillan, 1977, p. 77).

[18] George Herbert Mead, in Wrong and Gracey, p. 63.

[19] Ionesco, *Notes et Contre Notes,* p. 162.

starting point was a short story whose publication in *Les Lettres nouvelles* (September 1957) preceded the London controversy. Is this apparent contradiction to be interpreted as a change of heart? Was Ionesco simply wavering between opposite positions, a pattern which, in his own words, he is prone to follow? Or else, was this the sign that Ionesco rejected politics as a theme *only* when politics turn into an ideological epidemic and when art becomes a means to an end?

Whatever the reason for his paradoxical behavior, he did turn to politics, even if he took the long way around. The theme he tackled was not one that was directly topical like the Algerian war which was then raging, or the invasion of Hungary (1956), which was still recent; nor did it illustrate a ready-made political system like Marxism or Capitalism. Actually, Ionesco turned to the past, to recreating in an original way, the nazification process of Europe without ever mentioning the word "Nazi." As he explained in his preface to the American College edition of the play, his starting point was Denis de Rougemont's remembrance of a hysterical mass demonstration for Hitler's visit to Nuremberg in 1938.[20] But, certainly, Ionesco also drew on his own experience as a youth in Roumania when his country turned into a camp of Iron Guards, and his own father rode with the tide. Yet, what he insisted upon was the universality of the phenomenon:

> *Rhinoceros* is certainly an anti-Nazi play, yet it is also and mainly an attack on collective hysteria and the epidemics that lurk beneath the surface of reason and ideas, but are nonetheless serious collective diseases passed off as ideologies. . . .[21]

The common denominator for all the forms of mass hysteria, is what he dubs "rhinoceritis." In this context, his endeavor appears quite different from that of Sartre for example, both in form and content. Ionesco does not attempt to recreate lifelike situations, but stands back, takes great pains to use *l'insolite*, to show the bizarre and irresistible metamorphosis of the characters. He is not writing to illustrate a system, an edifice based on deductive logic, but to debunk idols. In this light, his behavior appears less contradictory than when he first crossed swords with Tynan. His intention was to stigmatize "collective hysteria," ideological epidemics, whether they be Nazism, Communism or what you will. He was determined to illustrate how they sprout, grow and flourish, and to denounce the crass stupidity and serious danger of all slogans and all ideological systems which, under the guise of scientific objectivity,

---

[20] Ionesco, *Notes*, p. 199.
[21] Ionesco, *Notes*, p. 199.

turn into fanaticism and terrorism. In short, to borrow Raymond Aron's witty expression, he shows "la raison déraisonnante" at work and warns against its cataclysmic consequences. In a humorous manner blended with derision and *reductio ad absurdum,* he focuses on the psychological rather than the political mechanism of collective contamination. As he told Claude Bonnefoy:

> En effet, avant de devenir idéologiques, le nazisme, le fascisme, etc., ce sont d'abord des sentiments. Toutes les idéologies, marxisme inclus, ne sont que les justifications et les alibis de certains sentiments, de certaines passions, d'instincts aussi issus de l'ordre biologique.[22]

The play is therefore an attempt to demystify and remain lucid. Here, Ionesco is accidentally close to a French tradition which includes *moralistes* and intellectuals as diverse as La Rochefoucault and Sartre. But he also comes close to Freud in his conceptualization of human nature: many actions are seen as mere rationalizations of our passions, aggressivity or self-interest. Hence, clichés-ridden philosophical systems which attempt to justify these actions are in fact empty utopias. Passionate systemic thinking and behavior are symptoms of instinctual and neurotic drives. Characters like the ludicrous logician, like the narrow-minded Botard who, in his own words, has "la clé des événements, un système d'interpretation infallible,"[23] and like Jean, who is superorganized, has a superiority complex, acts like a robot, and considers himself to be the recipient of universal Truth, all illustrate his point. They all suffer from rhinoceritis, and the other characters are too weak to resist the epidemic, too conformist to resist the herd instinct. Here myth is coming to life.

When myths are predicated on simplistic manicheism they release the destructive energy of the unconscious: violence is justified when transgression of the sacred occurs. We go back to barbarism. As Jung remarked, modern man "is blind to the fact that with all his rationality and efficiency, he is possessed by powers that are beyond his control. His gods and demons have not disappeared at all; they have merely got new names."[24] From this perspective, it is remarkable that Ionesco's approach, admittedly amateurish, sometimes coincides with Jung's and Eliade's. The terminology and conceptual apparatus may be different, but the explanation is *basically* the same. Thus, Ionesco's political opinion, which had appeared reactionary to some, in fact partly coincides with a relatively new view of man. It would be more

---

[22] Bonnefoy, p. 25.
[23] *Rhinocéros,* in *Théâtre III* (Paris: Gallimard, 1963), p. 63.
[24] Carl Jung, *Man and his Symbols* (New York: Doubleday, 1964), p. 82.

accurate, however, to add that his views owe something to a variety of sources: not only to his friend Mircea Eliade, and to Jung, but also to Denis de Rougemont and Emmanuel Mounier, whom he admired, and perhaps to Camus, whom he frequently mentions. But first and foremost, Ionesco's political reaction derives from experience: he remembered the spread of Fascism over Roumania and kept the haunting memory of a loved and hated father, who flung himself into the arms of every new ideology and followed every new leader. (In this sense, his political approach seems closer to American pragmaticism than to the modern European passion for systems; or, for those who wish to go back further, his reaction appears *grosso modo,* akin to the political liberalism of the 18th century *philosophes,* who, like him, lived in different countries and compared different political systems.)[25] He has enough animal instinct to sense when he is threatened. His reactions are echoed by Bérenger: "Ils sont tous devenus fous. Le monde est malade."[26] And, Bérenger characteristically concludes:

> Eh bien tant pis! Je me défendrai contre tout le monde! Ma carabine, ma carabine! Contre tout le monde, je me défendrai, contre tout le monde, je me défendrai! Je suis le dernier homme, je le resterai jusqu'au bout! Je ne capitule pas![27]

Although Ionesco's opponents would grant him that the theatre is an art which must simplify and magnify to be effective, they could point out that this kind of determination is totally unrealistic, and would have had no chance of success in Nazi Germany or Soviet Russia. To which he could reply that the belief in individualism may indeed seem ludicrous, but it was held by such tenacious "hommes de bonne volonté" as Solzhenitzin or Sakharov, and a host of others who dared oppose a horribly repressive system, and made use of the leverage offered by international opinion.

In any case, his philosophy goes beyond his mere support of individualism. What he stands for appears implicitly as a counterpoint to the preposterous remarks of the brainwashed villains or puppets. The logician asserts for example: "La peur est irrationnelle. La raison doit la vaincre."[28] Needless to say, this is overestimating the power of reason and underrating man's physical nature. As to Jean, who is less of a caricature than the logician, he makes a series of objectional statements, for example:

---

[25] Ionesco, *Notes,* pp. 198–199.
[26] Ionesco, *Rhinocéros,* p. 114.
[27] Ionesco, *Rhinocéros,* p. 117.
[28] Ionesco, *Rhinocéros,* p. 16.

'L'amitié n'existe pas. Je ne crois pas en votre amitié.'[29]
'L'homme. . . Ne prononcez plus ce mot! . . . L'humanisme est périmé.'[30]

His ideas are couched in an axiomatic language where the use of the definite article plays a crucial role. They create an impression of rashness and overgeneralization, especially when they have a pseudo-Nietzschean or Nazi ring to them, as when Jean flouts ethics: "La morale! Parlons-en de la morale, j'en ai assez de la morale, elle est belle la morale! Il faut dépasser la morale."[31] Yet, the founding of a code of ethics was no luxury in the history of mankind, but the very cornerstone of society. It is not by chance that the Bible has stressed the Ten Commandments, or that Freud, in *Civilization and Its Discontents,* considered that the rise of civilization was made possible by restraining man's instinctual impulses with a code of ethics, with rules to prevent aggression and destruction. In this context, Jean's contempt for man and the past, and his will to break boundaries, are based on ignorance as much as on irrationality.

In contrast, Ionesco holds on to time-honored values, to the hard-won principles of democracy, to the legacy of decades of "civilization," and to human nature's basic need for warmth and freedom. This is not to be confused with narrow conservatism. His amateurish, but healthy, approach to politics remains close to man's vital needs, and subsumes a belief in experience and common sense, as well as a call to action.

Although not a problematic play, *Rhinoceros* was variously interpreted by the critics. Some saw it as purely anti-Nazi but Ionesco's comments on the subject include Marxism. One of Botard's statements which may have been overlooked indeed echoes Lenin: "Psychose collective! C'est comme la religion qui est l'opium des peuples."[33] Other statements of his endorse the ideological connotations Marxists give to words like "myth," "mystification" or "propaganda."[33] In brief, without being an abstraction, *Rhinoceros* is a parable of sorts condemning all totalitarian regimes. This is why it contains no references which can be associated with a specific time and place. This device, which is one of Ionesco's favorites, reflects his aspiration to universality rather than a flight from action.

As Ionesco's political itinerary unfolded, the occasional satirical references to Marxism gave way to blitzkrieg attacks, especially in *A Stroll in the Air*

[29] Ionesco, *Rhinocéros*, p. 72.
[30] Ionesco, *Rhinocéros*, p. 76.
[31] Ionesco, *Rhinocéros*, p. 75.
[32] Ionesco, *Rhinocéros*, p. 52.
[33] Ionesco, *Rhinocéros*, pp. 52-54.

(1963) and *What a Hell of a Mess* (1973). Although not dealing exclusively with this theme, the first play contains several revealing passages where Bérenger becomes Ionesco's spokesman. Totalitarian regimes, be they Fascist or Marxist, are again taken to task. *A Stroll,* which premiered in Dusseldorf, contains a passage which caricatures Fascist principles, and is also highly reminiscent of Nietzsche's *Twilight of the Idols:* friendship is equated with weakness, shyness, delusion, sentimentality and hypocrisy, whereas energy, which is what matters, feeds on hatred of course. It is the life force, as the naive, brainwashed journalist explains:

> Comprenez-vous, Monsieur, l'amitié, l'amitié c'était une duperie. En outre, elle tue lentement. La détestation, c'est cela l'ambiance vitale favorable. Elle seule peut nous donner des forces. La détestation c'est l'énergie. L'énergie même.[34]

There is another didactic episode in *A Stroll* where Ionesco caricatures the Marxist idolatry of history. If history has something to teach us, it is not that it is the Truth, and the only salvation. On the contrary, Ionesco's spokesman, Bérenger, declares unequivocally:

> Ils considèrent que l'Histoire a raison alors qu'elle ne fait que déraisonner. Mais pour eux, l'Histoire, c'est tout simplement la raison du plus fort, l'idéologie d'un régime qui s'installe et qui triomphe. Que ce soit n'importe lequel. On trouve toujours les meilleures raisons pour justifier une idéologie triomphante.[35]

This statement, which has been repeated almost verbatim to Claude Bonnefoy,[36] considers that, far from being based on the use of enlightened reason, the course of events shows the triumph of aggressivity and ambition. The pious reasons Marxist theorists put forward, the ideology they have dreamed up, are mere rationalizations. They are but one example of a more general phenomenon that Arthur Herzog characterizes as hyperrationality:

> Hyperrationality denotes the overreliance on "scientific" approaches to "Problem solving." It has to do with what can be called the "fallacy of scientific method"—drawing a generalization from an incomplete induction. Hyperrationalist inductions tend to be incomplete because they ignore, or minimize, activity that is random, unplanned unplannable. Contrary evidence, unanswered questions, alternate explanations, even authentic facts,

---

[34] Ionesco, *Le Piéton de l'air, Théâtre III,* pp. 179-180.
[35] Ionesco, *Le Piéton,* p. 126.
[36] Bonnefoy, p. 149.

are safely stored out of sight by the Hyperrationalist. By reducing the world to abstractions, the Hyperrationalist blocks out that which causes interference, falls short of requirements, or just gets in the way. The result is a vacuum-sealed, highly structured view of reality.[37]

Thus, the hyperrationalist predicates his logical conclusions on overly neat premises which History simply cannot offer. Needless to say, Ionesco does not trouble himself with such theoretical questions. As a matter of fact, in a cynical vein not unworthy of La Rochefoucault, he bluntly asserts that Marxist ideology is an alibi to placate the Marxist's conscience and fulfill his dreams. Yesterday people believed in God's will, today they believe in the myth of History—a mysteriously objective, powerful, but impersonal power which would govern socio-economic forces and bring about the triumph of justice and the proletariat. Ionesco remains unconvinced, but stops short of claiming that History is "toujours déraisonnable."[38] What he does claim, however, is: "La plupart des écrivains d'aujourd'hui pensent être de l'avant alors que l'Histoire les a justement dépassés. Ils sont bêtes et ne sont pas courageux."[39] They believe in naive ideological fairytales, or lack the courage to go against the tide, to expose modern bad faith and injustice. Such is Bérenger's message, as the ridiculous journalist in *Stroll in the Air* points out.

Another point worth noting here is that Bérenger thinks that ideally art should remain free from political commitment. Like Ionesco, he feels dissatisfied with the compromise he had to make. "Hélas, dit-il, c'est bien malgré moi [que je donne un message]."[40]

After having dealt a blow to Fascism and Marxism, the dramatist turned to a third hot topic: Revolution as myth, revolution as mass delusion. France's 1968 aborted revolution very likely provided the starting point, or the political background, for *What a Hell of a Mess* (1973), which came ten years after *A Stroll in the Air*. But just like Ionesco's other socio-political plays, this one deals with many questions besides the social one upon which we are now focussing. Ionesco is here particularly sensitive to the magnetic fascination that revolutions have for leftists in France and elsewhere. This fascination has been analyzed by a specialist, Raymond Aron, whose opinion I will briefly exemplify:

> Pas plus que le concept de gauche, le concept de révolution ne tombera en désuétude. Il exprime, lui aussi, une nostalgie, qui durera aussi longtemps

---

[37] Arthur Herzog, *The B. S. Factor* (New York: Penguin, 1975), p. 89.
[38] Bonnefoy, p. 150.
[39] Ionesco, *Le Piéton*, p. 127.
[40] Ionesco, *Le Piéton*, p. 127.

> que les sociétés demeureront imparfaites et les hommes avides de réformer. (. . .) On connaît des révolutionnaires par haine du monde, par désir de la catastrophe; plus souvent, les révolutionnaires pèchent par optimisme. Tous les régimes connus sont condamnables si on les rapporte à un idéal abstrait d'égalité ou de liberté. Seule la Révolution, parce qu'elle ouvre une aventure, ou un régime révolutionnaire parce qu'il consent à l'usage permanent de la violence, semble capable de rejoindre le sublime. Le mythe de la révolution, sert de refuge à la pensée utopique, il devient l'intercesseur mystérieux, imprévisible, entre le réel et l'idéal. La violence elle-même attire, fascine, plutôt qu'elle ne repousse.[41]

Needless to say, Aron's opinion does not totally coincide with Ionesco's, but it perceives some of the same elements at play: uptopia and myth, violence, excessive optimism, and a fascination for adventure. But there is more to it than that. Like Camus, whom he admired, Ionesco sees revolutions as necessarily betrayed. Historical examples are not lacking: "les justes," the pure at heart, end up defeated or turn into tyrants. This is echoed by the concierge in *What a Hell of a Mess:* "Deux siècles de revolutions ont-elles jamais engendré autre chose?"[42] But Ionesco does not really walk in Camus' footsteps, because as a playwright, he is more interested in the man in the street than in leaders and theoreticians. The few pages of dialogue he devotes to revolution (more reminiscent of 1968 than 1789 or 1848) exude bitterness and disillusionment. The title, *Ce formidable bordel,* says it all.

This caricature, this gem of a caricature, is a cornucopia brimming over with Marxist slogans and utopian beliefs. Here we rediscover the cliché juggler, the master of accumulation and proliferation used as magnifying and satirizing devices. In typical fashion, the rebellious couple denounce Capitalism, the "sales bourgeois," "l'exploitation de l'homme par l'homme," "la société de consommation," "la société malsaine," and long for the apocalyptic collapse of the old hopeless world of corruption and injustice. Very often, Ionesco delights in loading the dice to reveal abruptly that clichés are at variance with the facts. For example, the two unruly and unsavory characters inveigh against dishonesty but refuse to pay for their drinks and even leave with bottles of alcohol taken from the café owner. Or we hear such nonsense as: "la dictature, oui, mais dans la liberté."[43] Or again, the ideal of brotherhood which is a leitmotiv uttered six times, clashes with the actual behavior of the bloodthirsty and sadistic female rebel who shouts "Du sang! des ventres crevés! Je veux voir les boyaux sortir de leur ventre;" "Il nous faut du sang,

---

[41] Raymond Aron, *L'Opium des intellectuels* (Paris: Gallimard, 1955, 1968), p. 105.
[42] Eugène Ionesco, *Ce formidable bordel* (Paris: Gallimard, 1973), p. 98.
[43] Ionesco, *Bordel,* p. 73.

de la volupté et de la mort."[44] Both rebels claim they want to set up a just society, but they do not give a hoot about children and women. They supposedly struggle for the working class, but insult and bully the waitress. They are vulgar, have no sense of decency, behave like vandals, obey their basest instincts, and give free rein to their ambition, agressivity and lust. As a young character remarks: "La révolution c'est l'explosion de nos désirs."[45] The female rebel is a lewd woman, with a robust Rabelaisian nature and utopian ideas which are summarized in her motto: "la révolution pour le plaisir."[46] Pleasure then also appears as a leitmotiv which is in fact uttered nine times in a row. All this ends up on a naive note summarizing their actual "philosophy:" "nous allons vivre dans la fête, la joie pour toujours."[47] Amen, the Golden Age has come.

Behind this caricature we feel Ionesco's bitterness. His views might be called reactionary by some, but this is not the proper approach to take. He looks around and does not see youth to be wiser than anyone else; what he sees is ambition, greed, aggressivity, a great deal of bad faith or inconsistency, and the pervasive rule of the unconscious. Both snappily and tongue-in-cheek, he concludes through the concierge:

> L'ère des révolutions est terminée. Tous les régimes sont mauvais (. . .). La politique est dépassée. La révolution n'est plus qu'une obsession, une fixation obsessionnelle, un bobo. On la fait encore, la révolution, mais elle ne sert plus à rien. C'est à la technique et à l'industrialisation de parler. (. . .) On a dit "Aimez-vous les uns les autres," c'est pas possible. Il faut dire que la verité c'est: "Mangez-vous les uns les autres." "Tout est conflit."[48]

This is Ionesco in one of his most pessimistic moods. All societies are bad, although not equally so; human nature is basically rotten, and the law of nature for man, as for other animals, is the survival of the fittest. And with disgust, annoyance and despondency he concludes: "Elle a assez duré l'aventure humaine. Que ça finisse, qu'on n'en parle plus. Le Créateur s'est gouré."[49] This is not the viewpoint of a politician or an ideologist, but rather of a moralist, a depressed and cynical one perhaps, but one who tries to remain lucid and truthful.

[44] Ionesco, *Bordel*, respectively p. 75 and p. 73.
[45] Ionesco, *Bordel*, p. 96.
[46] Ionesco, *Bordel*, p. 75.
[47] Ionesco, *Bordel*, p. 76.
[48] Ionesco, *Bordel*, p. 98.
[49] Ionesco, *Bordel*, p. 99.

What seems interesting in his general outlook on revolution, Communism and Fascism is their common underlying basis. In this respect, he shares a great deal with Jung and especially with one of the foremost historians of religions, his friend Mircea Eliade. Like them, he finds that ideologies rest on mythical thinking. Modern non-religious man regards himself as the sole agent of history. He wants to desacralize the world and to be free of the taboos and superstitions of the past. However, in Eliade's words, he "still retains a large stock of camouflaged myths and rituals."[50] In *Aspects du Mythe,* Eliade explicitly states:

> La mythologie eschatologique et millénariste a fait sa réapparition ces derniers temps en Europe, dans deux mouvements politiques totalitaires. Bien que radicalement sécularisés en apparence, le nazisme et le communisme sont chargés d'éléments eschatologiques; ils annoncent la Fin de ce monde-ci et le début d'une ère d'abondance et de béatitude.[51]

Behind their ideological and pseudo-scientific jargon, behind their rhetoric of power, Fascism and Communism unwittingly revive the archetypes of the struggle between the Elect and the armies of the devil: in the present case, the Aryans against the Jews, and the Proletarians against the Bourgeois. Nazism attributes a great amount of prestige to the racist myth of the noble origin of the Aryan who is gifted with wonderful qualities: superiority, purity, strength and heroism. In *Rhinoceros,* this is echoed in Daisy's exclamation: "Ce sont des dieux."[52] As to Marxism, according to Eliade, it revives the redeeming role of the Just (the proletariat), and the myth of the Golden Age: a classless society, and the final triumph of History.

There are other reasons why Ionesco refuses political myths, reasons to be found in the works of a man he admired for his humanistic objectivity: Emmanuel Mounier. Both writers share some of the same feelings and ideas: an aversion to bovaryzing ideologies, a rejection of fuzzy or wishful thinking, a denunciation of conformity and ready-made systems of thought. In fact, in spite of many points of divergence, Mounier's philosophy comes close to Ionesco's when the former writes:

> Avec les périodes de combat nous voyons avancer le règne du Mensonge qui est le propre des combats modernes. L'évènement grave (. . .) c'est la pro-

---

[50] Mircea Eliade, *The Sacred and the Profane,* trans. Willard Trask (New York: Harcourt Brace, 1959), p. 204.

[51] Mircea Eliade, *Aspects du mythe* (Paris: Gallimard, 1963), p. 88.

[52] Ionesco, *Rhinocéros,* p. 114. Cf. also the passage where she praises energy and downgrades love, p. 113.

lifération massive du mensonge. (. . .) La forme la plus dangereuse en est le mythe.[53]

As stated here by Mounier, the problem seems deceptively simple, but, in fact, we are dealing with a complex phenomenon taking place on at least three levels. On the conscious level, governments and political parties use to varying degrees a deliberate strategy to cheat and manipulate. They resort to hyperboles and euphemisms, to sophistry and verbal cloudiness; they administer language placebos, sell promises, images and myths, and take advantage of people's hatred or gullibility. Here a strong dose of verbicide would do wonders, or as Herzog puts it: "words ought to be protected from human predators like some rare species of wildlife.."[54]

On the semi-conscious level, *la mauvaise foi,* or rationalization, plays a major role. People end up half believing in what they want to believe, or what they want *you* to believe. And, on the third level, deep down in the unconscious where obsessions, passions and the irrational rule supreme, individuals rally around cult words and utopias, giving in to mesmerization or intoxication. "Although the group needs a leader, says Freud, he must himself be held in fascination by a strong faith."[55] Images become reality, abstractions become facts. Here, as Ionesco has shown so often, language becomes alienating or oppressive.

For those theoretically inclined, a variation on the same explanation could be found thanks to Ogden's and Richards' well-known view of the triangular relation between signifier, signified and referend. Against this background, rhinoceritis develops whenever the signified is confused with the referend. The truth is that language symbolizes and categorizes reality, but can never replace reality itself. Believing otherwise amounts to mental malpractice. In this context, Ionesco could rightly assert in *Antidotes* that statesmen and politicians themselves are alienated,[56] that systems become prisons for the mind. The path to serfdom rambles through the land of mythodiscourse.

At times, Ionesco is so weary of all systems that he would gladly get rid of all of them. This reaction underlies *Hunger and Thirst* (1964) which, he feels, has been misunderstood. The play was somewhat inspired by Zen Buddhism because, as Ionesco explained: "Le Zen, c'est la libération de

---

[53] Emmanuel Mounier, "Leçons de l'émeute ou la révolution contre les mythes," in *Oeuvres, I,* Paris, Le Seuil, 1961, p. 361.

[54] Arthur Herzog, p. 54.

[55] *Group Psychology and the Analysis of the Ego,* ed. James Strachey (New York: Norton, 1959), p. 13.

[56] Eugène Ionesco, *Antidotes* (Paris: Gallimard, 1967), p. 137.

l'homme, la destruction de son aliénation non pas par le refus mais par le dépassement de toute pensée systématisée."[57] The last episode, which takes place in a prison-monastery-barracks, portrays two clowns: Tripp and Brechtoll. Brechtoll is a portmanteau word combining Bertold and Brecht, whereas Tripp seems to be a spoonerism on *pitre* (clown, buffoon), and perhaps a reference to Peter (Latin *Petrus*, Greek *Petros* = rock, stone) the head of the apostles but also the one who thrice denied Christ (Matthew XXVI, 34). Simone Benmusa took Tripp to mean *tripes*, the bowels of one who is always hungry. In any case, Tripp conceives of existence as having religious transcendence, and his opposite, Brechtoll, is a philosopher whose views are based on dialectical materialism. Both characters, who switch roles every night, are imprisoned in separate cages—which symbolize man's predicament—and starved until they recant their beliefs and espouse opposite views. Some spectators and critics were quick to conjure up the various images of the Inquisition, the KGB or the Gestapo, and the political or religious sadism of fake trials. However, on a higher level, beyond this satirical brainwashing session which derides visionaries, pedagogues and dogmatists, Ionesco also aims at undermining all "systèmes, doctrines, dogmes, mythes, tics, automatismes mentaux qui nous accablent."[58] As Friar Tarabas remarks:

> La vraie prison, c'est l'aliénation de l'esprit."[59] Si vous êtes enfermé, c'est parce que c'est vous qui avez une croyance, un critère, un dogme ou (. . .) une morale. Bref des préjugés. (. . .) C'est votre pensée qui vous enferme.[60]

This situation, defined by Tarabas (a likely reminder of Barabas, the prisoner who was released in preference to Jesus), is presented as universal. Sometimes, we manage to free ourselves, but only for a short while: "il n'y a de liberté que provisoire."[61] The fundamental reason is that we cannot get rid of our thirst for an absolute. Ionesco's denunciation of the partiality and failure of all systems to account for the complexity and fluidity of reality certainly sounds typical. What is rather untypical here, although we are dealing with a caricature, is his levelling of all values—a total nihilism which goes well beyond what the author usually asserts. The protagonist Jean, whose quest was predicated upon a spiritual solution to life, ends up in this mental prison like everyone else.

[57]Gilbert Tarrab, *Ionesco à coeur ouvert* (Montreal: Le Cercle du Livre de France), pp. 103–104.
[58]Eugène Ionesco, *La soif et la faim*, in *Théâtre IV* (Paris: Gallimard, 1966), p. 140.
[59]Ionesco, *La soif*, p. 139.
[60]Ionesco, *La soif*, p. 150.
[61]Ionesco, *La soif*, p. 139.

Let us now pause for a moment and place Ionesco's ideas in perspective. We have already noted that they partly coincide, or flirt with, those of Mounier, Denis de Rougemont, Camus, Aron, Jung and Eliade. Although Ionesco has occasionally been seen as a dilettante, he stands side by side with scholarly specialists in psychoanalysis, mythology, political science and philosophy. This appears as a rather surprising spiritual family, all the more so as this family includes another member, a representative of the New French Philosophers whose views Ionesco claims are sometimes similar to his own. He is thinking of Bernard-Henri Lévy, who, like him, has refused what Julien Benda would have called "la trahison des clercs."

Barbarism with a Human Face (1977), which makes no mention of the dramatist, has chapters with revealing titles: "History Does not Exist," "The Encyclopedia of Lies," "Faces of Barbarism," "Faces of Totalitarianism," "Marxism: The Opium of the People," "May 1968, or the Defeat of Life." The superficial similarities with Ionesco's views reflected in these titles, become deeper upon examination of some of Lévy's statements. In the philosopher's own words, the chief political problem of our time is the totalitarian state. which "is not quite a secular state without faith; it is more precisely *a state which secularizes religion and creates profane beliefs."*[62] As a matter of fact, he adds, "Politics is, and has always been, nothing but another face of religion."[63] Does not all this sound familiar? Well, the epilogue presents a number of points which are even more akin to Ionesco's views, and which can easily be summarized: 1) Like Bérenger in *Rhinoceros,* we have to learn to say "no," to surrender: "No matter where it comes from, resist the barbarian threat."[64] 2) Lévy has attempted to set down the foundations of "pessimism in history," 3) his ethics is one of *"lucidity* and *truth,"* 4) Perennial guides always end up justifying "massacre and repression," 5) the antibarbarian intellectual is a metaphysician, an artist, and a *moraliste.* Ionesco could endorse every one of these points. In fact, he has made these points, in his plays, editorials and journals.

If we had more space, more could be said about his recent writings, particularly *Antidotes* and *Un Homme en question.* Yet, in this controversial area a consensus would not be reached. And this is just as well. Ionesco has convinced a few, entertained or depressed many, and left others shocked or unconvinced. The latter feel they cannot take seriously his delight in paradoxes, his sweeping and seemingly naive statements, least of all his contradictions. Certainly he did contradict himself, but who has not? Granted, he

---

[62] Bernard-Henri Lévy, *Barbarism with a Human Face*, p. 137.
[63] Lévy, p. 134.
[64] This quotation and all subsequent ones from Lévy are taken from the epilogue, pp. 191–197.

goes further than most of us when he vindicates the right to contradict himself. However, this vindication of the right to contradiction is no mere challenge, but also a reflection of the genuine belief that man can never become a totally logical being, a pure intellect free from the foibles of his physical nature. At best, this is a sign of tolerance and clear-sightedness. Indeed, deep down, he refuses to delude himself, and he is successful at it when he sees himself, and man in general, as necessarily imprisoned in subjectivity, when he sees that our opinions often reflect what we want, what we need, what serves our own interests.[65] As Nietzsche said in one of his better moments, ultimately there are no facts, only interpretations. Pure reality can not be directly perceived, or, as Saussure profoundly expressed in an arresting phrase: "c'est le point de vue qui crée l'objet." My own interpretation is no exception, and so be it.

The way Ionesco ultimately views himself is summarized in his *Fragments of a Journal:*

> Ni masochiste, ni sadique, ni fanatique politique, je crois avoir été toujours lucide, d'une lucidité un peu simple, peut-être insuffisante, mais, en gros, j'ai vu juste. Je comprends pourquoi ils se font la guerre, pourquoi ils se débattent, je comprends qu'ils ne veuillent pas le comprendre, je sais parfaitement que les idéologies, philosophies, autres raisons qu'ils se donnent, ne sont que des alibis et des justifications, inconscientes, mi-conscientes, de leurs passions, d'un désepoir caché. . . . Je sais, je sais ausi qu'ils ne l'admettront jamais et refuseront toujours de se démystifier. . . .[66]

Well, this thorough individualist who refuses to howl with the wolves, or rather, to run with the rhinos, this *moraliste* with a partiality to metaphysics, this simple man who speaks his mind, stumbles, strays, laments, wavers and yet asserts, this optimistic pessimist with a vivid imagination and a good sense of humor, this man who wants to understand and be lucid, this living paradox who believes in the enlightening power of dreams, knows, and so do we, that life is a losing proposition for nobody ever came out of it alive. Hence, he can write on the first page of *Un Homme en question:* "Je n'ai cru que moyennement à tout ce que j'ai écrit."[67] This may be a trifle depressing, but it is certainly better than an inferno built on *Mein Kampf* or patterned after *The Gulag Archipelago*.

University of Houston

---

[65] Ionesco, *Antidotes*, p. 271.
[66] Ionesco, *Journal en miettes*, Paris, Gallimard, 1967, p. 145.
[67] Ionesco, *Un Homme en question*, p. 7.

IONESCO: SYMPTOM AND VICTIM

David I. Grossvogel

Not unexpectedly for a dramatist, Ionesco is a creature of dialogue—his critical trajectory, a happening. In 1956, much of his play *Improvisation* derides the then-popular Brecht, his method and his ideology. But over the years, Brecht becomes for Ionesco something more than merely left-wing didacticism: by the time of his dialogues with Claude Bonnefoy (*Entre la vie et le rêve*, Paris: Belfond, 1977), Brecht is one of the accepted axes around which a certain kind of theater revolves. Similarly, at some time before 1975, Ionesco tells Robert Jouanny that he does "not like what Samuel Beckett writes" (*La Cantatrice chauve, La Leçon d'Eugène Ionesco*, Paris: Hachette, 1975). But in the 1977 version of those same *entretiens* with Bonnefoy, he calls him "le grand Beckett" (p. 178) and says of him, "I like him very much" (p. 185). However, even within this second and seemingly contradictory affirmation, a dialectical tension subsists. What Ionesco still does not like about Beckett is what he terms Beckett's "non-participation with others" (p. 178). There is a kind of serenity in Beckett that irritates Ionesco:

> In *Waiting for Godot*, in *Endgame*, in *Happy Days*, there is a waiting, an agony within the wilderness and, when all is said and done, within tranquillity. A disconsolate tranquillity, but tranquillity nonetheless. Yet these days, death is not quiet—one dies amid sound and fury. There are wars, revolutions, repressions [. . .]. Writers like Beckett separate themselves from the rest of humanity and find a place, that I would not quite call comfortable, in which to agonize and die. But the very realistic literature of the Gulag Archipelago, among others, has shown us how very evident are the collectivity and fraternity of despair and death. (p. 178)

Ionesco amplifies this criticism of Beckett by extending it to the *nouveau roman*: "[in] the *nouveau roman* . . . the soul is canceled out" (p. 178). "Take

Last Year at Marienbad by Robbe-Grillet and Resnais. I think that after awhile one will laugh at the film's characters because they are empty" (p. 179).

This would seem to indicate that Ionesco favors drama that probes the individual quandary with a greater intensity born of human sympathy. And also one that would do its probing with greater excitement. Sensing the first, Bonnefoy suggests, "What you tax the *nouveau roman* with is having abolished tragedy?" To which Ionesco responds, "That's it" (pp. 179-80). Having posited tragedy as the somber lodestone that will indicate one of the polarities of his drama, it becomes necessary to understand just what Ionesco has in mind when he considers tragedy—or, at least, a stage informed with a sense of the tragic.

At the onset, it appears to be a pathology that affects even the process that describes it: "I believe that literature is neurosis. Health is neither poetic nor literary" (p. 37). In fact, Ionesco speculates that he may have been led to writing through an inner nihilism. "Why did I write my first play? Maybe to prove that nothing had any deep value, that nothing was viable, neither literature, nor the theater; neither life, nor values" (p. 53).

Ionesco acknowledges that, for him, writing remains very much an intimate exercise, a form of personal catharsis, a "défoulement"—the release of repression (p. 68). Ionesco criticizes someone like Sartre in part because Sartre, as playwright, *talks* about the absurd but doesn't *live* it. Ionesco feels that an existential anguish felt by the author must possess his whole stage, not merely the words of his characters.

Looking for a unifying theme that will subsume this intimate projection of Ionesco onto his stage, Bonnefoy suggests the anxiety of death, to which Ionesco answers, "I think you are right" (p. 79). But this gracious accession on Ionesco's part runs counter to the evidence that Bonnefoy elicits from him; the bulk of their conversation makes it clear that Ionesco feels that existence is informed by another, and at least equally strong, perception—a sense of what Freud would term the "uncanny" and which Ionesco names "l'insolite"— a term he prefers to the more popular "absurd."

> I write theater to express a sense of surprise, of stupefaction. Why and who are we? What does it mean? No, I don't even ask the why or wherefore, I don't ask what it means. It's an unspoken question but more compelling than if it had been articulated, a kind of feeling that is altogether fundamental, primal, before the evidence that something is there that moves or seems to move. (p. 60)

This sense of a strange world derives from a separation which is, by its very nature, a form of perception, of insight, of understanding. To be outside the event, to see it with surprise, as strange, is to evidence the acuity of one's seeing. And Ionesco, far from thinking that his perception is idiosyncratic, is able to find extended resonances for it; he likens his 1973 play *A Hell of a Mess* (or rather his first novel, from which the play is drawn, *The Hermit*), to Zen teaching that gives as ontological revlation the fact that we are God's joke (p. 163).

This ontological distancing has two immediate consequences. First, in that his writing affords Ionesco a personal catharsis, it allows him to alleviate a part of the absurd anxiety (p. 140). Second, it suggests quite naturally the comic as a point of departure for a more frightening sense of the world. Seen from an outer, alienated point of vantage, that is to say without the possibility of incorporating, of "taking in" the event, a disturbance or derangement ("dérèglement") is first of all comical—what might have been alive becomes, through the percipience of the distanced onlooker, mechanical, setting in motion the Bergsonian process of laughter; something mechanical is imposed upon the living reality. But in proportion as that dernagement becomes greater than the object that demonstrates it, the mechanical assertion becomes frightening. As such times, as happens in *The New Tenant* or *The Lesson* (to quote Ionesco), "the comic is frightening, the comic is tragic" (p. 51). Ionesco locates his drama at the point beyond which comic amplification becomes scary. "For me, the theater is the exposition of something that is quite rare, quite strange, quite monstrous. It is something terrible that reveals itself gradually, not as the action progresses . . . but rather a series of events, or more or less complex states of being" (p. 152).

These dual consequences of a levitation away from the normalcy of constraining bounds and the consequent entry into a world that is alive with the threatening freedom of growth unrestrained, whether through expansion, multiplication or illogicality, are akin to those of the dream. And indeed, an oneiric consciousness informs a considerable part of Ionesco's musings. First, the personal catharsis: "The stuff of my plays is often made of dreams," says Ionesco. "I attach great importance to dreams, because they give me a more acute, a more penetrating awareness of myself" (p. 12) For *A Stroll in the Air*, "I used one of my dreams. The dream of flight" (p. 63). But the dream may comprehend worlds that extend beyond moments of the author's private rehearsals. *Rhinoceros* starts with a nightmare, "a distant, assimilated nightmare" (p. 69), which issues onto the world of ideas: *Rhinoceros* becomes "phenomonologically, the process of collective transformation. I was doing it in an altogether lucid way, with this sense of the nightmare as ground" (p. 69). Writing the preface to an American edition of the play (New York: Holt, Rinehart and Winston, 1961), Ionesco suggests that a scene of Nazi mass hysteria described by Denis de Rougement might have been at the starting point of *Rhinoceros*.

The temptation of the idea, even though it seems to run counter to the freedom of the oneiric, remains constant in Ionesco. He gives as one of the influences that marked him that of Kafka (along with de Chirico and Borges). And more particularly, in Kafka, he mentions "The Metamorphosis." But given the choice between a phenomenological interpretation of the short story (one that would locate it in an oneiric mood, thus emphasizing the "uncanny" forces that confront Gregor Samsa), or a symbolic reading, Ionesco opts for the latter, reading the tale as an idea, a moral allegory:

> The monster can spring out of us. We can have the face of the monster. That is to say, what is monstrous in us can get the upper hand; mobs, entire nations, are periodically dehumanized; wars, uprisings, pogroms, collective fury and crimes, tyrannies and oppressions. These are only a part of the evidence of our monstrousness. . . . Our monstrousness has countless faces, collective or not, more or less striking, more or less evident. (p. 40)

This seeming contradiction in Ionesco is not crucial—it may even result from the dialectics of the interviewing process. Moreover, a playwright is first and foremost the plays he writes, not what he says about them (nor, for that matter, what he says about himself or his colleagues). But repeated reference to "ideas" in a theater whose source is supposed to be the dream, or nightmare, gives pause. (The dream is, after all, the redeeming virtue strong enough to rescue even an occasional *nouveau romancier*, such as the latter Butor who interests Ionesco "much more" because of his attempt "to speak the language of dreams," p. 180.) One wonders whether, in feeling the need to bolster oneiric vision with the weight of "ideas," Ionesco is not acknowledging that displacement of his drama's motor force from the tragic to the oneiric represents a reduction of its assertion and power.

Certainly, that reduction is not Ionesco's alone; it is characteristic of far more than just his theater. It corresponds to a kind of formal concern not unlike that already identified by Nietzsche. Following Feuerbach, Nietzsche notes in *The Birth of Tragedy* that appreciation of classical tragedy requires a fullness of all the senses; its power is like that of nature in its vernal rebirth. Nietzsche feels that this power *realizes* and binds together all its participants. Tragedy does not provide, at the start, a character who masks himself in order to effect an illusion for others—this would represent too small an act: *all* the participants will be brought to feel *beside themselves*, quite properly in ecstasy—"out of themselves." It is an experience wherein the indissolubility and fixity of the individual is abolished, wherein each feels himself under a spell, transformed and magnified. Nietzsche contrasts this fullness of ecstasy with the need of the modern sensitivity to analyze the full sensory experience, to break it down into more assimilable parts. Examining how the French classical age effected this analysis and reduction of its models, he notes their containment within formal concerns—they acquire shape through *plot*, which is in fact an enigma addressed to intelligence and a field open to *small* passions which, in the end, are not tragic at all.

One might wonder why, in view of his appeal to an oneiric source and his need to demonstrate an address to intelligence, Ionesco was tempted by the tragic suggestion in the first place: his subsequent emendation of the concept acknowledges at least indirectly how difficult it is to use tragedy today as even a critical label applied to modern drama. Be that as it may, it is clear that between the extreme of tragedy and the need of a mental reduction that Nietzsche speaks of, the personal, oneiric world would occupy an awkward middle ground.

When asked about "the events, the reflections, the sensations, the discoveries" that went into making the man who made the plays, Ionesco suggests as most telling for him "the sadness of my mother," "the awareness of death," "solitude." And, on the sunny side, "days of plenitude, happiness, light" (pp. 12-13). Sadness, death, solitude on the one hand; exultation, fullness, radiance on the other: these are indeed states of intensity of the kind that sustain the tragic sweep. And when Ionesco places himself within an historical perspective, he sees the French stage suffering from what he calls a "kind of logic" that inhibits this tragic intensity: "In spite of Dullin, in spite of Jouvet, in spite of Pitoëff, [French directors] were still not very far from Antoine. Literature, painting, music had experimented in surprising ways: surrealism, Picasso's painting, non-objective painting, new music, etc. Psychology had made tremendous strides. The theater was behind. There was always a sort of conventional realism in the theater" (pp. 89-90).

But, in contrasting with these conservative inhibitions the freedom of the modern stage, Ionesco does not refer to the kind of fullness envisaged by Nietzsche; he does not even refer to the kind of emotional intensity he recalls from childhood. He speaks instead of the dramatist's freedom that affords him, through novel departures, an "aggression of the public"—he shifts his argument from content to strategy. When he speaks of his first play, *The Bald Soprano*, he has in mind not human truth but the dementia of an anti-human mask: "I began with clichés, with automatisms, with ready-made truths. At a given moment, those truths go mad" (p. 147). We recognize here the mechanism of proliferation: a mechanical process of multiplication and enlargement which, even though it may intend metaphysical echoes, is first of all perceived as an actual threat. Novelty may indeed be spiritually aggressive, but here, aggression is first a physical act: the spectator feels discomfort. In 1950, at the end of *Jack, or the Submission*, we will be reminded explicitly of this fact as the final curtain falls, "All this must provoke in the spectator a feeling of discomfort, a malaise, a shame." (Ionesco himself reminds us that his first childhood "play" was the fictional realization of a tantrum: "What I remember is that it ended this way: everything was broken in the house. Seven or eight children got together, had their *goûter,* and then broke their cups; they broke all their dishes, they broke their furniture, they threw their parents out the window," p. 55.)

Bonnefoy summarizes this tendency in Ionesco as the temptation of "acceleration, proliferation, destruction" (p. 55), and Ionesco acknowledges that "acceleration and proliferation may well be a part of my rhythm, of my vision" (p. 56). The ambiguity of this vision is that it either reduces the tragic to a sense of jeopardy derived from a comic mechanism gone out of control, or that it lends to the comic element a sense of anger: in either case, tragic intensity gives way to threat and the comic moment is fraught with irritation. Likewise, the "radiant" moment of which Ionesco speaks, and which tragedy allows, is jeopardized by Ionesco's more intimate brooding. Ionesco believes that he has created such a moment in the so-called "cité radieuse" of *The Killer:* "In the first act, Bérenger enters a radiant city. He discovers a world transfigured that had been disfigured: he rediscovers paradise after having left the rainy city" (p. 31). But Ionesco also complains that this privileged moment went unnoticed: "people weren't able to understand the nature of the radiant city of which I spoke in that play. . . There has been much misinterpretation" (pp. 30-31). Evidently because he was not quite on the side of the angels either, Bonnefoy then asked a rather logical question and provoked a rather interesting exchange.

> Bonnefoy: What is disturbing is that this paradise should be inhabited by a criminal. What can be the meaning of such a luminous yet menaced world?
> Ionesco: It's a degradation, the fall.
> Bonnefoy: It's the summit.
> Ionesco: It's the fall.
> Bonnefoy: It's the summit, the point from which one falls.
> Ionesco: That's it. (p. 31)

Even the moment of exaltation is constrained by the kind of jeopardy that informs all other moments of this drama: the aspirational as well as the somber intensities of tragedy are hemmed in by the contingencies of Ionesco's drama.

That drama is evidence of a humanistic propensity, about which Sartre complains, that nurtures an intuition of defeat and degeneration which it assumes to be humanly defining (one is reminded of Pozzo's philosophical wryness as he relights his pipe in *Waiting for Godot* and says, with what one might have hoped would be a sigh of well-being, "the second one is always less good than the first"). This sense of a grim witnessing, this demonstration of an irreversible destruction, is explicitly stated by Madeleine towards the end of *Victims of Duty* (a play which is in part a commentary on the theater): "There is always something to be said. Since the modern world is in a state of decomposition, you can be a witness of decomposition." The words are ironic in their intent but echo yet a deeper irony inasmuch as the mocking comment is unable to raise the play to its commenting distance: the play remains evidence of the destruction and witnessing about which Madeleine ironizes. Madeleine, unknowingly and ineffectually, defines the kind of theater of which she is a part but which she cannot alter even through her insights.

This sense of a fall, for which the *physical* evidence is always clearly evident, and the personal nature of that sense, make of Ionesco's writing the fruitful consequence of a "disequilibrium":

> At a given moment, things seem clear to me. I can discourse more readily, but I do not write. At other moments, it is as if there were an earthquake in my microcosm, as if everything were collapsing, and there is a kind of night, or rather a mixture of light and darkness, a chaotic world. That is where creation begins, as in the great macrocosm. . . . On the level of artistic creation, there is a genesis too. *Mutatis mutandis,* it is just about the same process, but in its own likeness. (p. 67)

That sense of a primal chaos, personalized, requires a peculiarized image. Once again, it is not the genetic myth with its abstract grandeur that we will be speaking of here, but the personal sense of an unbalancing. That private sense requires individual figures, not the abstract figure of the tragic hero, who is less than the god, against whom he contends *only* through the very limited cause of his fall. And these figures are subject to the same laws of gravity as govern the metaphysical parts of the world: they are not magnified by their fate; instead, they remain singular people that have become unsightly, ungainly or decayed (the adjectives are Bonnefoy's) through the effect of the particular threat that confronts them.

The question is whether we should speak at all about a tragic sense when we keep coming up against these idiosyncratic limitations. Ionesco says of his stage that its theatrical tension derives from the "opposition of . . . the comic and the tragic" (p. 122); whereupon Bonnefoy asks,

> Why did you, who give such importance to the dream, to life, and, consequently, to the tragic significance of life, why did you start with a play, *The Bald Soprano*, where the mechanical and the comic dominate, at least in appearance?

To which Ionesco replies,

> Because mechanistic theater was what was most contrary to me. Even in *The Bald Soprano*, the comic is not as comical as all that. It is a comedy for others. In reality, it is the expression of an anxiety. And is the comic not the start of the tragic? All you need do is speed up the tempo, for the comic; slow it down for the tragic. (p. 122)

There seems to be a contradiction here. It may be true that the tragic is a *rallentando,* a slowing of the dramatic tempo. But we have seen that Ionesco's sense of a personal jeopardy derives from a force that has broken loose from its bounds through intensification, through a *crescendo* that we associate with either proliferation or some other kind of unarrestable growth. And we have noted as well that it is this tempo that Ionesco most frequently indulges in his drama.

But we cannot be sure that we are speaking here about the conventionally comic either. It is true that the comic requires a necessary human *recognition* prior to the distancing of laughter, that laughter requires a human evidence to subvert. But Ionesco's self-projections onto his stage are figures of a more intimate *Angst* that cannot afford the distancing that comes from at least the common parlance nature of the comic. The opposition of the comic and the tragic is most likely not possible if one accepts the human reality implicit in both terms. Certainly, in Ionesco, we seem to be closer to a theater whose darkness is more personal than tragic, and whose lighter side remains forever within a part of that personal gloom.

Some twenty years ago, when I was beginning to speculate publicly on the theatre of Ionesco, I suggested that Ionesco had been mistakenly classified within the theater of the absurd (this was in 1962 and Esslin's book had just come out the year before). I believed at the time that what I identified as the repetition of a dehumanizing mechanism could only alienate the spectator. It is clear that in the intervening years, Ionesco has not lost his audience. In order for a critic to subsist, he must find more encompassing reasons for what might appear to be otherwise mere lapses of prescience: I must do likewise— since Ionesco did not lose his spectator as I thought he should have, I am compelled to ask myself something about that spectator, about that spectator's expectations. I am encouraged to do so by Ionesco himself who believes that he may yet lose his audience. Speculating on the possibility of his theater to endure, Ionesco tells Bonnefoy that he has "self-contradictory" feelings on the subject (p. 96). But later, in an unguarded moment, he considers his work inadequate to witness the human dilemma-as-futility:

> Some months ago, I was ill. When I was being operated, before receiving the anesthetic needle, I said to myself that maybe I would die, but I felt no fear. I don't know if at the moment of actual death I will see things the same way, but there I had the very strong feeling that all I had done, that everything that was behind me had absolutely no importance. The whole social component had dropped out. All my acts, the history of mankind had turned into a basket of ashes. At the same time, I also had the disagreeable feeling that ahead of me there was nothing. I fell asleep. I awoke, and for a long time thereafter, that feeling stayed with me. I would say to myself: I am alive, all right. One would speak to me of what is called my work and it seemed ridiculous to me that it should be spoken of. (p. 113)

Clearly, Ionesco is speaking about more than his work here: he is describing a state of mind before the world. Still, this is not the first time that he has alluded to the negligibility of his work; if Robert Jouanny is reliable, Ionesco is supposed to have had the following afterthought about his plays: "You know, Sir, that I do not like what Samuel Beckett writes. . . . Well, what I write is not worth even what Mr. Samuel Beckett has written: it is dust." And at this point, Ionesco is supposed to have sought confirmation from Mrs. Ionesco, "Isn't that so? Not even dust"; which elicited, according to Jouanny, a supportive response from Mrs. Ionesco that sounds very nearly like lèse-majesté: "No, Eugène, it is not even dust," thereby confirming Ionesco in his most mournful self-assessment: "No, it's just rubbish, it doesn't mean a thing" (op. cit., p. 9).

I would not wish to be as harsh on Ionesco as he is on himself in a moment of despondency, but I would like to use the evidence of that despondency as a symptom through which to begin the analysis of a malady that affects our times and, consequently, our stage and our theater goers. It is a malady of which Ionesco is both an instance and a victim—or, if you prefer, a witness. We have said previously that although Ionesco believes that he has occasionally modulated his stage in the direction of light, he himself is aware that this modulation has not always been successful, that it has been missed by his spectator. Bonnefoy suggested that there may be a perfectly plausible reason for this: Ionesco's radiant city is, after all, the space of a lurking threat. Conversely, we have noted that although Ionesco places himself under the sign of tragedy, his stage seldom claims the kind of exultation which we associate with tragedy: instead, we have within the darker side of this theater, once again, the suggestion of a lurking threat.

This persistence of the reduction of a greater (Nietzschean) seizure to the dimension of a physical threat may result from Ionesco's intuitive sense of his spectator, from a delicate perception of the modern sensitivity. For although Ionesco uses freely the word "tragedy," it is clear that he has something else in mind. The writer in him seems to know that the concept which Nietzsche prized for its sacred fullness conveys to the modern ear and mind unseemly grandiloquence and abstraction. As Nietzsche himself surmised, the modern sensitivity feels more comfortable with the more intimate and limited assertions of a personal dilemma. We have followed Ionesco through the analysis of how his stage becomes a kind of personal exorcism. We should note further that the self-consciousness that rejects grandiloquence and abstraction will more readily accept the reductive particularization of the comic mask—even though its laughter, to borrow Ghelderode's term, gnashes its teeth. One understands without having to refer to Nietzsche—or Freud—the reasons that brought the tragic spectator to the tragic stage: the tragic protagonist shed his personal demons on stage in an act of ritual grandeur sufficient to sweep up its spectator. It is not as easy to understand just what it is that drives the modern sensitivity to its stages, if it is given to witness only a personal exorcism that expels intimate demons *onto* a stage where they remain to exacerbate the spectator's own malaise.

What is lost with the possibility of tragedy is the possibility of human assertion. An optimistic and egocentric belief that sees man as the ultimate measure of all things gives way to a belief that displaces man from the center to a marginal position on the edge of darkness, the object of threatening and malevolent forces. The theater that conveys this latter image of man shows him mutilated and humiliated, rather than equal at least to his jeopardy. The exception that comes to mind in the theater of Ionesco is the last scene in *Rhinoceros*, the one in which Bérenger takes his stand—and his gun. Yet even this optimistic ending remains less than satisfying—perhaps because of that very gun that Bérenger grabs as the final curtain comes down. In order for us to grant Bérenger our tragic sense—assuming that such commitments are still possible—we must be able to move from the gun back to Bérenger: we must internalize his otherwise ridiculous weapon. It is only if we can sense that the gun will be ineffective and that Bérenger, knowing this, takes his stand nevertheless, that we are moved and magnified by the character. If we remain with the gun, we remain in a world of more limited symbols: the rhinoceros becomes Nazis, or some other finite threat that can be disposed of, in the end, by a gun—or something like a gun.

What tragedy once intended to assert was the perdurability of the human spirit against the multiple forms of a continuous threat—not a partial threat, but a threat as total as was the human totality required to counter it. Tragedy cannot entertain any lesser threat; therefore it cannot entertain either spiritual mutilation or a reductive analysis of the tragic hero's integrity. Perhaps for this reason, that hero's stage is bare—guns, or their equivalents, disappear along with other transitory symbols: the human assertion has no peculiarities, neither in the face that it turns towards jeopardy, nor in the jeopardy itself. The modern stage is baroque alongside that barrenness, since each form of the jeopardy wears its distinctive face.

That proliferative force constitutes the peculiar strength and tempo of the modern stage. But that stage is in danger by virtue of its very acceptance. At a time when a tight, overbearing stage constrained itself and its spectator within a rigid set of rules, that strength and tempo were as real and as powerful as the obstacles in their path. Publics had to be educated, habits and expectations disrupted, conventions overturned. But once those obstacles had been made to collapse, and the stage found itself ready to display only the great force that had cleansed it, that force no longer had any object against which to direct itself. Having effected a dramatic renewal through the freedom that it claimed for itself, this theater finds its own renewal to be problematic: it has eliminated, along with the former oppression, its *raison d'être*. Its efforts to maintain itself as a simple dynamics are more reminiscent of the capitalist market that will renew itself artificially if it must (out of a tautological desire to keep merchandizing its product) than of the revolutionary force that swept aside a previous constraint through a power superior to that constraint.

At the social, or political, level, this theater becomes one of denial and rejection, alongside which form, history and values are denied. The multiple shapes that this denial require eventually reduce the strength of the denial to the superficiality of the value analyzed (hence reduced) and denounced: the particularization of the attack causes its weakness. We are left once again with a quantity of energy spending itself in the gratuitous and wasteful fashion of an uncapped oil well. That random energy finally conceives of itself as a desperate freedom, with no object to give it shape, with no sense of its purpose or future.

At the end of their talk, Bonnefoy asks Ionesco if there is no hope for literature. After suggesting that "the novel is no longer possible, . . . poetry is no longer anything but word play, . . . theater is frequently inferior literature" (p. 197), Ionesco sees possible salvation in a change of form: "I hope . . . literature will be reborn. . . . But it will have another aspect." When Bonnefoy asks what that aspect might be for the theater, Ionesco responds with the ideal of the happening.

> I think for example of the new American theater, the theater of the event where all of a sudden people are on stage and begin not only to imagine but to live what they imagine, to conjure things, events that are altogether unexpected for them as well as for the spectators. In the best of cases, the spectators participating, it would be necessary for all to be authors. Formerly, authors would propose an imaginary mode of life. Now, the art of theater must give to each the possibility of living, of being a poet, of bringing on his own unforeseen. (p. 197)

This ultimate freedom in the theater is freedom through the abandonment of theater. So we move from the overbearing constraints of a past theater to simple existential continuance. This is freedom indeed: in the arts, it dismisses, along with the constraints out of which the artifact was created, the artifact itself. That is to be expected when the novel can no longer endure as simply an expression of the need to narrate, of the need to tell something important about the human condition; when poetry is no longer the *necessary* form of a human outcry; when theater is no longer the desire of a communal ritual that asserts, in its pain and its exaltation, the fullest human dimension.

Cornell University

JOURNEY TO THE KINGDOM OF THE DEAD
Ionesco's Gnostic Dream Play

Rosette C. Lamont

Journey to the Kingdom of the Dead—Theme and Variations, may appear at first glance to still belong to the genre of the Metaphysical Farce, and to be as deeply rooted in Dadaism, Surrealism, and Jungian analysis as the penultimate *Man with Bags,* the first tablet of this diptych, when it is in fact a fascinating new departure.

In *Journey,* the dream material is transmitted raw, in an astonishingly direct, simple manner. Were this the principal aspect of this oneiric drama it would already qualify as a daring dramaturgic enterprise. "These are family quarrels," Ionesco stated in the course of the Symposium held at the University of Southern California, "and although the contenders are no longer among the living, and the contentions as dead as they are, the inveterate strife continues. Night after night I dream of the same members of my family, night after night they feud." We recognize in the play scenes from Ionesco's journals: confessional passages, *pensées,* meditations on politics and culture, anxiety attacks, and, above all, dream images jotted down over the years. Concretized upon the stage, states of mind and tropisms become, despite their highly personal character, universal, archetypal effigies. They allow us to explore what Joseph Campbell calls "the mythogenetic zone of the individual heart."[1]

The myth of the visit to the underworld is as ancient as human consciousness. We cannot help but connect Jean's search to Odysseus' encounter on the mist-enshrouded shore of the land of the Cimmerians with Tiresias, the

---

[1] Joseph Campbell, *The Masks of God, Creative Mythology* (New York: Viking Press, 1968–70), p. 677.

seer who reveals to Homer's hero how the latter is to make his way back home. Nor was the author of the *Odyssey* the first inventor of infernal voyages. He himself inherited an ancient tradition the remnants of which can still be observed today in the hypnotic trances of shamans, voodoo practices, the "magic" healings of witch doctors. Cartographers of the Beyond have left their maps upon sarcophagi. Nor are these explorations necessarily katabases. In primitive cultures, dead ancestors are periodically invited to visit the living, and to partake of a feast prepared in their honor. The way is open for the living and the dead to make contact; its path is traced through ritual and art. As W.H. Auden once said in public, shortly before he died: "Art is breaking bread with the dead."

Ionesco's "Nekyia" is as ancient as the beginnings of man, yet the language of the play is as modern, and at times self-consciously trite, as the conversations of the Martins and the Smiths in *The Bald Soprano*. The dramatist, however, carefully plants a series of clues within the surface of absurdisms that compose many sections of the text. He indulges in a charmingly perverse game, misleading his audience on the one hand while guiding the receptive listener on the other. Thus, a passage which might easily be taken for a bit of surrealist delirium turns out to be, if properly analyzed, a time capsule enclosing a coded message.

At the end of a profoundly painful confrontation between Jean, the protagonist of *Journey,* and the latter's dead father, or one ought perhaps to say, between their two dream doubles, Jean's glorious achievements (so much like those of Ionesco himself), at last acknowledged not only by society but by his family, are being scrutinized. Upon close examination Jean's writings turn out to be nothing but old, dirty notebooks, their pages covered with doodles. Bits of rusty wire, a cook book, soiled rags, broken pencils fill the protagonist's desk drawers. The bottle of ink he takes out opens, and its contents spill upon the stage. Horrified and dismayed Jean exclaims:

> Everything must be re-examined, done over again. But I'll go on fighting to protect the Occident, to champion the venerability of the Greek cosmos, the liberty conferred upon us by the planets, Existentialism, Gnosticism, the right to infer, the Valentinian speculation, the song of the pearl. The defense of the Occident, the defense of the Occident, the jig of the departing, the Italian campaign, the march on Rome, the defense of the Occident, the Occident of the defense, dental defense, the defense of the Occident, the defense of the occiput, and my political itinerary. The status of man, of

culture, of Oriental cults, the defense of the Occident, dental defense, the Fens of dent.[2]

These ravings are not merely the discourse of an anguished mind; there is much method to this madness.

Earlier in the play, Ionesco refers to "the Last Knights of the Occident" (NRF, I, p. 5). The dramatist has never been neutral politically, even as he kept on affirming that he was apolitical, and that his work was free of ideological content. From his journals we learn that he scorned his father's chameleonic propensities, his accomodations with each and every changing regime. Ionesco and his wife left Rumania when the rise of fascism started to infect every sphere, including that of familial ties and personal relations. The break with his father, and his country, was to be a final one; it clearly haunts the writer. In France, as soon as the dramatist became a well-known literary figure, he began publishing essays and articles denouncing the new fascism, that of the Left. Russian imperialism disguised as Soviet protectivism, the horror of slave labor camps and of psychiatric wards used to "re-educate" dissidents, the violation of human rights in the Soviet Union and its satellite countries, literary censorship, official anti-semitism masked as anti-Zionism, the oppression of religious groups, the uprooting of nationalities, all of these evils came under Ionesco's systematic, lucidly phrased denunciation. Nor did his irony spare the members of the capitalist intelligentsia who wished to blind themselves to the existence of the *gulags*. Together with two other famous Rumanian exiles, Mircea Eliade, and Cioran, Ionesco can be seen as a champion fighting in the only way he knows how, by means of his pen. Ionesco, Eliade and Cioran are three of "the Last Knights of the Occident," a chivalric order dedicated to the preservation of humanism.

If "the Greek cosmos, the liberty conferred upon us by the planets, and Existentialism" belong to various periods of the latter, the reference to "the

---

[2] Eugène Ionesco, *Theme and Variations or Journey to the Kingdom of the Dead, La Nouvelle Revue Française,* 1er janvier 1980, No 324, 25. All quotations from the play have been translated by the writer of this essay. They will be referred to in the body of the text in the following manner: NRF for *La Nouvelle Revue Française,* and I, II, III for the three issues which add up to the complete version of the play: I for January 1st, 1980, No 324; II for February 1st, 1980, No 325; III for March 1st, 1980, No 326. The essay is an expanded version of the lecture on the play delivered at the University of Southern California in the course of a three-day Symposium on the works of Eugène Ionesco. Since Ionesco participated in the Symposium some of the remarks quoted in this essay were made by the dramatist at some time during the Symposium. *Voyages chez les morts* was first presented at the Guggenheim Museum in New York (September 22–November 2, 1980).

Valentinian speculation," and to "the song of the pearl" hint at a different order of knowledge. None of this ought to come as a surprise to those who have been aware over the years of Ionesco's ever-growing fascination with Eastern philosophies, mystery religions, Neoplatonism, alchemy, astrology, the Egyptian and the Tibetan Books of the Dead, and his general tendency to syncretism. Like the Neoplatonists, this Knight of the Occident would like to reconcile the best aspects of the teachings of Plato and Aristotle with Oriental mysticism. Thus, if the word "Gnosticism" appears right next to "Existentialism" in the passage quoted above, it is not merely for oxymoronic effect. Indeed, it becomes obvious that one of the keys to a deeper reading of *Journey to the Kingdom of the Dead* is the Valentinian doctrine.

The "song of the pearl," or *Song of the Soul,* as it is perhaps better known, is a magnificent Gnostic text attributed to Bardesanes. It is one of the few actual writings of the Gnostics that survived. As to the Valentinus of "the Valentinian speculation," he was the most prominent leader of the movement, the only one to have formed disciples. Perhaps for Ionesco, the writer of words to be spoken from the stage, there is a something deeply moving about the old Gnostic myth preserved by Valentinus of man's creation by angels, and of the subsequent penetration into this creature of the seed of the spirit, resulting in the faculty of speech. It is speech that will allow man to rise above the world-creating angels.

In *Découvertes* Ionesco describes the infant's discovery of the world, the baby's attempt to invent sounds and words for the things he sees and feels. From the start man is a giver of names, an inventor of speech. Ionesco starts with the faculty of astonishment, a mixture of delight and anxiety, a sense of awe. Unlike *l'homme moyen sensuel,* the artist is able to retain a child-like sense of wonder allowing it to permeate his creative sphere. Poetic language parallels the word-inventions of the child since neither the artist nor the infant recognize dividing lines separating the real from the imaginary. Not unlike Plotinus whom he admires and studies, Ionesco feels that the soul is a stranger among the visible world of appearances, and that the spirit must not choose to dwell amid the shadows of the so-called real despite the imperatives of that great deadener, habit. The adult, the aging man is trapped in what Ionesco often refers to as "the warm slime" of existence. By sinking into matter man is no longer able to free himself for the mystical flight of "the alone to the Alone" (to quote Porphyry's famous definition of the aims inherent in his master's teachings). If moments of illumination are rare—Porphyry counted four occasions during the six years of his association with Plotinus when the latter reached an ecstatic union with the deity—they are all the more precious. Ionesco mentions such epiphanies when one is visited by a light that has nothing in common with that of day, even of the brightest and most joyous of days. The mysterious glow seems to emanate from an invisible sun; it lingers in the mind, and those who have seen it once live in hope of the return of bliss.

In his essay "Eugène Ionesco and 'La nostalgie du Paradis,'" Mircea Eliade detects an influence on the dramatist of the Byzantine mystics, "particularly the Hesychasts and Gregory Palmas. . . ."[3] In a footnote Eliade explains: "Like so many Rumanian writers of his generation, Eugène Ionesco was, in the 30's, attracted by the Byzantine spirituality and the eastern-orthodox traditions. For a number of intellectuals, such preoccupations were part of their endeavor to connect modern Rumanian culture to its 'autochthonous,' i.e. 'Oriental' roots, in order to counterbalance the powerful influence of Western, particularly French, culture. . . ."[4] Later, as this pursuit became associated with the chauvinism of the right, Ionesco seemed to retreat from it. With the defeat of fascism his perspective shifted once more, so that it appeared desirable to fuse the philosophies of east and west.

"The defense of the Occident" Ionesco's protagonist pledges himself to effect can be carried out only by one able to bridge the two cultures, the Occidental and the Oriental, that is by a Neoplatonist of today. By virtue of having been born at the crossroads of civilizations, in the Balkans, the dramatist hopes that he can achieve the Janusian look, the ability to see two directions simultaneously.

To have been born and raised at the crossroads of civilizations is a very privileged situation. Here is how Elias Canetti describes it in his journal, *The Tongue Set Free, Remembrance of a European Childhood*:

> Ruschuk, on the lower Danube, where I came into the world, was a marvelous city for a child, and if I say that Ruschuk is in Bulgaria, then I am giving an inadequate picture of it. For people of the most varied backgrounds lived there, on any one day you could hear seven or eight languages. Aside from Bulgarians who often came from the countryside, there were many Turks who lived in their own neighborhood, and next to it was the neighborhood of the Sephardim, the Spanish Jews—our neighborhood. There were Greeks, Albanians, Armenians, Gypsies. From the opposite side of the Danube came Rumanians; my wetnurse, whom I no longer remember, was a Rumanian. There were also Russians here and there. . . .

---

[3] Mircea Eliade, "Eugène Ionesco and 'la Nostalgie du Paradis Perdu,'" in *The Two Faces of Ionesco*, ed. Rosette C. Lamont and Melvin J. Friedman (Troy, New York: Whitston Publishing Company, 1978), p. 23

[4] Eliade, p. 28.

> It would be hard to give a full picture of the colorful time of those early years in Ruschuk, the passions and the terrors. Anything I subsequently experienced had already happened in Ruschuk. There, the rest of the world was known as "Europe," and if someone sailed up the Danube to Vienna, people said he was going to Europe.. Europe began where the Turkish empire had once ended. . . .[5]

Ionesco often says about himself: "I'm only a peasant from the Danube." The adverb carries treasure troves of irony.

In a beautiful and mysterious passage at the beginning of *Journey*, the scene of the first dream encounter between Jean and his father, a city is evoked by the two men; it is not unlike Canetti's Ruschuk, or the "cité radieuse" of Ionesco's *The Killer*. It seems to be of no place and of every place, harmonious, complete, a totality. This is how Jean describes it:

> What never stops surprising me is the discoveries I make in the course of my travels, the unexpected cities, cities I've never heard about. I've never been a good student of geography, but I knew the essentials. And there, all at once, in the midddle of the desert, a new city arises. It must have been a French colony once upon a time. It was extremely harmonious. There were tiny public squares, streets that were not too narrow, boulevards not too wide, houses pleasing in their proportions neither too high nor too low. One somehow sensed that inside these houses the apartments were comfortable. There were many balconies. The streets were not overcrowded. It must have been due to the fact that the inhabitants of this town felt good about staying home where they had all they needed (NRF, I, p. 5).

Jean's father has heard of this former French colony in China, "somewhere in the North" (p. 5). He adds: "The men are great riders; they are known as the Last Knights of the Occident" (p. 5). Yet they live in the Far East. Extremes touch, fuse, as Ionesco always says. "You failed to see them because they were out in the fields when you visited their country" (p. 5), the father explains.

What is this oasis in the desert where men go out in the surrounding fields? It seems to be inland, yet Jean claims to have caught sight of a sea as blue as that of the Côte d'Azur, or of the waters of the bay of San Francisco. The name of the country is Boganda, and its capital is Bocal, a metropolis standing in the plain of Bocala. The initial "B" cannot fail to suggest Bucharest, although the word "Bocal" evokes the *vas* of the alchemists, the vessel

---

[5]Elias Canetti, *The Tongue Set Free, Remembrances of a European Childhood*, trans. by Joachim Neugroschel (New York: Seabury Press, 1979), pp. 4–5.

in which all foul matter undergoes the process of transubstantiation. This dream city could be the New Jerusalem where opposites are reconciled, where East and West merge, where only the One reigns.

The father who knows that his son has not come in search of him, but of his first wife, Jean's mother, whispers the untranslatable: "J'ai depassé l'amertume" (p. 6). The French word for bitterness contains the word for sea ("mer"), and/or the word mother ("mère"). Since Jean's mother was deserted by her husband, who subsequently remarried, the father's confession reveals a truth he might have been hiding from himself: He has gone beyond Jean's mother, leaving her stranded on some distant shore of memory. It will now be up to Jean to track down her weary ghost.

Ionesco's study of Gnosticism must have taught him that the origin of evil coincides with that of creation. To effect the latter, the Demiurge swallowed part of the true Father's infinite light. Yet, according to Valentinian Gnosticism, Primal Man can be redeemed, and he will rise again. To free the light, Jean must visit the realm of shades there to encounter the dual image of the Great Mother, Demeter-Kore, and to enter once again, on a spiritual plane, into the sacramental relationship of the Heavenly marriage. To issue whole from this exploration, Jean will have to perform what Ionesco calls "the jig of the departing." Such an exit is no easy task, even for a hero. Here is the way the Sibyl of Cumae describes it to Aeneas:

> . . . day and night the door of darkest Dis is open. But to recall your steps, to rise again into the upper air; that is the labor; that is the task. A few, whom Jupiter has loved in kindness or whom blazing worth has raised to heaven as god's sons, returned. (vi. 176–181)[6]

Like "pious Aeneas," Ionesco's protagonist will have to step through the gate of polished ivory, "les dents de la défense."—We must recall that in French the word "défense" can also refer to the elephant's tusk.—In Book XIX of the *Odyssey*, Penelope describes to Odysseus, whom she has failed to identify under his protective disguise as a beggar, the mysterious gates of the world of dreams: one is made of horn, one of polished elephant's tooth. "The elephant's tooth is full of untruth; it cheats with a burden of vain hope. But carven horn is not forsworn; a dream coming through that gate forecasts the truth of days to come."[7] If dreams must pass through the gate of horn in order to come true, Aeneas can exit only through that of polished elephant's tooth for he is no phantom but a flesh and blood hero who was granted entry into

---

[6] Virgil, *The Aeneid*, trans. by Allen Mandelbaum (New York: Bantam Books, 1961), p. 137.
[7] Homer, *The Odyssey*, Book XIX, trans. by W.H.D. Rouse (New York: New American Library, 1949), p. 224.

the underworld. Book VI of *The Aeneid* ends with an interesting reinterpretation of Penelope's soothsayer's art:

> There are two gates of Sleep: the one is said to be of horn, through it an easy exit is given to true Shades; the other is made of polished ivory, perfect, glittering, but through that way the Spirits send false dreams into the world above. And here Anchises, when he is done with words, accompanies the Sibyl and his son together; and he sends them through the gate of ivory. (vi. 1191–1199)[8]

"The elephant's tooth" of the Greek and Roman epic has become in Jean's deceptively irrational monologue "la dent de la défense." To defend Occidental culture, to uphold the traditions of Humanism, Jean will have to follow in the footsteps of the departing ("l'exitant"), the Eastern hero par excellence, Trojean Aeneas, on his way to Latium, and therefore to the creation by an Eastern people of the future Roman empire, and thus, of Occidental culture.

From this point on, the monologue's strong inner logic becomes easier to follow since all the references are to familiar landmarks of western culture. "The Italian campaign" (the French "campagne italienne" is richer in allusions since it suggests the Italian countryside as well as military prowess) brings to mind the "Guerres d'Italie" waged by successive French kings— Charles VIII, Louis XII, François Ier—to conquer Naples and the Duchy of Milan. The finest by-product of these senseless invasions was the discovery of Italian Renaissance art and architecture, and the great changes brought about in France as a result of these discoveries. What is perhaps suggested here, with a good deal of irony, is that wars brings culture. "The march on Rome" deepens the irony further evoking as it does Napoleonic invasions; it is a vivid reminder of the Emperor's dream of uniting the Occident and the Orient under his domination. Thus, the Humanism imported into France by François Ier was to become Bonaparte's official export in his imperialist wars. Ionesco tells us in his own oblique way that conquerors have "la dent longue," as long as "une défense d'éléphant," against which one cannot defend oneself.

Flight, exile are often the only forms of self-defense. Ionesco's "political itinerary" took him away from the sharp teeth, the hungry jaws of the rhinoceroses. As one who spent an equal number of years in France and in Rumania until he left the latter, Ionesco is particularly able to bridge the gap between two cultures. He is aware that it is up to him to "re-examine" everything, as he states at the start of Jean's monologue. He also feels that this process is doomed to failure. His realization that humanistic values are

[8]*Aeneid*, p. 162.

disappearing, even from the "Free World," is concretized in the deconstruction of language at the end of the soliloquy. Since in Ionesco's *oeuvre* language is one of the principal *dramatis personae,* the topsy-turvy transformation of "la dent de la défense" into the meaningless "la fense de la dent" (which I translated above as "the Fens of dent") concretizes more eloquently than any action could hope to do the dramatist's apprehension that both the life of the spirit (for him Eastern Gnosticism), and that of the mind (Occidental rationalism) are now fossils. The boldness of Jean's rhetoric throughout his monologue, his attempts at reaffirmation, are deflated, destroyed, by the very tool man uses to establish his dignity as "roseau pensant." Language itself, Ionesco suggests, may be as antiquated as the old-fashioned pistols Bérenger aims at the assassin in *The Killer* and which he finally lowers, accepting his defeat at the hands of gratuitous evil.

In the space of a short monologue, Ionesco is able to comment on the development of civilization, the course of history, and the brutishness of our own epoch. The secret message is not in what Jean says but in how he says it.

If the ancient dream of the reconciliation of opposites has become an impossibility how can the individual soul achieve wholeness? This is perhaps the central question in this most confessional of all Ionesco's plays. *Journey to the Kingdom of the Dead* is the dramatized story of a realized individual, a writer (not unlike Ionesco himself) who has achieved world renown but who must face his ghosts, put to rest numerous grudges, transcend his bitterness, and, above all, be re-united with his *anima,* his dead mother. The play is a process similar to that tested by C.G. Jung when he began to set down some of the archetypal visions that came to him. Jung speaks of it as "writing letters to the anima."[8] *Journey to the Kingdom of the Dead* is Ionesco's letters to his dead mother, and, by extension, to himself.

Ionesco's play begins in a simple, almost child-like fashion. It is as though the protagonist, a mature man and a respected writer, had regressed to the state of being a timid child, an experience that is not unusual under hypnosis, or for a person dreaming.

We see Jean enter a low room where an old man, his head covered by a skull-cap, is stretched out upon a pallet. Jean addresses him with respect, and yet as casually as though they had parted a short while ago: "Hello, grandfather" (NRF, I, p. 1). The old man, however, will have none of this familiarity, or at least he seems to prefer another kind of social address: "I'm your maternal grandfather, but I wish to be called by my first name, Leon" (p. 1).

---

[9]C.G. Jung, *Memories, Dreams, Reflections* (New York: Vintage Books, 1965), p. 186.

Clearly this crank does not relish the role of dignified ancestor. After death, age no longer matters, nor any kind of precedence. Jean, sensing that he must now tread carefully, inquires about "Emma," his grandmother. Why isn't she there, with her husband? The reason is provided without hesitation: "She died a widow, she's free" (p. 2).

Ionesco's Beyond is neither the Elysian Fields, nor the Christian paradise; it is a land of the unexpected, of shifting relations, of the relativity of the concept of aging. As his grandfather invites his visitor to step through a door, into the next room, Jean finds himself face to face with a younger man, sitting on a bed, reading the paper; it is his maternal uncle. The latter seems furious at having been discovered. "Who gave you my address?" (p. 2), he keeps on asking. He also protests that he is not dead. "I simply reached the age of ninety, that's all, and I decided to stop there, to keep on being ninety. I could be my father's father" (p. 2).

The fact that a son, if he reaches old age, can in fact be "older" than his own father, if the latter died young, should not surprise any reader of Ionesco. In *Man with Bags* we were made to witness the tragi-comic encounter between a decrepit old hag and a beautiful young woman. The hag rushes towards the lovely apparition calling her "ma petite maman." Those who die young, or disappear from our life while in the blush of youth, retain, like the Greek and Roman goddesses, eternal loveliness. Virgil expressed in moving terms the all too human bewilderment of Aeneas when, upon encountering a beautiful young huntress in the forest, the Trojan hero realizes that it is his mother, the goddess Venus, up to one of her usual tricks of assuming a disguise. The pain of being only half-divine, or perhaps suffering confinement within the existential injustice of human mortality, draws from Aeneas an exclamation which is a cry of pain:

> Why do you mock your son—so often and so cruelly—with these lying apparitions? Why can't I ever join you, hand to hand, to hear, to answer you with honest words? (I, 581–584)[10]

The Trojan hero's grief echoes the sorrow of Odysseus when, in the underworld, the King of Ithaca attempts to clasp the ghost of his dear mother in an embrace she thrice eludes, she who died of despair at their long separation. Later, in Ionesco's *Journey,* we will find Jean similarly distressed. In the meanwhile, it is his maternal uncle who does not welcome any expression of intimacy. He does not, however, wish to be called by his first name, but orders his nephew to address him with all due formality as "Uncle." Perhaps

---

[10]*Aeneid,* p. 15.

this is due to the fact that he is older than the grandfather, that he cannot be treated as a contemporary. Jean's father is also "younger" than his son, or rather Jean, still living, is now older than his father was when he died. In a long talk they have together, Jean expresses his puzzlement, particularly at the fact that though this be so, face to face with this strict disciplinarian, he, a mature man, a famous writer, is once again "the unhappy child, thrashed and severely restricted" (NRF, I, p. 12) by his father. Death freezes certain memories, girds us in the attitudes we had in relation to those who have gone beyond our reach. What was done cannot be undone. Is this why the dead seem so perturbed? Jean, sensing the anger of his grandfather and of his uncle, inquires: "What's the matter with both of you? Is it having died that makes you furious?" (p. 2). This question remains unanswered.

One of the main themes, perhaps the main theme of *Journey to the Kingdom of the Dead,* is that of the quest of the mother. Little is told us about her disappearance. We know that one day she went to the station, and purchased "une couchette" (a berth) in a sleeping-car. Her husband cannot even recall in what direction the train was leaving. Having left, she wrote no one. Jean says accusingly: "I think you were glad to see her go. You did everything to have this happen. You didn't try to hold her back. You could have, so easily, with one word." The Father seems to speak in riddles: "She must have gone far away, where no one can be seen, to a place beyond the scrutiny of human eyes, or of mechanical devices" (NRF, I, p. 7). What is this mysterious *locus*? We must recall that death and disappearance stood at the center of the Eleusinian mysteries. Ionesco blends here the realistic fact of his parents' separation with the mythical journey of the Mother Goddess to the land of the dead. Stretched out on her "couchette," carried within a sleeping car, the mother sails to eternity, as in one of the barges of ancient Egypt. Jean mourns her departure, and he is profoundly offended by the fact that his father has replaced her, marrying a woman of his people, one who spoke his language.— We must recall here that Ionesco's mother was French, and that when the dramatist's father took a second wife it was back in his country.—Now the second wife is dead also, and Jean is to meet both women in the underworld when he enters the realm of The Mothers.

After much questioning and searching, Jean finally reaches his mother. At first he does not recognize her for she has grown as old as her own parents who are accompanying her. When the protagonist expresses his dismay, his mother explains: "I've caught up with my parents' age. One grows old in the Beyond. We get to be a hundred years old and then we stop. You'll age also once you'll be among us" (NRF, I, p. 17). A woman, perhaps Jean's wife (he himself is not sure whether she is his wife, his sister, or his daughter), states that if the mother has aged after death it is because she feels ill at ease in the underworld. The woman adds by way of explanation: "When you feel good over there, time proceeds backwards. It's not true that one keeps on aging in the Beyond" (p. 18). Perhaps those who grow old, or older, in the Beyond are people with unfinished business on this earth, unsettled accounts with the living. Even after death ancient rivalries continue. The Father's two wives squabble over which was the one he loved the best. It is suggested, although they do not know this, that he was probably truly happy only after his second wife's death, when he lived with his maid, a gypsy. The love rivalry between two wives, both dead, lends a grotesque and infinitely tragic character to all such doubts. If love is tied to ambition, pride, greed, if it becomes a matter of competition rather than compassion, then it is vitiated. Jean Paul Sartre wrote at the end of *No Exit:* "Hell is other people." Ionesco shows us this hell:

> The Grandmother (to Jean): Your mother ought to remarry your father.
> The Grandmother: Right now, let's at least try to get Ernest out of debt.
> The Stepmother: This is my home. No one will remove me from here. No one will take my husband away from me.
> The Wife: (to the Stepmother): He doesn't love you all that much. In fact not at all any more. He must be with his concubine at this very moment, the gypsy girl.
> The Stepmother: Don't talk nonsense. He's chosen to be with me forever in the family vault. He wants nothing to do with you.
> The Mother: Nor with you.
>
> The Stepmother: If he's with the gypsy girl it's to have a good time, that's all. I know his deep feelings. He made his choice; he chose me and that's irrevocable. (To Jean) Your mother's family belongs to another species of humanity. He had to sever those ties. With me, with my brothers and my cousins, he gets along well. We speak the same language. . . .
> The telephone rings, and yet no telephone is visible.
> The Voice: Hello, Jean?
> The Stepmother: Are you being called?
> Jean: Who is speaking? Who's there? An anonymous voice that does not wish to identify itself.
> The Stepmother: What are those voices calling you? As if this were your home! This is my home.
> The Wife: What you call your home has been appropriated. It belongs to each and everyone.
> The Stepmother: Everything here belongs to me since it is my husband's property.

Jean: Nothing belongs to anyone, or rather, everything belongs to everyone (NRF, I, pp. 21–22).

The ceaseless quarrels about property rights, ludicrously out-of-date in the face of a communist take-over, the debate about gradations of feelings made equally futile by the father's last love for a servant girl, freeze the characters who, like the fratricidal traitors of Dante's *Inferno,* remain entangled in the icy web of their ever-repeated, relived, insoluble recriminations. Nor does the resemblance stop there for they share, after all, the misty clime of the Danube so eloquently evoked in Canto XXXII by the great Florentine exile:

> Danube in Austria never could disguise
> His wintry course beneath a shroud so thick
> As this, nor Tanais under frozen skies,
> Afar. . . .   (p. 25–28)[11]

Even the accusations of the Grandmother against the second wife, and her family, echo the moral wrath and the prophetic tone of the *Commedia:* "Your brother has gotten rich through ill-secured gains, through theft. This is how he was named to high office. Many were killed by him, many condemned to death. It is unjust, but the Lord God will know whom to punish" (NRF, I, p. 20).

As the Mother's family begins to make its exit, the grieving ghost turns to Jean uttering these final words: "I kiss you my child. We will await you, without much hope, but we will still await you indefinitely" (ibid). Profound longing, the pain of separation, are movingly suggested in these brief lines. They echo the words of wisdom of Odysseus' mother: "As soon as the spirit leaves the white bones, the sinews no longer hold bones and flesh together—the blazing fire consumes them all; but the soul flits away, fluttering like a dream. Make haste back to the light, but do not forget all this. . . ."[12]

Jean must also find his way home, and it will take him to rue Claude Terrasse, the address of one of Ionesco's first apartments in Paris. It is not easy to make one's way into the past. Jean's wife suggests that he take a horse-drawn carriage since there is "no direct train" (NRF, I, p. 21). Although there are no buses, nor taxis that would go there, coaches and troikas can be secured. "Once there used to be streetcars" (p. 21), Jean sighs. The homeward journey is an imaginary voyage into the past, *a recherche du temps perdu.*

---

[11] Dante, *The Divine Comedy, Hell,* trans. by Dorothy L. Sayers (Penguin Books, 1949), p. 272.

[12] *Odyssey,* Book XI, p. 128

The way has been mapped in books Jean finds on his desk, but he is unable to decipher the archaic writing. "They must be books explaining what is to be done when one is about to die, or has just died... These are ancient books in which one finds transmitted experiences handed down from a remote past; they are so ancient I can't make them out. I've forgotten the language" (p. 21).

The theme of forgetfulness, of the disappearance of a certain kind of *gnosis,* and of the codes by which it can be transmitted, is repeated over and over again. Man's mind, his memory, are full of holes, *lacunae.* These gaps—we must recall that one of Ionesco's most amusing and at the same time terrifying metaphysical farces is entitled *La Lacune*—open onto the greater gap, or hole, the abyss of death. The books Jean is leafing through could be *The Egyptian Book of the Dead,* and *The Tibetan Book of the Dead.* Were the protagonist able to decipher the latter, he would read therein that a gap is a basic psychological experience, one that has to do with the notion of the Between, the *bardo,* an interval between life and death. It is also applicable to the world of the living. The experience of uncertainty yields a rich apprehension that restores to the one who undergoes it fully the sense of wonder human beings lose in the process of daily living.

To find again the "rez-de-chaussée" apartment on the rue Claude Terasse, a low, humid dwelling, such as his mother seemed to favor despite their obvious proximity to the confines of the underworld, Jean will have to step through just such a gap. It is difficult for him who "changed beds every night" (NRF, I, p. 21), to understand why anyone would elect this kind of abode. Now it seems to be occupied by a couple of strangers. They invite Jean to spend the night; they have three beds. Now the apartment seems to suffer a metamorphosis: it is the old mill of the Chapelle-Anthenaise, the village where Ionesco was sent as a child by his mother and where he was extremely happy. It is also the large château of Cerisy-la-Salle, the property of Ionesco's close friends, now a summer retreat for writers, and the *locus* of literary symposia, *les décades.* It is as though the many places where Jean/Ionesco lived had floated through space, amalgamated, forming a photographic montage. These familiar rooms, pieces of furniture, colors, shapes, form a reassuring décor, one that serves to mask the terror, the knowledge of the black hole under one's feet, the memory of Nothingness. Perhaps it was to outsmart death that Jean kept on shifting from one dwelling to another, from a bed to another bed. Or did he feel, like Baudelaire, that "cette vie est un hôpital où chaque malade est possédé du désir de changer de lit."[13] At any rate, in a lengthy speech addressed to the woman who occupies the composite apartment, city dweller/

---

[13] Charles Baudelaire, "Any Where Out of the World, N'importe où hors du monde," *Le Spleen de Paris, Oeuvres,* I (Paris: NRF, Bibliothèque de la Pléiade, 1944), p. 487.

farmer/châtelaine, Jean speaks of how "the abnormal became the norm" (NRF, II, p. 51), and how, on the other hand, the habitual acquired a monstrous aspect.

> I felt at home, after a while, when there were forms, objects in space, and then, all of a sudden, these objects took on monstrous forms, perhaps in order to remind me that I was not at home. Where was I then? The chair was a two-headed dragon, and the armoire looked like a lake. A funny lake! Where did it all come from (NRF, II, p. 51).

Jean finds it difficult to distinguish between the real and the imaginary. The chair he sees now seems the archetypal chair, those he glimpsed earlier were "shadows of chairs" (p. 51). It is as though Jean had reached at last the world of Platonic essences: "This is a real chair, the essence of chair, and this a real table, the essence of table. One feels all of this is real. Their presence is sufficient to make you believe in eternity, in reality" (p. 52). Every armchair, every table is varnished by the patina of time. The château of Cerisy is a magic place, a zone of peace and quiet, a space out of time, Baudelaire's "chambre double."

Earlier in the play, Jean makes contact with a film maker who has come to see him about writing a scenario. The protagonist is excited about this possibility, and he cannot stop apologizing for the shabby quarters in which he is forced to receive his visitor: "Please forgive me for having you call on me here, in this dilapidated old palace. Once, long ago, when I lived here with my wife and daughter, it was much neater. Now I return here only occasionally. I no longer inhabit this dark, ground floor apartment. . . . My ample quarters on rue Pathé are infinitely roomier, but at present they are being renovated. . . ." (NRF, II, p. 46). For Ionesco, the rue Pathé may echo the name of a familiar street in Bucharest, Paké, but for his French audience it is as evocative of cinema as the MGM Lion would be for Americans. The great house, however, is not a real place; it is a dream house, or perhaps, with special reference to movie palaces, it is the house of dreams.

Although Jean often speaks of vast, palatial residences, the house he is looking for is an intimate space, one that is connected to his childhood. As Henri Frankfort explains in his *Kingship and the Gods*, "'house,' 'town,' or 'country' may stand as symbols of the mother."[15] Later in the play, Jean will state: "Real houses are those that live in one's memory, those one finds again and enters in dream" (NRF, III, p. 51). A friend with whom he is having this

---

[14] Baudelaire, p. 409.
[15] Joseph Campbell, *The Masks of God, Oriental Mythology* (New York: Viking Press, 1970), p. 53.

conversation adds: "The house that's real for you is the one in which you lived with your mother" (p. 51). Houses are nests, and by remembering houses and rooms we learn something about ourselves, we abide within ourselves. Most of us recall exploring secret corners of a house we lived in as children, climbing up to a warm attic full of treasures, toys, old clothes, treasures, or making our way to a damp cellar full of goodies, bottles of wine, preserves, barrels of pickles. In *La Terre et les rêveries du repos*, Gaston Bachelard writes: "Le retour au pays natal, la rentrée dans la maison natale, avec tout l'onirisme qui le dynamise, a été caractérisé par la psychanalyse classique comme un retour à la mère."[16]

The country estate, or château, however, is less a home than a self-contained universe. As Ionesco describes it to the film maker it seems to be made up of rooms within rooms, worlds within worlds, like nests of Chinese boxes, or the chambers of an Egyptian pyramid. Since Jean has been offered 20% of the profits for writing the scenario, and is bargaining for more—Ionesco caricatures here the impoverished *châtelain* who must think up gimmicks to restore his crumbling estate—he suggests that the film need not be made in a studio but within his vast house which contains all one would require: not only sound stages, a theatre in one of the numerous attics, storage and backstage space, doors for entrances and exits, but even trees planted under the roof, and an artificial lake. Jean's château sounds like the bizarre, heraldic, composite set envisioned by Alfred Jarry for his *guignolade, Ubu Roi*. Jean continues with mounting enthusiasm: plains and meadows could be created inside for exteriors to be shot within the confines of his intérieur. The monologue acquires delirious speed, much like the proliferation of objects of Ionesco's earlier plays; Jean's wild imaginings, his so-called practical schemes, try to keep pace with his mushrooming desire for lucre. Nor do we feel that this is Jean's sin alone; he is as sinned against as sinning. Caught within our materialistic society he is simply trying to keep up, like Alice in Wonderland who is told by the Red Queen that on the other side of the "Looking-Glass" one must run as fast as one can merely to keep in the same place. Jean also senses that "to get somewhere else, you must run twice as fast as that!"[17] The monologue is a race of words and images; it culminates in the breathless: "You understand me, we're going to sign a contract" (NRF, II, p. 46).

The surface wit, the irony of this passage do not conceal its philosophical allegory. The latter becomes clear in a later scene in which Jean describes the same or a similar estate:

[16] Gaston Bachelard, *La terre et les rêveries du repos* (Paris: Librairie José Corti, 1948), p. 121.
[17] Lewis Carroll, *Through the Looking Glass* (New York: Random House, 1946), p. 32.

Yes, dear friend, I own in the country, between the sea and the mountains, a very handsome house, quite different from the one in which I really live. It is a palace with vast reception halls, Louis XVI furniture, and Empire sofas. I'm sure that Louis XIII lived in it, but it is a house I see in my dreams. Since I see it in a dream state, it must be a real house, a palace, as I just said, but it contains castles larger than palaces, and these castles have land reaching to the ocean, and beyond. How can castles be held within palaces; it is a mystery of the In-Between-Two-Worlds, or In-Between-Three-Worlds. These spaces fit one into the other, or on top of one another. This makes sense only in the state of dreaming, and since I see this house often in my dreams, I know it has to be real, utterly real. (NRF, III, p. 50)

Jean's country palace with its many levels and floors, rooms within rooms, houses inside of houses, suggests the Tower of Babel, or the Babylonian representation of Heaven as a seven-story mountain. For the ancient Hebrews the Underworld was the reverse image of the pyramid, a down-pointing mountain made of earth and minerals. If Heaven had seven tiers of airy architecture, Sheol is made up of seven cellars. This teeming, self-contained universe is also connected with the literature of Mahayana Buddhism, the "Western Paradise" of the Buddha Amida. Thus, the dream palace, an amalgam of western history (Louis XIII, Louis XVI, Empire furniture), and of the Oriental myths of creation and destruction, is typical of the Ionesco kind of syncretism. It also serves to deepen the Gnostic coloring of the play.

On the realistic plane, Ionesco was inspired by the architecture and furnishings of the lovely château of Cerisy-la-Salle where he spent many a summer in the company of his wife and daughter, and where, in August of 1978, a "décade Ionesco" was held. Ionesco has a great fondness for large, mysterious spaces. In the summer of 1969, when the Ionescos were invited to Stockbridge for the American production of *La soif et la faim,* they were housed in the decrepit, but quite wonderful hotel called Heaton Hall (it was torn down soon after). Ionesco used to walk through the rooms saying: "Ces pièces sont vastes et mystiques." As to the suggestion that a film be made in his own home, it parallels the filming of *La Vase* in Ionesco's *"résidence secondaire,"* "Le Moulin," formerly a mill, which must remind the dramatist of his beloved Chapelle-Anthenaise. Since a number of legal problems spoiled the charm of this property, Jean's anguished need to make money reflects some of the dramatist's urgent concerns.

Even without these links to biography, or to religious and philosophical traditions, one recognizes in the ideal world painted by Jean Baudelaire's "chambre double":

> Une chambre qui ressemble à une rêverie, une chambre véritablement *spirituelle*, où l'atmosphere stagnante est légèrement teintée de rose et de bleu. L'âme y prend un bain de paresse, aromatisé par le regret et le désir.—C'est quelque chose de crépusculaire, de bleuâtre et de rosâtre; un rêve de volupté pendant une éclipse. Les meubles ont l'air de rêver; on les dirait doués d'une vie somnambulique comme le végétal et le minéral. Les étoffes parlent une langue muette, comme les fleurs, comme les ciels, comme les soleils couchants. . .
>
> A quel démon bienveillant dois-je d'être ainsi entouré de mystère, de silence, de paix et de parfums? O béatitude! ce que nous nommons généralement la vie, même dans son expansion la plus heureuse, n'a rien de commun avec cette vie suprême dont j'ai maintenant connaissance et que je savoure minute par minute, seconde par seconde! Non! il n'est plus de minutes, il n'est plus de secondes! Le temps a disparu; c'est l'éternité qui règne, une éternité de délices![18]

Ionesco, who has a profound admiration and love for Baudelaire—he came to France on a scholarship to write a thesis on the theme of death in the poetry of Baudelaire and the symbolist poets—is just as prone as the author of *Les Fleurs du Mal* to experience the "vertiges de l'infini."[19] Both the symbolist French poet, and the contemporary dramatist are as "amoureux du beau en toute chose,"[20] as was Edgar Allen Poe, that master of what Baudelaire calls "l'absurde s'installant dans l'intelligence. . ."[21] What Baudelaire found particularly fascinating about Poe was "l'art de transformer une chaumière en un palais d'une espèce nouvelle."[22]

The study of affinities is not without importance in this instance. In the case of Poe, Baudelaire, and Ionesco there is a common longing for the absent or dead mother. The protective walls of the house, its nurturing innerness, suggest the womb. In *Le Peintre de la vie moderne* Baudelaire states: "Tout ce qui orne la femme, tout ce qui sert à illustrer sa beauté, fait partie d'elle-même; et les artistes qui se sont particulièrement appliqués à l'étude de cet être énigmatique raffolent autant de tout le *mundus muliebris* que de la femme elle-même."[23]

---

[18] Baudelaire, pp. 409–410.
[19] Charles Baudelaire, "Edgar Allan Poe, sa vie et ses ouvrages," *Oeuvres Completes: Préface, Présentation et Notes de Marcel A. Ruff.* (Paris Aux Editions du Seuil, 1968), p. 328
[20] Baudelaire, "Edgar Allan Poe," p. 342.
[21] Baudelaire, "Edgar Allan Poe," p. 345.
[22] Baudelaire, "Edgar Allan Poe," p. 342.
[23] Charles Baudelaire, "La Femme," *Le Peintre de la Vie Moderne, Oeuvres II* (Paris: NRF, Bibliothèque de la Pléiade, 1951), p. 353.

The absent or dead mother can still be sensed in the home that was hers. In his quest for his mother Jean reaches an empty house which is the effigy of the woman he remembers:

> Look, the house is empty; there's only a small table so that we won't waste time looking for her behind armchairs and chairs. For some peculiar reason the house resembles her; her invisible gestures have lingered here, as has her sad countenance. On the floor one can still see traces of her tears that will not dry (NRF, III, p. 51).

The friend with whom Jean entered the house claims to hear "sobs and moans falling from the ceiling drop by drop" (ibid). Jean calls out to his mother, begging her to come down. When she finally answers his plea, it is not as a poetic ghost, an angel from heaven. Images of decay fill her mournful speech; they echo the Metaphysical Poets, or Baudelaire's *Une Charogne*.

> The Mother: I'm afraid on the ground floor, the boards are rotten. Cockroaches were bred by tears. Vermin infested the decaying floor boards. Below is the grave. I don't wish to fall into it, turn to dust together with all my relations. Up here I was safe from dust and death (NRF, III, p. 52)

Refusing to honor her request to linger in the attic, in hiding, Jean and his friend proceed to pull down an armchair whose underside is seen from below. Slowly the piece of furniture is lowered; it holds a terrified old woman. It is not Jean's mother, as his friend points out, for she was soft and sweet; this is his grandmother, or great grandmother. The armchair she sits in suggests a throne. A key to this bizarre scene can be found in Erich Neumann's book, *The Great Mother*. Neumann writes:

> The seated Great Mother is the original form of the "enthroned Goddess," and the throne itself.
>
> . . . It is no accident that the greatest Mother Goddess of the early cults was named Isis, "the seat," "the throne," the symbol of which she bears on her head. . . .[24]

The Mother who is both herself and her own mother is the unified Demeter and Kore. Again Neumann is enlightening: "In the unique relief of a feminine cult both enthroned goddesses appear as the twofold aspect of the mother-

---

[24] Erich Neumann, *The Great Mother*, trans. by Ralph Manheim (Princeton: Princeton University Press, Bollingen Series XLVII, 1972), pp. 98–99.

daughter unity. . . . The whole is permeated by the self-contained transformative unity of mother and daughter. . . ."[25] Jean who is well aware of the sacral symbol of the enthroned mother exclaims: "I'll take you away, clothed in purple, lying in a magnificent glass sarcophagus, like that of the Italian Popes" (NRF, III, p. 52).

This promise fails to calm the old woman who keeps on complaining that she has been abandoned, left to her own devices. Jean explains: I looked for you in all the cemeteries, in old age homes, at your sister's home, and that of your cousin, among the living and the dead. I looked through church registers, and I did not find your name, mamma" (NRF, III, P. 53). Not only did the mother disappear, but her identity, her name vanished also. The motif of the changed name, the hidden national identity, was already formulated in *Man with Bags*. Here something else is added: a secret sense of shame, perhaps remorse. The Mother says: "You were frightened, ashamed, and yet I'm the one, yes your own mother. I'd recognize you through the ages, until the end of the world, after the world's end, and I'd find you again in Limbo, or higher still, in the pleroma" (p. 53).

On January 29, 1970, André Bourin of *Les Nouvelles Littéraires* interviewed Ionesco, who had entered the Académie Française a week before. The journalist asked the new academician many questions, among them whether he liked to stroll, to re-visit places where he had lived. The answer he received was quite extensive, and it seems not unrelated to the theme of the search for the mother, for lost origins:

> When I used to live in the Marais, the Saint-Paul quarter, I used to enjoy walking over to Montparnasse. Now that I live in Montparnasse I go for walks in the Marais. It's a neighborhood for which I feel a deep affection. I particularly like the rue des Rosiers, and the rue des Francs-Bourgeois. When I'm there, I feel that I'm in another world. The rue des Rosiers in particular is very beautiful. When I walk along that street it is as if I had traveled a great distance, gone very far away. I go to look at the hotel where I lived when I was four years old. Memories of things half lost surface in my mind. I sense that there is something utterly familiar about this place, but I don't quite know why."

The ancient Jewish quarter of Paris, the rue des Rosiers, now an Arab neighborhood except for some kosher restaurants, and a few inhabitants not wiped out by the Holocaust, is indeed a strange universe. One would not be surprised to meet there the two women Jean questions early in the play, when

---

[25] Neumann, p. 307.

he first begins to look for his mother. They look like her, and yet they are not her, nor her sisters. The First Woman states: "We all look the same. All of us who belong to this community," and the Second Woman echoes: "We're not even related, we're not her sisters, monsieur. All there is between us is spiritual affinities" (NRF, I, p. 10). The haunted, weeping house at the end of the play could be standing on the rue des Rosiers, its moldy floor covering the entrance to the Kingdom of the Dead, those who perished in the camps of the Holocaust. In Ionesco's dream play the house and the mother have merged.

At the end of the play, as Jean pursues his conversation with the woman he takes to be his mother, the latter's voice and manner suffer an extraordinary transformation. The sweet, elegiac mood of the early exchanges, the gentle reproaches, turn to violent wrath: "I'll fill the pleroma with turmoil; chaos will invade it" (NRF, III, p. 53). The woman who enters is a harpy, with long, sharp nails. She orders a table, covered by a black cloth be brought in, together with an armchair, "the judge's seat" (p. 54). A trial is about to begin; it is no ordinary court, but that of the Last Judgment. Jean is invited to sit on the right of the female judge, not unlike Hades, the Lord of the realm of the dead. The Old Woman declares: "I am the Judgment, the delegate of the judges. God may be just, but he is also fierce. You didn't know that God is a man who does not forgive" (p. 54). The legal training of Ionesco's Persephone seems to have been effected by the Demiurge. The Gnostic infrastructure detected at the start of the play, in the first long monologue, reappears with renewed vigor in the final scenes.

It will be the Great Mother's task to put on trial the second wife of Jean's father, and that woman's entire family. On the primary level one is aware of a strong autobiographical element as Ionesco crystallizes here his own mother's grievances, but the scene quickly transcends the personal level, opening upon the greater subject of man's inhumanity to man.

As the accused file in, the first to appear is the second wife. She is now an ugly old woman dressed and made-up to look like a young whore. The harpy cries out: "Here you are at last, you witch! You drove my daughter out of her own home. I'll sink my talons into your throat and they will be sharper and stronger than living claws, more painful also to the non-living who have no blood to spare for blood clots, as you are bloodless" (NRF, III, p. 54). This torture seems to issue straight out of Dante's *Inferno* where the non-living suffer eternally, and where the same pain is inflicted over and over again, without respite. Even the way in which the avenging figure describes herself echoes Dante's lines about the Harpies:

[26]Dante, p. 149

> Wide-winged like birds and lady-faced are these,
> With feathered belly broad and claws of steel;
> And there they sit and shriek on the strange trees (*Inferno*, XIII, 13–15).

These are the creatures Aeneas and his companions saw swooping down on food, devouring and defiling it. They represent the active will of destruction. Here the Mother/Grandmother will bring to final judgment those who tried to destroy civilization.

Next comes the Captain, the second wife's brother. He is to be judged for the murder of innocent people, for his genocidal exterminations. Not unlike Eichmann at his trial in Jerusalem, the Captain claims that he merely followed orders: "I was given the order to kill those who were not of my race. I was respected, saluted, decorated. I felt proud of what I was doing, yes, I knew that I had to exterminate people of a race different from mine so that my own race could live" (NRF, III, p. 55). These words are an unmistakable echo of the third Reich's definition of the Final Solution. Here is what Lucy S. Dawidowicz has to say about it in *The War Against the Jews, 1933–1945*:

> The Final Solution transcended the bounds of modern historical experience. Never before in modern history had one people made the killing of another the fulfillment of an ideology, in whose pursuit means were identical with the ends. . . .
>
> The German state, deciding that the Jews should not live, arrogated to itself the judgment as to whether a whole people had the right to existence, a judgment that no man and no state have the right to make. "Anyone who on the basis of such a judgment," said Karl Jaspers, "plans the organized slaughter of a people and participates in it, does something that is fundamentally different from all crimes that have existed in the past."
>
> . . . The Final Solution destroyed the East European Jews. In doing so, it subverted fundamental moral principles and every system of law that had governed, however imperfectly, human society for millenia.[27]

The Captain, the compliant tool of ideologies used as excuses for mass murder, will have to pay for his crimes. "I am Vengeance!" proclaims this avatar of Nemesis (NRF, III, p. 55). Turning to the accused, she calls him "a Superdead" (p. 55). Capital punishment will not suffice as a form of retribution; he will have to endure the eternal punishment of Dante's traitors in Nether Hell. The Old Woman sinks her claws into his head, chanting: "Your brain is black and

---

[27] Lucy S. Dawidowicz, *The War Against the Jews, 1933–1945 (New York: Bantam Books, 1976), xxiii-xxiv.*

red; I smear it on your eyes, your nose, your throat. . . . I pluck your monocoled eye leaving the other one in for just a second so that it can see what's happening to you" (p. 56). The red and black suggest the colors of the Nazi emblem (the black swastika, the field of red around it). The frightful torture, however, so similar to those inflicted by the "physicians" of the camps upon their experimental subjects, also echoes the wild cruelty of Tydeus, king of Calydon, who, mortally wounded by Manalippus, had his opponent killed, and, having ordered that he be beheaded, gnawed the scalp and tore out the brains. In Dante's *Inferno,* the two men, frozen together in a single hole, are Count Ugolino and Archbishop Roger.

>   I saw two frozen together in one hole
>   So that the one head capped the other head;
> And as starved men tear bread, this tore the poll
>   O' the one beneath, chewing with ravenous jaw,
>   Where brain meets marrow, just beneath the skull.
> With no more furious zest did Tydeus gnaw
>   The scalp of Menalippus, than he ate
>   The brain-pan and the other tissues raw (Inferno, XXXII, 1.125–132).[28]

Ugolino's tale of his slow death, preceded by that of his four sons, imprisoned with him in "the Tower of Famine," is perhaps the most famous scene in the *Inferno*. Ionesco's description matches the violence of this scene as it also alludes to the bestialities perpetrated in the camps. Never has Ionesco come closer to unleashing on the stage that dark force of "the plague" which Antonin Artaud felt was the basis of all great theatre.

We recognize the Old Woman and the Terrible Mother Goddess who "devours the souls that have not withstood the midnight judgment of the dead in the underworld."[29] She is the mistress of destruction, but nevertheless it is also through her purifying vengeance that rebirth can take place. She is also the ancient "Lady of the Beasts" who, according to Neumann, "is close to the wild, early nature of man, i.e., to the savage instinct-governed being who lived with the beasts and the free-growing plants."[30] As shaman, priestess, anima figure, the Old Woman must uncover all hidden vices.

Her next victim is the Father's second wife whose physical and spiritual ugliness are artfully disguised by make-up, wig, and all manner of devices. By knocking off her hat, rending her dress, tearing off her false nose, touching

---

[28] *Divine Comedy,* p. 274.
[29] Neumann, p. 156
[30] Neumann, p. 277

her with her cane—her magic wand—the Old Woman reveals that the "Witch" is not really a young woman but a hag. A subtle exchange seems to take place: as the younger woman is metamorphosed into a vile hunchback, the Old Woman visibly grows in stature and in strength. The latter declares: "I've taken from you your fake youth. . . . You've lost your strength, and given me mine back" (NRF, III, p. 57).

It is with renewed vigor that she turns to the High Official who seems to have persecuted some defenseless peasants. Now he hopes that those he spared will come to testify for him. This cannot be since they are now dead, turned to dust. As the High Official reaches inside his pockets, hoping to find some evidence, he finds that they are full of earth. The Old Woman intones: "Let earth testify. This earth will not speak. It is no longer earth. Look under your feet, the earth is not there. There is no earth, no sky, no world" (p. 58). The Judgment is taking place in the Beyond; our planet has disappeared. It is as though a shamanic trance had lifted the whole trial scene into eternity and infinity.

As the Old Woman gains ascendency she is revealed as a Sophia, a vessel of transformation. The spirit of destruction and vengeance is about to be transformed into the goddess of the beginning, "of the Whole, who governs the transformation from the elementary to the spiritual level; who desires whole men knowing life in all its breadth, from the elementary phase to the phase of spiritual transformation."[31] As a vessel of rebirth she is like the Gnostic *krater*. Now she must hand her judgment to the Demiurge, the fruit of her repentance. She speaks mysterious words: "I don't see any innocence, and the Demiurge is laughing at this very moment of the trial. I hand him this judgment so that he can laugh all the more" (NRF, III, p. 55). Real vengeance is senseless, but what can be achieved is an anarchic, transcendent, gnostic laughter. As one of the inventors of the Metaphysical Farce, Ionesco knows the healing powers of comic catharsis.

The judgment scene ends with a *renovatio,* a kind of resurrection. Having turned a seemingly younger woman into a hag, the Old Woman proceeds to strip herself of her tattered clothing, to remove her huge nose, her white hair. She emerges as a beautiful creature, and as this takes place she sings and shouts with joy in a voice of unearthly ecstasy. Now she is no longer Persephone, or Ereshkigal, goddesses of death and sterility, but Ishtar, goddess of life and fertility. When the latter decides to visit her sister in the Underworld her robes and garments are stripped from her one by one. Ereshkigal has her put to death, but she is finally released, together with her lover Tammuz.

---

[31] Neumann, p. 331

Jean's mother, wronged by her husband, forgotten by husband and son, dead, is at last released to be reunited with her repentant child.

Ionesco's play, however, does not end with a positive statement. Jean is not the luminous son of ancient mythologies, the sun-child who will fecundate the dark. We see him, alone after the disappearance of the woman, seated in the same armchair he occupied by her side during the trial scene. Like Heracles and Christ he has emerged from his journey to the realm of the dead. He is, however, no heroic figure like Odysseus, Aeneas, or Dante. The play ends in a long soliloquy which begins and ends with "I do not know" (NRF, III, p. 59 and p. 63). This final monologue is composed to a major extent of neologisms, free associations, sounds rather than complete words. It is as if all the books the protagonist had read and written served only to feed his doubting mind. Montaigne's "que sais-je?" becomes the negative "je ne sais pas." "Words say things, but do things say words?" Jean wonders (p. 63). Doctrines, philosophical speculations whirl in the heavens where everything is both right and wrong. Jean claims to be certain of one thing only, something he has kept on his person, "the fragments, the crumbs of cells" (p. 63).

Jean's final monologue is an exercise in deconstruction. On the level of *le discours,* of language games, Ionesco is the heir of Rabelais. For both Rabelais and Ionesco language is experienced as a phenomenon not containable within any strict code. Linear discourse is fractured, dislocated. No inner logic governs the sequences of certain words; they come together called by sound alone. Signifier and signified fall apart, broken asunder. Ionesco conveys his astonishment vis-a-vis things, objects, the decor of our life by means of his questioning of both vocabulary and syntax. Again, what might be taken for surrealist free associations, for a text dictated by the unconscious, is a planned attack on language as means of control, propaganda. Neologisms, as Leo Spitzer explained, may be rooted in the known, but they journey towards the new, the unknown. As the Professor of *The Lesson* carefully explains to the Pupil:

> If you utter several sounds at an accelerated speed, they will automatically cling to each other, constituting thus syllables, words, even sentences, that is to say groupings of various importance, purely irrational assemblages of sounds denuded of all sense, but for that very reason capable of maintaining themselves without danger at a high altitude in the air. By themselves, words charged with significance will fall, weighted down by their meaning, and in the end they always collapse, fall. . . .[32]

---

[32] Eugène Ionesco, *The Lesson,* in *Four Plays,* trans. by Donald M. Allen (New York: Grove Press Inc., 1958), pp. 62–63.

It is interesting to note that in the final monologue of *Journey* Ionesco returns to the device he used at the end of *The Bald Soprano,* as though he wished to come full circle. In both instances Ionesco derealizes the signifier in order to sever language from any practical material intent. Assonance is privileged over logic and syntax. Our faith in what is behind the word, at the core of discourse, is shaken, as is that of Ionesco himself. In *Fragments of a Journal* he writes:

> What a flood of images, words, characters, symbolic figures, signs, all at the same time and meaning more or less the same thing, though never exactly the same, a chaotic jumble of messages that I may perhaps end by understanding but which tells me no more about the fundamental problem: what is this world? . . .[33]

The above passage could have been spoken by Jean who says: "I no longer have my language. The more I speak, the less I say. The more I say, the less I speak. What do the thinkers of yesteryear who reasoned without reason do?" (NRF, III, pp. 59-60).

The language of the monologue cannot be reduced to any structure. Jean recalls that he used to "respect the categories he had inflicted upon himself" (NRF, III, p. 62). Now it is a thing of the past. By demonstrating the autonomous functioning of speech, Ionesco affirms the ultimate freedom of words from the Word. It is as though the Last Judgment of the Old/Young Woman had liberated him. He may not know the answers, but he is aware of the questions. Coherence, harmony, linguistic order are concepts of the past. A confusion of meaning and sound does not suggest, as it once did, a transcendent unity. If a monstrous hybrid emerges it does not point to any reality outside of itself. Thus, "Jean le Sel d'Alsace Sablons" is an absurd geographico-gastronomic amalgam. Ionesco's fantastic isomorphisms, his grotesque onomatopoeias, enumerations, numerologies, pseudo-Pythagorean calculations, mock-Chomskian theories of linguistics may constitute a supreme kind of intellectual balancing act, but the tight rope he walks is stretched over the void, that "black hole" which haunts Jean at the very end of the monologue. Perhaps, however, when Ionesco's protagonist claims to know nothing, he demonstrates at that very moment his profound knowledge and insight.

Journey to the Kingdom of the Dead is the most philosophical and the

---

[33] Eugène Ionesco, *Fragments of a Journal*, trans. by Jean Stewart (New York: Grove Press Inc., 1968), p. 119.

most personal of all of Ionesco's plays. Were it rooted in ontological considerations alone it would prove dry and abstract; were it purely confessional and private, it might become self-indulgent. Because Ionesco is able to blend the two, he speaks of himself as Man, and, in so doing, he also creates the myth of modern man. Jean may have fears that "the moths of myths" (NRF, III, p. 63) are making holes in his brain, but Ionesco demonstrates that he can probe the abyss.

In "breaking bread with (his) dead," the dramatist has also come to terms with long buried grief and remorse. Perhaps the definition of the new hero, the anti-heroic hero of our troubled epoch, is the following: One who, having forgiven others, is finally able to forgive himself.

The Graduate School of CUNY

IONESCO, OR A PREGNANT DEATH

Jan Kott

We all know that we shall die. But Ionesco knows it even as he eagerly reaches for a menu in a restaurant. Even while he eats, he knows he is dying. Each of Ionesco's doubles, the Bérengers in his comedies, knows it too. Not only is death constantly present in everything Ionesco writes, but it is present as *dying*—one's own and other people's, universal and incessant.

"When the bells toll for a funeral I am overcome with a mysterious anguish, a sort of fascination. We know all the people who die."[1] This is one of the earliest entries in "Scattered Images of Childhood" from Ionesco's *Fragments of a Journal*. A few pages later, he writes ". . . when I was four or five years old I realized that I should grow older and older and that I should die. At about seven or eight, I said to myself that my mother would die some day and the thought terrified me."[2] And once again: ". . . the only thing one can know is that death is there waiting for my mother, my family, myself."[3]

Many years later, in his reminiscences of the Vaugirard Square, close to where he spent his Parisian childhood, Ionesco wrote: "When memory brings back a picture of that street, when I think that almost all those people are now dead, everything does indeed seem to me to be a shadow and evanescence. My head spins with anguish. Really, that *is* the world: a desert of fading shadows."[4] And the following two lines, which could have concluded Bérenger's long monologue at his last meeting with the Killer: "It's to Death,

---

*This essay was translated from the Polish by Michael Kott.

[1] Eugène Ionesco, *Fragments of a Journal,* trans. Jean Stewart (New York: Grove Press, 1968), p. 8.

[2] Ionesco, *Fragments,* p. 10.

[3] Ionesco, *Fragments,* p. 20.

[4] Eugène Ionesco, *Notes and Counter Notes: Writings on the Theatre,* trans. Donald Watson (New York: Grove Press, 1964), p. 154.

above all, that I say 'Why?' with such terror. Death alone can, and will, close my mouth."[5]

Ionesco's double in *The Killer* says: "We shall all die, this is the only serious alienation." In *Fragments of a Journal* we read: "The human condition is beyond bearing."[6] And further: "I cannot understand how it should be that for hundreds and hundreds and hundreds of years men have accepted life and death in these intolerable conditions: have accepted an existence haunted by the fear of death, amid war and pain, without showing any real, open decisive reaction against it. . . . We are caught in a sort of collective trap and we don't even rebel seriously against it."[7]

One could go on and on citing such quotations, but they are tiresome in their monotony: death is the process of dying, there is no cure for it and no reconciliation. It is as if there were nothing else to say. Ionesco had intended to write his dissertation at the Sorbonne on "Sin and Death in Poetry After Baudelaire." He never completed his thesis. Smitten by death, he became an author of comedies.

According to my simple definition of this theatrical genre, comedy is a spectacle which evokes laughter. "Nothing is more difficult," wrote Molière, "than to amuse *les honnêtes gens*." Ionesco is one of the finest, if not the finest of modern playwrights who make us laugh. His plays amuse me and amuse us all. The comic power of *The Bald Soprano*, *The Lesson* and *Amédée* compares only with that of Chaplin's early films. They arouse and continue to arouse loud laughter.

What kind of laughter is it, and what is its object? "When I say: is life worth dying for? I am still using words. But at least they are comic."[8] In other words, dying can be amusing when it is talked about or performed. "For my part," Ionesco explains, "I have never understood the difference people make between the comic and the tragic. As the 'comic' is an intuitive perception of the absurd, it seems to me more hopeless than the 'tragic.' The 'comic' offers no escape. I say 'hopeless' but in reality it lies outside the boundaries of hope and despair. . . . For it seems to me that the comic is tragic, and that the tragedy of man is pure derision."[9]

The tragic is a source of metaphysical consolation. The tragic without metaphysics—ordinary dying which nothing will justify, the absurd without hope—is ridiculous. "Pure derision," writes Ionesco. And where does it

---

[5] Ionesco, *Fragments*, p. 27.
[6] Ionesco, *Fragments*, p. 21.
[7] Ionesco, *Fragments*, p. 31.
[8] Ionesco, *Fragments*, p. 73.
[9] Ionesco, *Notes*, p. 27.

occur? On stage. The *ridiculous-tragic* is a theatrical genre. In 1960 he wrote: "But when these older writers use the comic and mix it with the tragic, in the end their characters are no longer funny: it is the tragic that prevails. In my plays it is just the opposite: they start by being comic, are tragic for a moment and end up in comedy or tragi-comedy."[10]

The term as well as the theatrical genre of tragi-comedy, or tragico-comedy, was invented by Mercury, the god of transformation. "What's that? Are you disappointed/To find it's a tragedy?" he chides Plautus' Amphitryo; "Well, I can easily change it./I am a god, after all./I can easily make a comedy,/And never alter a line."[11] Ionesco called *The Bald Soprano* an anti-play, *The Lesson* a comic drama, *The Chairs* a tragic farce. In *Victims of Duty,* Nicolas explains to the Detective: "No more drama nor tragedy, the tragic's turning comic, the comic is tragic and life's getting more cheerful . . . more cheerful."[12]

"Tragi-comedy" would in this case be a misleading term. The "cheerful life" Nicolas envisions for the Detective is a "tragic farce." Using Aristotelian terms, we would say that terror is to be accompanied by laughter rather than by pity and compassion.[12a] The tragic hero must first perform his role clownishly. As a result of this clownish mockery, the terror of his tragic situation is revealed for a moment, only to be overcome by laughter so that life can become "more cheerful" again.

Ionesco has been transforming the *ridiculous-tragic* into the *tragic-ridiculous*, both in his reflections, and in his plays from *The Chairs, Jack, or the Submission* and *Amédée,* to *The Killer* and *Exit the King.* This dual exchange of theatrical signs, the inverted sequence of the tragic and the ridiculous, seems to give the formula for tragic buffoonery. The best and perhaps the oldest description of this theatrical genre, was given by Peter Quince in *A Midsummer Night's Dream* after he assembles his actors for the first rehearsal. "Marry, our play is 'The most lamentable comedy and most cruel death of Pyramus and Thisby.'"(I,ii,11–12)

The "most cruel death of Pyramus and Thisby," as the long title indicates, is a "comedy," but it is a "most lamentable" one. This little play, performed by Athenian craftsmen is a burlesque of *Romeo and Juliet,* which one of the

---

[10] Ionesco, *Notes,* p. 119.

[11] Plautus, "Amphitryo" in *The Rope And Other Plays,* trans. E. F. Watling (London: Penguin Books, 1965), p. 230.

[12] Eugène Ionesco, "Victims of Duty," in *Plays II,* trans. Donald Watson (London: John Calder, 1958), p. 309.

[12a] J. S. Doubrovsky, "Ionesco and the Comic of Absurdity," *Yale French Studies* (23, 1959), p. 9. "This non-Aristotelian theater presents us with a problem which Aristotle had not foreseen: that of pity and fear for which *laughter* is a catharsis."

Quartos called "The most excellent and lamentable tragedie." The most cruel death of Romeo and Juliet as well as the most cruel death of Bérenger in *The Killer* and in *Exit the King* have been made comic. Nevertheless these comedies are "most lamentable." "Take a tragedy;" Ionesco wrote in his *Notes and Counter Notes;* "accelerate the movement and you will have a comic play . . . ," and more emphatically: "A burlesque text, play it dramatic. A dramatic text, play it burlesque."[13]

The first performances of Ionesco's plays in the 50's aroused simultaneous delight and resistance, admiration and horror at their astounding novelty. And yet, most astounding in Ionesco's tragic farces was their reversion to the most ancient and the most persistent tradition of comic theatre and carnival pageantry: the world is set on its head, the beggar is proclaimed king, the ship of fools represents the human condition, clowns conduct laical and religious rites, death struts in a procession of masks through city streets, dying is equated with breeding, and life becomes "more cheerful."

> The darkness has scarcely descended into the narrow, highwalled street before lights are seen moving in the windows and on the stands; in next to no time the fire has circulated far and wide, and the whole street is lit up by burning candles. . . . It becomes everyone's duty to carry a lighted candle in his hand, and the favorite imprecation of the Romans, "Sia ammazzato," is heard repeatedly on all sides.
>
> "Sia ammazzato chi non porta moccolo:" "Death to anyone who is not carrying a candle." This is what you say to others, while at the same time you try to blow out their candles.

In this way, Goethe begins his description in *Italian Journey* of the 1788 Carnival in Rome.

> The louder the cries of *Sia ammazzato,* the more these words lose their sinister meaning and you forget that you are in Rome, where, at any other time but Carnival, and for a trifling reason, the wish expressed by these words might be literally fulfilled.
>
> Just as in other languages curses and obscene words are often used as expressions of joy or admiration, so, on this evening, the true meaning of *Sia amazzato* is completely forgotten, and it becomes a password, a cry of joy, a refrain added to all jokes and compliments. . . .
>
> All ages and all classes contend furiously with each other. Carriage steps are climbed; no chandelier and scarcely a paper lantern is safe. A boy blows

---

[13] Ionesco, *Notes*, p. 228; p. 182.

out his father's candle, shouting "Sia amazzato il Signore Padre!" In vain the old man scolds him for this outrageous behaviour; the boy claims the freedom of the evening and curses his father all the more vehemently.[14]

Ionesco wrote in his *Notes,* ". . . laughter alone respects no taboo . . . the comic alone is able to give us the strength to beat the tragedy of existence."[15] His earlier "intuition of the absurd," like his "tragedy of existence," is a debt paid to the philosophy fashionable in the 50's. Ionesco's true "intuition," however, was the return to carnival celebration where, like in the ancient Saturnalias, our modern *Angst* was present, but where masks of Death were accompanied by masks adorned with phalluses, and with this inversion of signs, funeral rites were turned into rites of wedding.

"There is nothing unfamiliar," continues Goethe, "about seeing figures in fancy dress or masks out in the streets under the clear sky. They can be seen every day of the year. No corpse is brought out to the grave without being accompanied by hooded religious fraternities. The monks in their many kinds of costumes accustom the eye to peculiar figures. There seems to be the Carnival all the year round. . . ."[16] I once watched in New Orleans an amateur theatre troupe which chose a funeral as the subject for a ballet. The rhythmic wailing to blues melodies gradually became more and more ecstatic. Voices rose to an ever higher pitch as a coffin was lifted higher and higher. From beneath long black skirts legs squiggled out as if they had a life of their own. A moment later the coffin swayed in the air, like the dancing hips and bellies.

New Orleans is one of the few places where old carnival traditions, which link together images of sex and death, still retain their compelling symbolism. As Goethe continues in his description of the Roman Carnival, "On the side streets are young fellows dressed up as women, one of whom seems to be far advanced in pregnancy. . . . As if from shock, the pregnant woman is taken ill, a chair is brought and the other women give her aid. She moans like a woman in labour, and the next thing you know, she has brought some misshapen thing into the world, to the great amusement of the onlookers."[17]

According to the oldest traditions of Saturnalia, the woman who gives birth is Death. "In the famous Kerch terracotta collection," writes Bakhtin in *Rabelais and His World,* "we find figurines of senile pregnant hags. More-

---

[14] J. W. Goethe, *Italian Journey,* trans. W. H. Auden and E. Mayer (New York: Pantheon Books, 1962), pp. 467–68.

[15] Ionesco, *Notes,* p. 144.

[16] Goethe, *Italian Journey,* p. 448.

[17] Goethe, *Italian Journey,* pp. 460–61.

over, the old hags are laughing. It is pregnant death, a death that gives birth. There is nothing completed, nothing calm and stable in the bodies of these old hags. They combine a senile, decaying and deformed flesh with the flesh of new life, conceived but as yet unformed."[18]

The body, Bakhtin writes, is shown in its two-fold contradictory process of decay and growth: a pregnant death. The Saturnalian and carnival signs epitomize the perpetuity and continuity of life and thereby negate completely Samuel Beckett's cruel vision of continuous dying: ". . . one day we were born, one day we shall die, the same day, the same second . . . they give birth astride of the grave. . . .'"[19]

The death that gives birth in a carnival farce is not a young woman, pregnant with a new death, but an old hag pregnant with a new foetus. The body, which is decaying, conceives. Awe occasions laughter: in the symbolism of carnival it is one and the same body.

> One of the fundamental tendencies of the grotesque image of the body is to show two bodies in one: the one giving birth and dying, the other conceived, generated, and born. This is the pregnant and begetting body, or at least a body ready for conception and fertilization. . . .
>
> In contrast to modern canons, the age of the body is most frequently represented in immediate proximity to birth or death, to infancy or old age, to the womb or the grave, to the bosom that gives life or swallows it up. But at their extreme limit the two bodies unite to form one. The individual is shown at the state when it is recast into a new mold. It is dying and yet unfinished; the body stands on the threshold of the grave and the crib.
>
> The unfinished and open body (dying, bringing forth and being born) is not separated from the world by clearly defined boundaries; it is blended with the world, with animals, with objects. It is cosmic, it represents the entire material bodily world in all its elements. It is an incarnation of this world at the absolute lower stratum, as the swallowing up and generating principle, as the bodily grave and bosom, as a field which has been sown and in which new shoots are preparing to sprout.[20]

Remarkably, this description of carnival imagination and wisdom which served Bakhin to introduce the world of Rabelais, is also a surprisingly apt introduction to the world of Ionesco's *Jack, or the Submission* and *The Future Is In Eggs*. In both plays, Ionesco appears to be reusing the old

---

[18] Mikhail Bakhtin, *Rabelais and His World*, trans. Helen Iswolsky (Cambridge, Massachusetts: The M.I.T. Press, 1968), pp. 25–26.
[19] Samuel Beckett, *Waiting for Godot* (New York: Grove Press, 1954), p. 57.
[20] Bakhtin, *Rabelais*, pp. 26–27.

formula for a comedy of manners about two families, a shy young man, an ugly miss, a matchmaker, an engagement, a wedding, and a long wait for progeny. But the "naturalistic comedy" becomes a carnival farce, almost an animal farm. The characters are all "Jacks" or "Robertas" with identical face-masks. Their bodies are unfinished, at once decaying and growing. Herded together, they begin to lose even their human shape. Body parts multiply as with the three noses of Roberta II or the nine fingers on her hand.

> Jack: . . . You're rich, I'll marry you. . . .
> [They put their arms around each other very awkwardly. Jack kisses the noses of Roberta II, one after the other, while Father Jack, Mother Jack, Jacqueline, the Grandparents, Father Robert, and Mother Robert enter without saying a word, one after the other, waddling along, in a sort of ridiculous dance, embarrassing, in a vague circle, around Jack and Roberta II who remain at stage center, awkwardly enlaced. Father Robert silently and slowly strikes his hands together. Mother Robert, her hands clasped behind her neck, makes pirouettes, smiling stupidly. Mother Jack, with an expressionless face, shakes her shoulders in a grotesque fashion. Father Jack pulls up his pants and walks on his heels. Jacqueline nods her head, then they continue to dance, squatting down, while Jack and Roberta II squat down too, and remain motionless. . . . The darkness increases. On stage, the actors utter vague miaows while turning around, bizarre moans, croakings. The darkness increases. We can still see the Jacks and the Roberts crawling on the stage. We can hear their animal noises, then we don't see them any more. We hear only their moans, their sighs, then all fades away, all is extinguished. Again, a gray light comes on. All the characters have disappeared, except Roberta, who is lying down, or rather squatting down, buried beneath her gown. We see only her pale face, with its three noses quivering, and her nine fingers moving like snakes.][21]

In *The Future Is In Eggs,* the barnyard changes into a chicken coop. Roberta II lays eggs, one after the other. She is oviparous. There is no limit to multiplying by way of eggs and the eggs are all the same. The future is in the eggs. Indistinguishable Jacko-Robertas will hatch from them. But even in this csrnival chicken coop of boundless fertility, where individuality has been eradicated and life is reduced to the egg, death is present. Even before the young wife begins to lay eggs in a basket, grandfather Jack dies. To "die" means to enter an empty frame. As a matter of fact, he will shock the whole family when he steps out of his frame for a moment to hum to himself.

[21] Eugène Ionesco, "Jack or the Submission," in *Four Plays,* trans. Donald M. Allen (New York: Grove Press, 1958), p. 109.

For Freud laughter is the bribe accepted by the censor of morals for permitting a joke that exposes prurient desires and forbidden wishes. However, more strictly prohibited and suppressed to the depths of the subconscious, is the dread of death, the fear that we will die. All of us. The bribe for revealing this dread and this fear is also laughter. The archaic pregnant Death laughs. Amidst piles of carnival litter, the begetting of a misshapen monster by a man dressed as a woman, evokes riotous laughter. Dread of the end spawns a jolly spectacle. "Death and death throes, labor, and childbirth are intimately interwoven. On the other hand, these images are closely linked to laughter. When death and birth are shown in their comic aspect, scatological images in various forms nearly always accompany the gay monsters created by laughter in order to replace the terror that has been defeated."[22]

With characteristic insight, Goethe perceived the same interwoven images of death, sex and birth in the carnival pantomimes performed on the streets of Rome: "In the course of all these follies our attention is drawn to the most important stages of human life: a vulgar Pulcinella recalls to us the pleasures of love to which we owe our existence; a Baubo profanes in a public place the mysteries of birth and motherhood, and the many lighted candles remind us of the ultimate ceremony."[23]

Pulcinella, as he left the *commedia dell'arte* for the streets, always wore a black leather mask with an enormous hooked nose over his eyes and brow. Harlequin had a similar mask, but his costume was different. Pulcinella wore a large white cylindrical hat, white breeches and jacket, a hump on his back and padding in his belly.

Entertainment for Children,[24] Domenico Tiepolo's ironic title for his series of a hundred wash drawings, is a great "tragic farce." This sad and cheerful, bitter and derisive story covers in a hundred scenes the life of Pulcinella— from his birth out of a turkey's egg to his banishment from eighteenth century Venice.

The title drawing of Tiepolo's *Divertimento per li Regazzi* shows old Pulcinella pensively gazing at a monument inscribed with the title of this series. Perched on his shoulder is a puppet of a beautiful Venetian woman who is smiling flirtatiously. Her head is inclined away from the tomb, in her hand is a fan. She is blithely swinging her legs, having drawn them out from beneath her dress. Possibly, the drawing symbolizes the death of Carnival and the approach of Lent. Or perhaps it is a burlesque parody of a passion play in which Christ arises from his grave.

[22] Bakhtin, *Rabelais*, p. 151.
[23] Goethe, *Italian Journey*,, p. 16.
[24] Marcia E. Vetrocq, ed., *Domenico Tiepolo's Punchinello Drawings* (Indiana University Art Museum, 1979).

Pulcinella dies, but not forever. In a Pier Leone Ghezzi drawing from the early eighteenth century, Pulcinella suddenly arises from his bier, terrifying a family of peasants. In one of the drawings from Tiepolo's *Divertimento*, Pulcinella's skeleton, wearing the same large white, cylindrical hat, leaps out of a Rococco grave. Death itself wears the clown hat of Pulcinella.

In Domenico Tiepolo's drawings, the streets of Venice are peopled with Pulcinellas. They paw young women under the ledges of terraced vineyards; dance at village celebrations, hunt for partridges, ride elephants in the circus, collect rent from peasants, and stare inquisitively at camels, which like Pulcinellas themselves, have humps on their backs. Not all of the Pulcinellas are male; women also wear the hooked-nosed masks. Pulcinellas have Pulcinella wives and Pulcinella children, who enter the world with potbellies, humps, and black noses. But the Pulcinella in Tiepolo drawings, and perhaps also in some lost story, is not merely the actor and hero in a Venetian comedy of manners or a carnival pantomime. Here he is incarcerated; other Pulcinellas visit him in prison. As in the paintings of Callot and Goya where the atrocities of the Napoleonic Wars are depicted, so in Tiepolo's *Entertainment for Children* we find scenes of hangings and executions. A blind-folded Pulcinella, still wearing a black-nosed mask, awaits execution bound to a stake. Another Pulcinella lies on the ground, already shot. The execution squad itself, rifles poised for firing, consists of Pulcinellas in white hats. In another drawing, Pulcinella, bereft of his hat, but still in his black-nosed mask, dangles from a scaffold where a crowd of Pulcinellas has gathered. The hangman is on a horse and wears the white Pulcinella hat; he, too, is Pulcinella. Pulcinella is the hangman and the hanged man; he is the executioner and the executed. Wars and revolutions are also a tragic farce: the actors and victims are Pulcinellas. Pulcinella is a new Everyman.

All Bérengers in Ionesco's plays are his doubles and at the same time, Everyman. In two small rooms in a basement of the Frick Collection in New York, where in the winter of 1980 *Entertainment for Children* was exhibited for the first time, I suddenly saw Ionesco's great theatre. Perhaps the Professor in *The Lesson* who rapes and murders his fourteenth pupil in a row, ought to wear the Pulcinella black mask with a hooked nose and the white hat. Perhaps the Pupil, who is able to multiply multi-digit numbers in her head but cannot subtract, and who suffers a sudden toothache, should wear not only the blouse and the short skirt of a school-girl, but also a little mask with a black hooked nose.

Perhaps the Old Man and the Old Woman in *Chairs* should also wear Pulcinella masks. Surely, the Orator who after the suicide of the Elders proclaims his final message to empty chairs, should be masked like Pulcinella and could display a hump as well as a potbelly. Wearing the white blouse of

Punch and Pierrot and a huge Pulcinella hat, he would draw letters on the blackboard and gesture with his hands like a deaf man. In *Amédée or How to Get Rid of It*, gigantic legs of a corpse gradually slide into Amédée's and Magdalena's dining room. This corpse may be a murdered lover or the Past. In any case, it is also Death. But here, Death is present only as the legs of a giant dummy. As in carnival imagery, this Death is "a gay monster created by laughter in order to replace the terror that has been defeated."

We "do die," writes Ionesco, "It is horrible and cannot be taken seriously. How can I trust in a world that has no stability, that flits away? One moment I can see Camus, I can see Atlan and suddenly they are gone. It's ridiculous. It almost makes me laugh. Anyway, King Solomon has already exhausted the subject."[25] Or, "King Solomon is my master," and yet again, "Yes, the leader I follow is King Solomon; and Job, that contemporary of Beckett."[26] Job and Beckett—the comparison is obvious, but what is Solomon's place in this company? "I am the most foolish of men,"[27] says Solomon in *Ecclesiastes*. Precisely this sentence is the one Folly cites with delight in Erasmus' *The Praise of Folly*.

King Solomon frequently appears in Medieval ribaldries as well as in Medieval and early Renaissance morality plays. His wisdom is always foolish. Ionesco could have written a tragic farce, "Solomon and Job Discourse on Death." In this "Dialogue of the Dead" we would hear again Lucian's derisive laughter.

The Death which comes to Bérenger in the epilogue to *The Killer*, does not utter a word. This is no longer the archaic pregnant Death, nor the gay carnival Death which gives birth to a new creature in order to overcome the terror. It is the Medieval Death which calls with a sickle on Everyman. Unbridable, irrevocable and ruthless, this Death has no respect for human honor or dignity. When the fifteenth century Everyman proposes a tribe, Death responds with indignation:

> Everyman, it may not be, by no way.
> I see not by gold, silver, nor riches,
> Ne by pope, emperor, king, duke, ne princes;
> For, and I would receive gifts great,
> All the world I might get;
> But my custom is clean contrary.
> I give thee no respite. Come hence, and not tarry.[28]

[25] Ionesco, *Notes*, p. 110.
[26] Ionesco, *Notes*, p. 156.
[27] Erasmus, "The Praise of Folly," in *The Essential Erasmus* (New York: New American Library, 1964), p. 164.
[28] "Everyman," in *Everyman and Medieval Miracle Plays*, ed. A. C. Cawley (New York: Dutton, 1959), p. 210.

In *The Killer,* Death is silent. Bérenger, all alone, must carry on a Medieval dialogue with Death:

> You're poor now, aren't you? Do you want some money? I can find you work, a decent job. . . . No. You're not poor? Rich then?. . . . Aaah, I see, neither rich nor poor! (Chuckle from the KILLER)[29]

According to Ionesco's stage directions Killer-Death is supposed to be ". . . very small and puny, ill-shaven with a torn hat on his head, and a shabby old gabardine; he has only one eye, which shines with a steely glitter. . . "[30] All Medieval texts talk about the hideousness of Death. Yet in folk drama, in the Sicilian Opera dei Puppi, and in the Polish folk theatre, Skeleton-Death is also quite funny. In the Italian theatre of marionettes, Death diligently saws off heads of sinners which then roll off stage to the merriment of the spectators. In Polish folk theatre, King Herod's head is a cabbage which Death reaps, like a peasant his crops. Death in Ionesco merely chuckles as it drowns its victims, in a basin in the Radiant City, where Death gathers its harvest to the perpetual accompaniment of *cris de Paris:* the banter of concierges, the mumbling of vagabonds, and the shouts of street vendors. Ionesco's chuckling Death could wear the mask of Harlequin with a hooked nose and have Pierrot's powdered white face. *The Killer* is a tragic farce performed on city streets.

We "do die," Ionesco repeats. "It is horrible and cannot be taken seriously." *Exit the King* is a comedy about dying. It is the only modern comedy about dying and the only *comedy* with a hero and the main actor who begins *dying* in the very first scene before he dies in the last one. If Bérenger were dying in a real bed, if he were mourned by a *real* wife and a *real* mistress, if he were treated and operated on by *real* doctors, if a *real* nurse rearranged *real* pillows for him, this *play* would be insufferable. But Bérenger, who is dying in Ionesco's comedy, is a King.

"The King," wrote Stanislaw Jerry Lec, "is naked . . . but under such splendid robes."[31] Bérenger is dying in splendid robes of royalty. He is King, a fairy tale King, a King in a palace assembled by children out of cards; he is King of a carnival masquarade.

Bérenger does not die. The King dies in the company of Queen Marguerite, who was his first wife, Queen Marie, his second wife, and the Doctor, who does not take care of him and who is at once, "a surgeon, a hangman, a bacteriologist, and an astrologer." Bérenger is dressed up as King so that he can die only as King.

[29] Eugène Ionesco, *The Killer and Other Plays,* trans. Donald Watson (New York: Grove Press, 1960), p. 105.
[30] Ionesco, *The Killer,* p. 97.
[31] S. J. Lec, *Unkempt Thoughts,* trans. Jack Galazka (New York: St. Martins Press, 1962), n.p.

Among the most enduring of carnival amusements is the crowning and uncrowning of the beggar enacted so that he can later be abused, scourged and chased. The beggar's coronation in the marketplace shows traces, according to Frazer, of an ancient ritual in which the king's substitute was killed annually in order to "resurrect" the real king. In the carnival travesty, death cannot be taken seriously. The inhabitants of the Isle of Winds in Rabelais' utopia emit gases when they die and their souls, like this unbecoming gas, leave their bodies *via rectum*. In Seneca's satire *Ludus Morte Claudii*, Caesar dies in the act of defecation.

In *Le roi se meurt, ou la cérémonie*, the ceremonies of dying are carnivalesque. ". . . we do die. It is horrible and cannot be taken seriously." Bérenger is Ionesco's double. King Bérenger dies to enable Ionesco not to die.

I saw *The Bald Soprano* and *The Lesson* for the first time when they opened in Warsaw. I think it was 1956. Subsequently, whenever I was in Paris I would go to the little theatre in the Rue de la Huchette, where *The Lesson* and *The Bald Soprano* were continually running. When I was there last in 1965, I was not sure whether the same actress was still playing the Pupil. She seemed less childish. After the performance I visited the Ionescos. I recorded my recollections from this evening in my diary, which was later published in *Theatre Notebook:*

> "Of course, it's the same actress," said Eugène. "*The Lesson* will go on being performed for another fifty or seventy years. One day the Pupil will die. I mean really die, not just on the stage. She will go to heaven, and St. Peter will sternly ask her: 'What did you do in life, my child?' And she will reply, 'What did I do? I was eighteen when I began to act the Pupil in M. Ionesco's play at the theatre in the rue de la Huchette. Then I got engaged, to be married, and I went on acting the Pupil. Then I got married. I went on acting the Pupil. Then I got pregnant for three months. I stopped acting the Pupil. Then my daughter was born. I went on acting the Pupil. Then I got a divorce. I went on acting the Pupil. Then I got married again. I went on acting the Pupil. Then my son was born. I went on acting the Pupil. Then I got divorced again. I went on acting the Pupil. Then my daughter had twins. I had to leave Paris for two weeks. Then I went on acting the Pupil.' And St. Peter will say, 'M. Ionesco can hardly wait for you; he is attending a rehearsal of *The Lesson*.'"
>
> Ionesco looked at me, became very sad all of a sudden and said in a choked whisper, "It's not true; I shall not die."[32]

State University of New York at Stony Brook

---

[32] Jan Kott, *Theatre Notebook 1947–1967*, trans. Boleslaw Taborski (New York: Doubleday, 1968), p. 220.

1. P. L. Ghezzi, *Punchinello Rising from his Bier*

2. Titlepage. *Divertimento per li Regazzi*

3. *The Apparition on Punchinello's Tomb*

4. *The Firing Squad*

THE PSYCHODRAMATIC STAGE: IONESCO AND HIS DOUBLES

Moshe Lazar

> "Everything can happen; everything is possible and likely. Time and space do not exist; on an insignificant basis of reality the imagination spins and weaves new patterns: a blending of memories, experiences, free inventions, absurdities, and improvisations. The characters split, double, redouble, evaporate, condense, scatter, and converge. But one consciousness remains above all of them: the dreamer's."
>
> August Strindberg, *A Dream Play*[1]

Ionesco belongs to that group of writers since Strindberg for whom the literary or dramatic artwork is not a tale of the objective and visible *persona*, or of its social behavioral patterns or its psychological motivations, but rather a metaphoric and dreamlike representation of the *psyche* in its labyrinthic, non-sequential, and disguised reality. The plays and novels of writers such as Strindberg, Kafka, Beckett, and Ionesco are not directly concerned with the socio-economic and the political situation of the world in which they happen to live, nor do they use their contemporary historical reality as a structural framework for a reproduction or imitation of life. They are rather fragmentary and kaleidoscopic mirrorings of existential anxieties, dreams and daymares, neurotic conflicts and traumas, dreadful or wishful projections, repressed emotions and discarded memories; their oneiric settings allow metamorphosed images to emerge into light—the visible artwork—from the darkness of the

---

[1] *A Dream Play and Four Chamber Plays*, trans. W. Johnson (Seattle: Univ. of Washington Press, 1973), p. 19.

soul, allow for muted voices to ascend from the groves of the unconscious into figures of speech, and allow for anthropomorphic and zoomorphic creatures of the psyche's underworld to be incarnated in narrative or dramatic beings which bear no resemblance to what traditionally is called a *character*. The works of these daymarers are obsessional in their circularity and in their spiral journeyings through an infernal underworld. The play, or the novel, is the journey itself or, rather, one of many similar stations along the *via dolorosa* of the splintered and embattled soul. Each and all of their writings, often including their diaries and letters, work out, act out, play out this ongoing *psychomachia*. The so-called "characters," especially the central ones, are the projected *doubles* of their creators: feared or wishful doubles, disguised or unmasked doubles, who are themselves sometimes mirrored in secondary doubles in the same text. If psychoanalysis started out as and still remains a "talking cure," then the expressionistic confessional monologues and dialogues of these authors are a "writing cure" of sorts, a *psychodramatic* performance in the narrative, pictorial, or theatrical mode. And because there are no definitive "cures" for these besieged souls, the journey into darkness and back into creativity is always starting all over again, repeating itself with variations, circling in a centrifugal manner around the Self, spinning around that mysterious center where "the end is in the beginning,"[2] the future is in the past, and where the only possible paradise is a "paradise lost."[3] Each individual work of these authors is a partial and temporary exorcism of their inner demons. The very personal psychodramatic process is transcended into an artwork, contrary to the irrational and hallucinatory narratives of a psychotic mind.[4]

---

[2] See S. Beckett, *Endgame* (New York: Grove Press, 1958), p. 69; also, Ionesco, *Fragments of a Journal*, trans. Jean Stewart (New York: Grove Press, 1968), p. 126; "The end is like the beginning."

[3] This is a central theme in Ionesco's plays. See, in particular on this point, J. Jacobsen and W. R. Mueller, *Ionesco and Genet, Playwrights of Silence* (New York: Hill & Wang, 1968), pp. 25–72.

[4] See Eugène Ionesco, *Entre la vie et le rêve. Entretiens avec Claude Bonnefoy* (Paris: Pierre Belfond, 1977), p. 37: "I believe that literature is neurosis. Without neurosis, there is no literature. Health is neither poetic nor literary . . . But is this neurosis meaningful or representative of human tragedy or is it only an individual case? If it is an individual case, it has certainly a limited interest." But if this neurosis represents metaphysical dread it is extremely interesting, meaningful, and worthwhile to delve into it. [This 1977 edition in France is very different from the preceding one published in 1966 and translated into English as *Conversation with Eugène Ionesco* (London: Faber & Faber, 1970). We translate from the French.] For the opposite view, that neurosis distorts creativity, see Lawrence S. Kubie, *Neurotic Distortion of the Creative Process* (New York: Noonday Press, 1977 [Univ. of Kansas Press, 1958].) We cannot agree with his basic assumption that "the neurosis is the most banal and undistinguished component of human nature. The statement

As a playwright, Ionesco is at the head of those who have contributed most in modern drama to the disintegration of the traditional structures of plot, character, and dialogue, and among those who have transformed the conventional stage into a metaphoric one which appears to be a double of their inner landscape, and a figurative projection of their intimate dream world. The challenge of giving shape to a shapeless and unnameable soul could not be met by using the stage of logic, reason, motivation and pseudodidactical entertainment. Verbal and visual metaphors, a different use of time and space, and a stage informed more by darkness and silences than by light and concepts were needed to express theatrically the *descensus ad inferos* of the anxious subject. Therefore, whatever enters the metaphoric field of this new stage—"characters," objects, props, sets—becomes in a way metaphorized. A chair is no longer a piece of functional furniture (*The Chairs*); a rhinoceros is not some zoological monster frightening innocent bystanders (*Rhinoceros*); the shrinking kingdom of Bérenger is not some historical empire of a dying emperor (*Exit the King*); and the policeman's interrogation of Choubert is not part of a detective story (*Victims of Duty*); in the same way the mushrooms growing on the floor of a living room and the corpse expanding into a gigantic presence are not just grotesque deviations of nature's norms (*Amédée*). The stage is the psyche of the writer, the "mindscreen" on which the Self (including the Others who inhabit its kingdom of darkness) projects its protean messengers and their ambiguous oracles. And it is only because we are prisoners of a traditional terminology that we continue to speak about the "characters" in Beckett and Ionesco as if they were of the same nature as Medea, Hamlet, Woyzeck, or Mother Courage. On the other hand, even though they are projections of the writer's inner world, they are not similar to the medieval personifications in the morality plays. These figures on the stage (masks, changing faces, puppets, grotesque icons) are *metaphorical personae* or *doubles*. The fact that they are embodied in "roles" within the drama and incarnated on stage by actors should not mislead us into believing that they evolve inside a given sociological, political, or psychological context. Their "realistic" features intensify the reality of the imaginary creatures, their surreality, and anchor these figures in a visible space and a verbal presence as images rather than people. The Stranger, doubling Stringberg in his play *To Damascus*,[5] declares: "Therefore I had to create a double, to add to my own personality

---

is true even for the symbolic language in which the neurosis expresses itself, whether in symptom, dream, or work of art or science." (p. 5). See also Ionesco, *A Stroll in the Air*, p. 21.

[5] August Strindberg, *To Damascus, I*, trans. Michael L. Meyer in *The Plays of Strindberg* (New York: Vintage Books, 1976), vol. II.

a being that could absorb in itself all that binds my spirit." In a text seeking to define a new type of psychological drama,[6] Strindberg alluded to the inadequacy of the traditional concept of "character": "In regard to the drawing of the characters, I have made my people somewhat 'characterless' for the following reasons. In the course of time the word character has assumed manifold meanings. It must have originally signified the dominating trait of the soul-complex, and this was confused with temperament. Later it became the middle-class term for the automaton, one whose nature had become fixed or who had adapted himself to a particular role in life. In fact, a person who had ceased to grow was called a character, while one continuing to develop . . . was called characterless, in a derogatory sense, of course, because he was so hard to catch, classify, and keep track of. This middle-class conception of the immobility of the soul was transferred to the stage where the middle-class has always ruled." Strindberg clearly distinguished between *persona* (character) and *anima* (soul): "I do not believe in simple stage characters . . . My souls (characters) are conglomerations of past and present stages of civilization, bits from books and newspapers, scraps of humanity, rags and tatters of fine clothing, patched together as is the human soul."[7]

The playwright, unless he decided to use solely pantomime or a silent puppet show to project the contradictory complexes of his psyche—which would be very simplistic—has no choice but to send out words to spy on the inner world and return to the stage as fragmented images. But once brought into light, these words and the metaphoric characters become obstacles between the writer and his Self. Pirandello, in his stories and plays (*Six Characters in Search of an Author*, in particular), was extremely anguished by the contradicting realities of *life* and *form, anima* and *persona,* face and mask. Ionesco has very often given similar expression to his own anguish: "I am lost in the thousands of words and unsuccessful acts that are 'my life,' which take my soul apart and destroy it. This life is between me and myself, I bear it along between me and myself, I do not recognize it as mine, and yet it is to this life that I ask to be revealed. How can you be revealed by what hides you? . . . And how, with the aid of words, can I express everything that words hide? How can I express what is inexpressible?"[8] And in the same way Pirandello once wrote, "For twenty years I have not lived my life, I have written it," and Ionesco despairingly confesses—in a style reminiscent of Bérenger,

---

[6] See the Author's Foreword to *Miss Julie,* trans. Elizabeth Sprigge in *Six Plays of Strindberg* (New York: Doubleday Anchor Books, 1955), p. 64.

[7] *Six Plays of Strindberg,* p. 65.

[8] Eugène Ionesco, *Present Past, Past Present,* trans. Helen R. Lane (New York: Grove Press, 1971), p. 168.

his double, in *Exit the King*—that even his psychodramatic plays had not succeeded in exorcising him of his deep-rooted anxieties and fear of death:

> I ought to have embarked long ago on this stubborn quest for knowledge and self-knowledge. If I'd set about it in time, I might have achieved something. Instead of writing literature! What a waste of time; I thought I had all of life ahead of me. Now time is pressing, the end is near, and haste is not favourable to my quest; indeed, it is because of literature that I can no longer understand anything at all. It's as though by writing books I had worn out all symbols without getting to the heart of them. They no longer speak to me with living voices. Words have killed images or concealed them. . . . But these words were like masks, or else like dead leaves fallen to the ground. The tree of life and death is still here, bare and black. Nothing can mask the deepest, most incurable distress. I am face to face with truth.[9]

But if these words no longer speak to Ionesco himself with "living voices"— because they have already been expressed and are buried in the past—they go on speaking with "living voices" to his dramatic doubles who exist in the eternal present of the written text, who continue to express their "incurable distress" from play to play and who endlessly dream their cosmonautical daydream of escaping death's gravity. It is with these doubles that this essay is concerned.

Ionesco has very often used his daymares and nightmares as primary materials of fantasy for many of his plays. The dreamer's psyche is a powerful stage in itself: with its disguised beings, their conflicting voices, and the marvelous independence from time and space. Ionesco has always been fascinated with this interior theater of the dreamer for which he was the playwright, the director, the various actors, the spectator, and sometimes the critic. Before analyzing the role and function of the dreamer's doubles in different plays, let us consider briefly Ionesco's deep-rooted interest in the play as a double of the dream, and his own existential experience as being double.

Throughout his plays, his narratives, and his journals, Ionesco projects a divided Self: the "I" of the past versus the "I" in the present; dreaming opposed to existing; literature as a double of the dreams masking the fear of death; wishful dreams antagonized by the acute consciousness of time; the desire to return to the womb contradicted by temptations of the future. If dying, dreaming, and writing are always woven in the fabric of Ionesco's works and constitute the backdrop of his stage, death anxiety is without any doubt the main source of both his neurosis and his creative act. Loss and

[9] Eugène Ionesco, *Fragments of a Journal*, p. 61.

separation appear as related motives in his fear of death and are contrasted with the nostalgia of a happy reunion with the mother. James McCarthy, in a recent study, has shown very convincingly how "birth and separation themes do override children's imagery of death,"[10] thus following Otto Rank's concept of "primal anxiety":

> Otto Rank's *The Trauma of Birth* constituted a significant departure from Freudian theory in its deemphasis of instinctual conflict as the source of neurotic anxiety. Rank saw intrauterine life as a psychic state akin to a blissful Garden of Eden. It is so satisfying that throughout his life man unconsciously strives to return to the womb. The birth process itself, hazardous though it may be, does not achieve a significance equal to that of the trauma of separation from the womb. Rank called the psychic pain of this separation "primal anxiety;" this was the origin of all anxiety. Such pain motivates man in a sense that is entirely different from Freud's drive for Thanatos.[11]

In the opening pages of Ionesco's *Fragments of a Journal*, while meditating on time and death, we are presented with a very revealing dream within a dream which could be the quintessence of Ionesco's existential and dramatic quest:

> I dream that I am told: "The revelation—the answer to all your questions—can only come to you in a dream. You must have a dream." So, in my dream, I fall asleep and I dream, in my dream, that I'm having the absolute dream. On waking, that's to say on really waking, I remember having dreamed that I'd dreamed, but I can remember nothing about the dream within a dream, the dream of absolute truth, the dream that explained everything.[12]

The splintered "I" in its multiple voices projects itself in the doubles of the narrator. Almost an echo of Calderón's verses in *La vida es sueño:* "life is a dream/ and dreams are only dreams." The division of the Self is frequently articulated in *Fragments of a Journal* in a clear analytical manner and with all the ingredients of a *psychomachia:*

> I have a sort of impression that events are taking place within me, that things and passions are conflicting within me; that I am watching myself and seeing

---

[10] See James B. McCarthy, *Death Anxiety: The Loss of the Self* (New York: Gardner Press, 1980), p. 51. This investigation is an excellent contribution to the undertanding of death anxiety as a major determining factor in existential and neurotic malaise. Its findings are based on psychoanalytical research and on the study of patients as well as of literary texts.

[11] James. B. McCarthy, *Death Anxiety*, pp. 50–51.

[12] Eugène Ionesco, *Fragments of a Journal*, p. 23.

Ionesco and His Doubles

> the struggle of these opposing forces, and that now one, now the other prevails: a *mêlée*, a mental battlefield, and that my real self is the "I" who watches the "myself" who am the scene of these happenings, these conflicts. I am not these passions, it seems, I am the one who beholds them, watches, comments, considers. I am also the one who yearns for a different self.[13]

Or, for example, along the same line:

> I am another.[14] The "I" is caught up in the "myself;" its root is myself. My "self" is the soil that feeds the "I," it is its very sap.[15]

In another passage, describing himself in a state of happiness and exaltation in some distant past, Ionesco remembers perceiving himself as double: "I was at the same time rooted in myself and detached from myself, as if I were both the actor and the spectator of myself. I could watch myself existing, in the June light."[16] The dread of death, the wishful thought of remaining young and the will to learn how to die are presented by Ionesco in a series of dreams and comments on their contents.[17] In one of them, where the deep-rooted desire to return to the womb is clearly manifest, Ionesco sees himself as a young child in a kind of translucent plastic bag floating in outer space; "in front of me is another child, in the same position, who looks like my *twin;* is he my double?"[18] Ionesco is very self-conscious of the death anxiety syndrome in his psyche, and its analysis by him (perhaps also some of his dreams) is reinforced by some readings in Freud, Jung, Mircea Eliade, and the *Tibetan Book of the Dead*. For example, in the following discourse:

> I know, I know; I shall be told that my disquiet comes from the fact that I am dissociated from myself. The theoretical explanation is familiar to anyone who has read even a little psychoanalytic writing, particularly Jung's. I suffer through dissociation from the mother-figure, from the feminine principle (anima), from the earth, from death. I therefore project myself on the non-self, making it into a self, extracting this rapacious self from the none-self

---

[13] *Fragments of a Journal*, p. 31.
[14] Compare with Rimbaud's "Je est un autre" (*I is another*).
[15] *Fragments of a Journal*, p. 31.
[16] *Fragments of a Journal*, p. 39.
[17] *Fragments of a Journal*, pp. 52–60.
[18] *Fragments of a Journal*, p. 54. We underline. Later, in the same dream: "I leave the station with a companion, that unknown companion of one's dreams who may perhaps be one's other self, one's severe, critical self." (p. 55). See, also, *Entre la vie et le rêve*, p. 35, where Ionesco speaks about this dream.

which is a more profound self, but which I am unwilling to admit as profoundly myself. Death, this non-self, is my truest, most essential self.[19]

In a dream, the Self can also project itself on a female character (becoming thus a representation of anima), dissociated in shadow and light, perceived as both good and evil, guardian angel and antagonist:

> R. appears in most of my dreams, in her own shape or else in some other shape, disguised, as if she didn't want to show herself, but I unmask her and recognize her. She is there, the perfect interlocutor, myself and another self both at once, sometimes like a shadow, sometimes reproachful and critical, sometimes my conscience, sometimes a formidable adversary.[20]

The double can take many disguises in a dream. The "I" may be projected as the dreamer himself, and at the same time as his companion, as his antagonist, as a bodyless voice, as an object. It is such a protean presence of the double that we are told about in a fragmentary dream by Ionesco:

> A few scraps of a dream: a friend of mine, Michel, is dead. He has died in peaceful resignation, and I see him lying there. The remaining images from this dream are hard to interpret: beside him lies his servant, who is his exact double . . . and then *this double is transformed into a page of writing from a notebook*. I learn that this double, this page of writing, died a week earlier. Michel tells me that he will send a message presently, bearing the number 139.[21]

From these few examples, and there are many more in *Fragments of a Journal* and other writings of Ionesco, emerges a clear picture of the centrality of the double in the thought and the dreams of Ionesco. The dreaming soul, the creative mind, and the disguised characters and objects in the dreams are all participants in the same drama, on the same stage; they are multiple voices of a single "primal scream," duplicated metaphors of a traumatic image. The splintering of the Self is not restricted to the dreamworld; it is also manifest in the daily experience of being one and multiple, of being alienated from past perceptions of the Self. In looking back upon himself, Ionesco writes:

---

[19] *Fragments of a Journal*, p. 58.

[20] *Fragments of a Journal*, p. 64. The literature on the *double* has grown considerably in the past decades. Among the more recent books, see R. Rogers, *The Double in Literature* (Detroit: Wayne State Univ. Press, 1970), and C. F. Keppler, *The Literature of the Second Self* (Tucson: Arizona Univ. Press, 1972).

[21] *Fragments of a Journal*, p. 66. We underline.

> A reverse metamorphosis: I became a caterpillar. Whatever became of the person I was, the person I still must be, the frail child, the brand-new being, and even the adolescent who still had something from his childhood left? Where have I disappeared to? . . . .
>
> I am in someone else's skin, in the layers of skin, and the folds of the layers of skin of someone else. I have personal knowledge of the following fact: one can become someone else. That may seem absurd. The only thing I have left is my regret at being someone else. It is this regret that makes me continue to be myself, or the child that I was, that I am. . . .
>
> I was a man, a child, and a wicked fairy or an evil magician turned me into a bear, into a boar, into a crocodile—why have I been punished this way? . . . It's a mistake, it's a nightmare, I want to be myself again, I'm that child . . .[22]

The doubles from the dreams and the conscious introspections from the daymares and the nightmares enter into the artwork as the multiple voices of the creator's psychodramatic agony. Their common identity is hidden behind their changing disguises. Ionesco has stated that he wrote diaries and a novel, *The Hermit*,[23] because he was tempted to show himself without disguise, without hiding behind his masked doubles in the plays, and because he wanted to express without mediation his "primal anxiety," his existential dread.[24] Ionesco himself points to our attention that not all his "characters" represent doubles of his Self; some stand for other people; but most of them are, in fact, doubles of himself, even when they are grotesque, exaggerated, and unlike his conscious Self:

> To be precise, I ought to say that my characters are not always *alter egos*; they are also other persons, they are also imagined; they are also a caricature of myself, that which I was afraid of becoming, that which I might have become and that which, fortunately, I didn't become; or they are but an exaggerated part of myself; or, as I said, other persons whom I pity, of whom I laugh, whom I dislike, whom I love; they are also, sometimes, those which I wished to be. Although they are rare. They are also the personifications of an anxiety. Dreamlike characters, also, very often.[25]

The "characters" representing the doubles of Ionesco fall into four main categories. There is a group of plays, a novel, and a film in which the central character constitutes a mirrored double of Ionesco, bearing his very name in

---

[22] *Present Past, Past Present*, p. 30.
[23] Eugène Ionesco, *The Hermit*, trans. Richard Seaver (New York: Viking Press, 1974).
[24] See, *Entre la vie et le rêve*, p. 56.
[25] *Entre la vie et le rêve*, p. 57.

Improvsiation or The Shepherd's Chameleon, or one of his official titles (i.e. the Academician) in *The Gap,*[26] or the role of narrator in *The Hermit*[27] (dramatized in *A Hell of a Mess*) and in *The Slough*[28]—the latter to become the basis for the film *La Vase* in which Ionesco as an actor assumes the role of his own double. A second group includes those plays whose main character transcends reality toward a metaphoric and symbolic context, representing a soul in quest of its form and meaning, always named Bérenger: *The Killer, Rhinoceros, Exit the King,* and *A Stroll in the Air.* In the short stories, from which three of these plays were derived, Bérenger is nameless and known only as the narrator's voice.[29] A third group of plays projects Ionesco into a character named Jean: as a negative double of Bérenger in *Rhinoceros,* or a very intimate double in *Hunger and Thirst* and in *Journeys to the Land of the Dead,* Ionesco's most recent play.[30] Finally, the fourth group includes a great variety of plays in which the principal character is a writer and dreamer, tormented by anxieties and the fear of failure, waiting for his artistic and existential redemption, and trying to liberate himself from matter, time and death:[31] the Old Man in *The Chairs*; Amédée in *Amédée or How to Get Rid of It*; Choubert in *Victims of Duty*;[32] the First Man in *Man with Bags*; the Character in *A Hell of a Mess*; the Old Man and probably also Emile in *The Killing Game.**

The doubles in the first group of texts are presented by Ionesco without any disguise. In *Improvisation,*[33] a sort of theatrical collage of fashionable ideas in the dramatic reviews of the early 1950's, the representation of the three pedantic theater critics (Bartholomeus I, II, and III) who try to brainwash with their dogmatic theories and doctrinarian ideologies a non-politicized playwright by the name of Ionesco, is but a grotesque parody of Brechtian and

[26] Translated from *La lacune* by Rosette Lamont, in "The Massachusetts Review," Vol. 10, No. 1 (Winter, 1969), pp. 119–127.

[27] The narrator's "I" becomes the Character in its dramatized version *A Hell of a Mess.*

[28] Published in *The Colonel's Photograph,* trans. Jean Stewart (New York: Grove Press, 1969), pp. 99–126. The French text had already been published in 1956.

[29] Published in *The Colonel's Photograph.*

[30] Eugène Ionesco, *Voyages chez les morts. Thèmes et variations* (Paris: Gallimard, 1981), Théâtre, vol. VII. It is worthy to note that Edouard and the drunken Man in *The Killer* are opposite doubles of Bérenger in the same way as Jean is the discarded double of Bérenger in *Rhinoceros.*

[31] See Bérenger in *A Stroll in the Air,* trans. Donald Watson (New York: Grove Press, 1965), p. 23: "I want to be cured of death."

[32] In the original narrative versions of the latter two plays (see *The Colonel's Photograph*) Amédée and Choubert were not so named, being the narrator's "I."

(*) Due to limitations of space we will not extend our study beyond the first two groups of doubles, reserving for a subsequent article the analysis of the other two categories.

[33] Eugène Ionesco, *The Killer and Other Plays,* trans. Donald Watson (New York: Grove Press, 1960), pp. 110–151.

pseudo-Brechtian texts.[34] In representing himself on the stage, in order to defend his idea of a theatre, Ionesco follows a well-established theatrical genre.[35] The playwright as a character in this Molieresque farce is victimized by these "theatrologists" and can hardly utter an opinion amidst the proliferation of trivialities. His only major speech, at the very end of the play, reiterates some of the ideas Ionesco had already expressed on various occasions, particularly in his polemic debate with Tynan and in his lecture at Helsinki on the avant-garde theatre. "For me," says Ionesco, "the theatre is the projection onto the stage of the world within: it is in my dreams, my anguish, my dark desires, my inner contradictions that I reserve the right to find the stuff of my plays."[36] The Academician in the farcical nightmare *The Gap* is again Ionesco himself, this time in his role as member of the French Academy, surrounded in his home (the one on the stage) by walls covered with a great number of Honorary Doctor Degrees from Universities around the world. The discovery that he lacks a baccalaureate diploma (hence, the *gap* in his social status and *persona*), his failure to pass now the necessary exams, and the fear of public scandal create in him a state of anger and frustration which put him on the brink of madness. This short one-act play represents a well-documented type of dream or nightmare experienced by writers and artists of fame, occurring frequently during a state of inner tension, of intense creativity or before an important event about to take place. They see themselves in their dream or nightmare subjected to an examination or trial by colleagues or some other jury, and they fail to answer the most elementary questions related to their area of knowledge. They experience a mental paralysis, guilt, shame and terrible dread.[37] Compared to the mirrored double

---

[34] Various texts published by Roland Barthes, Bernard Dort, and Berthold Brecht in the 1950's, particularly in the theatrical review *Théâtre Populaire*, are only slightly distorted in the play and are, very often, quoted almost verbatim. A satirical piece on Brecht's *Little Organon*, titled "L'Ecolier Limousin et le petit organon," written by Jacques Lemarchand (*NNRF*, May 1, 1955), might have been directly influential on Ionesco's parody. For a detailed and excellent study of the sources of this play, see Peter Ronge, *Polemik, Parodie und Satire bei Ionesco* (Berlin: Gehlen, 1967). There is also a grotesque playlet by Maurice Fickelson, *Eugène ou l'insoumission*, "Cahier des Saisons," No. 15, Winter 1959, pp. 268–273.

[35] See, among others: Molière, *Impromptu de Versailles* (1663); Duke of Buckingham, *The Rehearsal* (1671); Fielding, *The Author's Farce* (1729); Sheridan, *The Critic* (1781); Goldoni, *Teatro Comico* (1750); Giraudoux, *Impromptu de Paris* (1937); and, after Ionesco's play, Cocteau, *Impromptu du Palais Royal* (1962).

[36] *The Killer and Other Plays*, p. 150.

[37] See, for example, in Strindberg's *Dream Play*, the Officer (one of the playwright's doubles), sitting in his dream besides a schoolboy in a classroom, being examined by a teacher and unable to figure out the sum of 2 and 2; also, in Ingmar Bergman's *Wild Strawberries*, Isaac Borg, a well-known physician about to receive a honorary degree, sees himself in a nightmare put to shame in front of his colleagues and students.

of *Improvisation* and the nightmarish double of *The Gap*, the narrator of *The Hermit* represents a sort of wishful double: Ionesco would have liked to resemble him in his serene isolation from the external world instead of being immersed in the slough of politics and obsessed by the existence of totalitarian ideologies and regimes. The narrator is not characterized as a double of Ionesco's "social Self" but as the "expression of [his] existential anxiety and reality."[38] The narrator, as Ionesco himself, experiences life as being caught in the net of Time like a fish out of his natural environment:

> Born in horror and pain, I also live in horrible dread of the end, the exit. I'm caught in an incredible, inadmissable, infernal trap, between two frightful events.[39]

The "metaphysical anxiety" which obsesses the narrator, who is in a way both Saint Anthony in the desert and Faust in his study, has been often described by Ionesco as his own existential *via dolorosa* in his various diaries and interviews. The dread of the "hermit," as Ionesco's own despair, is not the result of a philosophical inquiry but of a psychological crucifixion. He confesses to the student-philosopher:

> I'm sure you're aware of these problems; you've read a lot, you have a great fount of knowledge. But for me these questions are crucial, they take me and shake me. For you, they're only cultural. You don't wake up every morning with fear and trembling, asking yourself what the answers are, then telling yourself there aren't any. But you know that everyone has asked himself these same qustions. . . . The only difference is that for you the whole thing is files and catalogues. . . . For you it's part of your culture. Despair has been domesticated; people have turned it into literature, into works of art.[40]

But as always in Ionesco's writings, the feeling of despair and of sinking in the slough (*enlisement*) is accompanied by a slight glimpse of hope and a desire to take off in a flight (*envol*): "Perhaps there will be a morning of grace for humanity. Perhaps there will be a morning of grace for me."[41] This moment of grace, so often described by Ionesco in his diaries and illustrated in his plays *The Killer, Amédée,* and *A Stroll in the Air,* seems to have descended

---

[38]*Entre la vie et le rêve*, p. 56. See also p. 112.

[39]*The Hermit*, p. 87. The feeling of being trapped in Time is powerfully described by the "hermit" (pp. 114–115). The dreadful experience of time is finally condensed in one question-answer sequence: "What is time anyway? The supplier of void."

[40]*The Hermit*, pp. 87–88.

[41]*The Hermit*, p. 88.

upon the "hermit" at one of the stations of his journey. The flourishing tree at the end of the novel, vanishing after having left behind three flowers to prove its visit, is not without resemblance—in its providing a feeling of ascent and exaltation—with the flourishing crysanthemum at the end of Strindberg's *Dream Play* or with the formerly bare tree sprouting leaves in the second act of *Waiting for Godot*.

> This was preceded by a long moment of silence: stretched out on my bed, I stared at the closet against the far walls, with its double doors. The doors swung open. They seemed to be two big gates. I couldn't see any clothing now, nor any linen. Only the bare wall. Now the wall disappeared. The doors wide-open, turned into two gilded columns. . . . A tree crowned with flowers and leaves appeared. Then another. Several. A long pathway. At the end, a light brighter than daylight. . . . Who was this meadow, this garden, this light for? The trees, in perfect rows, stretched into the distance. Between them, in the foreground, a tree sprang up. A tree or a big bush? To its right, that is to my left, a silver ladder, whose base stood a good three feet off the ground, rose and disappeared into the blue sky.
>
> . . . . Years passed, or seconds. The ladder came toward me. It hovered just above my head. Years passed, or seconds. It began to recede, to melt. The ladder disappeared, then the bush, then the trees. Then the columns with the triumphal arch. Some part of that light that had entered into me remained. I took that for a sign.[42]

The apocalyptic landscape and the vision of paradise are the backdrop of the stage on which many of Ionesco's doubles evolve. In *The Slough* (*La Vase*) Ionesco has added a new dimension to his double in the film version by playing himself the role of his double. The film, following the short story, describes with a greater intensity the slow process of descent and sinking into matter and darkness. It presents a bad death, without grace, a harrowing of Hell. Contrary to *The Killer*, which has at its center a radiant city, or *The Hermit* with its Edenic garden and its silver ladder, everything here is marshland, rotten food, filth, stench, degradation: a sort of "endgame" in a luciferian underworld. The experience of playing his own double in the film proved to be a very peculiar ordeal for Ionesco and at the same time a cathartic process, as if Ionesco had become the double of his fictional character. "When I wrote the script," confesses Ionesco to Claude Bonnefoy, "and I had a hard time writing it, I had the impression that it was a fictional story. No doubt, it is an invented story, but when you write literature you always ask yourself whether

---

[42] *The Hermit*, pp. 168–169. See, also, *Fragments of a Journal*, p. 69.

it is not true. Acting in the film, I had the impression that it was not fictional, but really true."[43] If it was exhausting for Ionesco as an actor (*persona*), it was even more dreadful for his *anima*: Almost like a death ritual without resurrection. If writing the story had partially exorcised him from a severe depression, incarnating his own double in the film meant a new descent into the underworld of his neurotic anxiety.

> This film is the story of a mental depression, and here I had to relive this depression. I thought that I had gotten rid of a character when writing *The Slough,* and now, because I was impersonating him, this character was falling on my back. I had to struggle with him, live his adventures, physically live my fantasies.[44]

The four representations of Bérenger in the second group of plays, as doubles of Ionesco's social and metaphysical Self, rather than being different one from another are various stages in the confrontation of Ionesco/Bérenger with the problem of evil, the nostalgia of paradise lost, the fear of death; they are also the various faces and masks of our contemporary Everyman, struggling with a divided mind and a splintered soul in the ongoing quest for a meaningful existence, experiencing the difficulty of surviving as a human being in a world devoured by evil from within. Bérenger, as a double, transcends Ionesco and becomes the metaphoric double of everybody. The four Bérengers combine in their projected image some of the attributes and qualities of both Don Quixote and Charlie Chaplin.

Ionesco has often told how in his childhood and adolescence the presence of light and spring had, on some exceptional occasions, flooded his soul with a quasi-mystical feeling of exaltation and absolute happiness. It is this rediscovery of an earthly paradise which haunts many of his doubles and constitutes the background and the central metaphor of *The Killer.*[45] Bérenger's journey through the Radiant City is a stroll through a fragile and ephemeral paradise which carries in its womb the seed of evil and doom. It is Dante's journey inverted: from Paradise to Hell, and his guide is not a compassionate poet but

---

[43] *Entre la vie et le rêve*, p. 105.
[44] *Entre la vie et le rêve*, p. 106.
[45] *The Killer and Other Plays*, p. 21. Bérenger to the Architect: "It's such an old story, I've almost forgotten, it might have been an illusion; and yet it can't be an illusion when I still feel the loss of it so badly. . . . I can't analyse the feeling, I don't even know if the experience I had can be communicated. It was not very frequent. It happened, five or six, ten times perhaps in my life. . . . When I was in a gloomy mood, the memory of that dazzling radiance, that glowing feeling, gave fresh life to the force within me, to the reasonless reason for living and loving." And see also, *Entre la vie et le rêve*, pp. 14–18 and 30–33.

a technocratic Architect. Bérenger's ecstasy and his poetic expressions are without echo in the scientific and bureaucratic brain of the city's mastermind. Or, rather, a technical echo answers the poetic voice:

> Bérenger: . . . Since this morning I'm a new man, I'm sure I'm becoming myself again. The world's becoming itself again; it's all thanks to *your* power. Your magic light. . . .
>
> Architect: My electric light!
>
> Bérenger: . . . Your radiant city.[46]

It will become apparent to the reader or spectator that the "smiling city"—inhabited by a dangerous killer—is smiling that morning for Bérenger alone and that it is his "inner" landscape which he sees projected around him. Like for Don Quixote, reality is transfigured in a personal dreamland in which he, Bérenger, thinks he is the only one awake. "Although I hadn't been here before, I recognized everything at once. . . Another universe, a world transfigured! And just that very short journey to get here, a journey that isn't *really,* since you might say it takes place in the same place."[47] This *don-quixotisation* of the outer landscape by the visionary eye creates a climate of happiness for Bérenger and at the same time, without him knowing it, blindfolds him and impedes him to recognize the real nature of the Architect and later that of the killer. The dream, perceived in the beginning of the play as reality, will remain but a dream at its end. To Bérenger's statement "No, no, it's not just a dream this time," the Architect answers with some irony: "Perhaps it would have been better if it had been a dream. It's all the same to me. . . . But for a lot of people, reality, unlike dreams, can turn into a nightmare. . . "[48] Walking through the deserted streets of the city, empty and soundless like a Chirico landscape, Bérenger represses a feeling of anxiety ("Why can't you see a single soul in the streets?") but can not give up his image of a rediscovered paradise: "It would be understandable in a dream, but not when it's real."[49] The slow build-up of discomfort first, and anxiety later, in Bérenger's mind parallels his slow awakening to the reality of the killer, to the reality of the world represented by a grey and rainy city, and to the real nature of people fascinated by demagogy and totalitarian ideologies. It is also an awakening to his own weakness and impotence. While the Architect, prototype of ambiguity

[46] *The Killer,* p. 15.
[47] *The Killer,* p. 17.
[48] *The Killer,* p. 26.
[49] *The Killer,* p. 30.

and Machiavellianism, transforms on the stage into the Chief of Police, Bérenger's visionary and utopian outlook on life is being shattered twice: the "smiling city" appears to be a dangerous place and his sudden love for the secretary Dany remains unanswered.[50] The "radiant city" is being terrorized by a killer and Dany has been found murdered while trying to free herself from the Architect's totalitarian realm. Bérenger's awakening at the end of Act I seems at first to be an expression of self-assertion and courageous involvement in political action.

> We can't, we mustn't let things go on like this! It's got to stop! It's got to stop! . . . It can't go on! We must do something! We must, we must, we must!

but these lines are echoed at the end of the play by an almost ritualistic submission to the killer's hypnotic power:

> Oh, God! There's nothing we can do. What can we do? What can we do?[51]

Bérenger's weakness and hesitancy are mainly a result of his idealistic and liberal nature which fails to recognize reality and humans for what they are. He tries to understand the other, to find arguments in his favor, to see himself guilty because he is different from him. Both Edouard in *The Killer* and Jean in *Rhinoceros* are good examples of *alter egos* of Bérenger: he identifies with them so blindly, guided by his innocent heart, that he lacks the lucidity to recognize that Edouard might have gone over to the camp of the Killer[52] and Jean to that of the rhinoceroses. Bérenger's naïveté and humanitarian concept of "morality" and "brotherhood" is best dramatized in that grotesque and tragic monologue in which Bérenger, at great length and with labyrinthic argumentation, tries to understand the Killer before collapsing into total

---

[50] In *Rhinoceros* Bérenger falls in love with Daisy but his dream is shattered with her joining the camp of the beasts. In both plays, Bérenger's idealized love for Dany and Daisy closely resembles Don Quixote's passion for Dulcinea.

[51] Confronted with many explosive and inhumane situations on the international scene, Ionesco has asked himself "what can I do?". And he then did, what he does best: write, without hesitation nor ambiguity, against any evil from right or from left. See his various Journals.

[52] Edouard has a briefcase similar to the Architect's one. When Bérenger discovers that Edouard's briefcase contains photographs of the Colonel and some other objects which could link him to the Killer, it does not ring an alarm in his mind: he does not question his friend's integrity because, as always, Bérenger never sees the worm in an apple. The proliferation of briefcases in *The Killer* parallels the multiplication of the beasts in *Rhinoceros*, both plays enacting metaphorically the spread of a totalitarian plague which contaminates society at large and infects the minds of the masses.

impotency.[53] He is hostage of his own language; as much a victim of the tyranny of his own proliferating vocabulary as the Young Pupil is the victim of the Professor's terrorizing language in *The Lesson*.

Bérenger in *Rhinoceros* is not so different from his double in *The Killer*: innocent, naive, friendly, in love, blind to the transformations in Jean, listening passionately to Daisy who is fascinated by the beasts ("They are like Gods!"), weighing the arguments of Dudard and the Logician, pondering whether he could convince the rhinos to change back to their human nature ("It would be a labour of Hercules, far beyond me. In any case, to convince them you'd have to talk to them. And to talk to them I'd have to learn their language. Or they'd have to learn mine. But what language do I speak? What is my language?")[54] He is overwhelmed by their power, by their number, by the fascination they exert on so many people. Bérenger feels totally different, isolated, somewhat ashamed of being "abnormal," without even a small horn:

> I'm not good-looking! . . . They're the good-looking ones! I was wrong! Oh, how I wish I was like them! I haven't got any horns, more's the pity! A smooth brow looks so ugly. I need one or two horns to give my sagging face a lift. Perhaps one will grow and I needn't be ashamed any more—then I could go on and join them. But it will never grow! . . . Oh I'd love to have a hard skin in that wonderful dull green colour—a skin that looks decent naked without any hair on it, like theirs! Their song is charming—a bit raucous, perhaps, but it does have charm![55]

Also here, as in *The Killer*, Bérenger is confronted at the end of the play with the monster himself: the one-horned beast being metaphorically equivalent to the one-eyed killer. But it is at that precise moment, when he realizes in a glimpse of self-reflexiveness that he might succumb to the temptation of becoming a rhinoceros—like Jean, his alter ego—that Bérenger assumes a different attitude than the one adopted by his double in *The Killer*: rather than being hypnotized and paralyzed by the monster, even ridiculous-looking with his two old-fashioned pistols, Bérenger calls for his carbine[56] and declares war on the beast:

---

[53] "Bérenger's speech to the Killer at the end of the play is one short act in itself. The text should be interpreted in such a way as to bring out the gradual breaking-down of Bérenger, his falling apart and the vacuity of his own rather commonplace morality, which collapses like a leaking balloon. In fact Bérenger finds within himself, in spite of himself and against his own will, arguments in favour of the Killer." These are Ionesco's own stage directions (*The Killer*, p. 9.)
[54] *Rhinoceros and Other Plays*, trans. Derek Prouse (New York: Grove press, 1960), p. 106.
[55] *Rhinoceros*, pp. 106–107.
[56] The English version of the play (see p. 107) unfortunately omits this crucial detail and

> People who try to hang on to their individuality always come to a bad end! Oh well, too bad! I'll take on the whole lot of them! [*My carbine, my carbine!*] I'll put up a fight against the lot of them, the whole lot of them! I'm the last man left, and I'm staying that way until the end. I'm not capitulating!

Edouard and Jean, as ugly doublings of Bérenger, represent human beings, gifted with intelligence and culture, who have accepted consciously and almost willingly to be changed in beasts; their transformation is not the sudden and nightmarish metamorphosis of Gregor Samsa in Kafka's novel. In their mirror Bérenger perceives his own image, the one he is about to become, the one he could become if he would weaken his resistance to brainwashing and massification. From this point of view alone, Bérenger is the double of Ionesco himself. In his conversations with Claude Bonnefoy, Ionesco has made this point very clear. Explaining his opposition to various kinds of totalitarian ideologies, on the left and on the right, his disgust with the "leftists" of today and the "fascists" of yesterday, Ionesco remembers the years 1932–1935 in Bucharest when many of his intellectual friends joined the ranks of the fascists, among them his own father, from whom he was going to break away.

> I felt more and more alone. We were a small number of people not to accept the slogans, the ideologies which were invading our lives. It was very difficult to resist, not so much in the context of political action (which would have been extremely difficult indeed), but in the simple confines of moral and intellectual resistance, even a silent one, because when you are twenty years old, and you have teachers who elaborate theories and scientific discourses—or pseudo-scientific ones, and you have newspapers, doctrines, the social ambiance, and an entire political movement against you, it becomes really very difficult to resist, not to be convinced; luckily, my wife was of great help to me.
> —But this is the story of Bérenger in "Rhinoceros" that you are telling me.
> —Precisely.[57]

In *A Stroll in the Air* we are faced with a different double of the preceding two Bérengers: he is now married and has a daughter, he is a playwright of great fame, he is wondering about the meaning of literature in general and of his own writing in particular, he is anxiety-ridden by the fear of death—"para-

---

deletes Bérenger's words "Ma carabine, ma carabine." It makes all the difference between this Bérenger and the one in *The Killer*. The stage versions of the play have blindly followed the translator's misinterpretation.

[57] *Entre la vie et le rêve*, pp. 24–25.

lyzed"—and his only real desire is "to be cured of death."[58] But who is this Bérenger we are speaking about? It is, without any doubt, the story of Ionesco again. The interview with the journalist, which opens the play, highlights several themes which Ionesco himself had already elaborated in some of his writings or in real-life interviews. Bérenger, away from the city, spends a vacation with his family in the English countryside—a sort of radiant landscape, functioning in the play as the inner dream landscape in which our playwright can transcend reality and realism.[59] As in *The Killer,* the radiant landscape is corrupted by images of death; but here, it seems that the inner dream landscape of Bérenger is blown into pieces by Mrs. Bérenger's nightmares (the tale of her father's death and her Kafkaesque trial) and by his own ascension to "where space and time come together" which enabled him to see the apocalyptic landscapes of this world and of the universe. The theme of death is explored on the personal and general level. While one Bérenger was paralyzed by death and the other was awakening to react, the last one is trying "to be cured of death" in a dreamworld. The dreamland, through which the Bérenger family strolls, is a mosaic of Ionesco's childhood memories, in particular those corresponding to his experience of absolute happiness in La Chappelle-Anthenaise.[59] This ephemeral childhood paradise has become the opening scene and the backdrop of Bérenger's fairytale-like adventures. Bérenger's ascension to dream and his landing in reality's nightmare are but Ionesco's own daydreams and daymares. Bérenger's disenchantment with literature and theater parallels Ionesco's quest for a renewed mode of writing after the success of his first plays, *The Bald Soprano, The Lesson, The Chairs,* and some other of his short dramatic pieces:

> For years it was a consolation for me to be able to say there was nothing to say. But now I feel far too sure I was right. I'm convinced of it. . . . Writing isn't a game for me any more, and it will never be a game again. It ought to lead to something else, but it doesn't.[61]

> Sometimes too I wonder whether literature and the theater can ever give a full account of reality; it's so complex, so overwhelming. . . We are living a horrible nightmare. Literature has never been so powerful, so vivid, or so

---

[58] *A Stroll in the Air,* pp. 20–23.

[59] It is therefore not astonishing that Ionesco should recommend that the stage design be in "the manner of Douanier Rousseau or perhaps Utrillo or even Chagall. . . . The dreamlike effect should be achieved rather by the methods used by a Primitive artist, consciously naive, than by those of a surrealist artist." (Introduction to *A Stroll in the Air.*)

[60] *Entre la vie et le rêve,* pp. 14–16; and see *supra,* note 45.

[61] *A Stroll in the Air,* p. 20.

intense as life. . . . What must we do to make literature an exciting voyage of discovery? Even imagination is not enough.[62]

Bérenger as a playwright, turning to his dreamworld in order to express the world of reality, mirrors Ionesco's gradual progression toward a type of Strindbergian dreamplay which will culminate in such works as *Man with Bags* and *Voyages to the Land of the Dead*; this psychodramatic process is already evident in *Victims of Duty, A Stroll in the Air*, and *Exit the King*. From dream-sequences interwoven with reality-sequences, Ionesco orients his writing toward plays entirely informed by his dreams and nightmares. Concerning the original tale from which he later derived *A Stroll in the Air*, Ionesco writes: "I used one of my dreams. The dream of flying. . . . At the source of this tale is, on one hand, a dream—dream of liberation, of power—and, on the other hand, a critique, a satire, a realistic description of the nightmarish life in totalitarian regimes, a prophecy of doom. . . . The dream is about that man who takes off in the air. The conscious part concerns that which he perceives thanks to his ascension. And what does he see? Simply that which happens in one half of the world and that which the other half, because of its blindness, indifference and prejudice, refuses to see."[63] These considerations, indeed, explain the point of departure of Ionesco's tale, but in dramatizing it he went far beyond his original intention of writing a sort of allegorical satire. By introducing in this play Bérenger and his young daughter Marthe and having them understand each other's oneiric language, Ionesco establishes a dialogue between Bérenger and his own childhood, paradise past becoming in Marthe paradise present, and allows for a glimpse of hope to survive the burning landscape, not in Bérenger's soul but in Marthe's innocent eyes only. The exploding bombs and the festive fireworks become a "kind of English Fourteenth of July." Marthe has the last words of the play:

> Perhaps that's all that's going to happen, just firecrackers. . . . Perhaps it will all come right in the end. . . . Perhaps the flames will die down, perhaps the ice will melt, perhaps the depths will rise. Perhaps the . . . the gardens . . . the gardens . . .[64]

Ionesco's personal fascination with the mysteries of the universe (the infinite of the inner and outer world, the physical and the mental, anti-matter, black holes, the riddle of death, space and time, void and nothingness) is projected

---

[62] *A Stroll in the Air*, p. 22.
[63] *Entre la vie et le rêve*, pp. 63–64.
[64] *A Stroll in the Air*, p. 117.

in Bérenger's vision of the Anti-World which is a pivotal scene in the play:[65] Bérenger's daydream is met with skepticism by all around him, including his wife, but is absorbed by the curious and imaginative mind of his young daughter

> ... the negative of our universe *does* exist ... Perhaps we can get a vague idea of this world when we see the turrets of a castle reflected in the water, or a fly upside down on the ceiling, or handwriting that you read from right to left or up the page, or an anagram, or a juggler or an acrobat, or the sun's rays shining through a crystal prism, reflected and broken up, disintegrating into a patchwork of colors and then put together again, you see, on this wall, on that screen, on your face, like a dazzling white light ... as though turned inside out ...[66]

Having established the world of his daydream, Bérenger is now presented with the vision of the mythical silver bridge in the landscape, spanning the abyss as those bridges of various mythologies which are meant to test the soul and spirit of the holy or knightly questing hero. The transformation of the silver bridge into a circus where Bérenger rides a bicycle in the air like an acrobat is shattered by the vision during the flight. The daydream has turned now into who are, without any doubt, doubles of the painter. The joy of the ascension is shattered by the vision during the fight. The daydream has turned now into a daymare. Like many other travelers to the other world before him (Aeneas, Dante, Tundale) and like Faust during his flight in company of Mephistopheles, Bérenger returns with his own vision of the netherworld which is but a mirror-image of the world he lives in. The apocalyptic landscape described by Bérenger is similar to that represented by Hieronymus Bosch in his visions of Hell:

> I saw ... I saw ... some geese ... Men with the heads of geese ... Men licking the monkeys behinds and drinking the sows' piss ... I saw whole continents of Paradise all in flames. And all the Blessed were being burned alive ... I saw some knives, I saw some graves ... In another place, the

---

[65] *A Stroll in the Air,* pp. 45–58.

[66] *A Stroll in the Air,* p. 52. There is an interesting parallel to Ionesco's vision of "a world turned upside down" in Strindberg's *Dream Play (Six Plays of Strindberg,* pp. 214–215): "*Daughter*: Do you know what I se in this mirror? The world as it should be. For as it is it's wrong way up. —*Lawyer*: How did it come to be wrong way up? —*Daughter*: When the copy was made. —*Lawyer*: Ah! You yourself have said it: the copy! I always felt this must be a poor copy, and when I began to remember its origin nothing satisfied me. Then they said I was cynical and had a jaundiced eye, and so forth. —*Daughter*: It is a mad world."

earth was cracking . . . the mountains were caving in and there were oceans of blood . . . of mud and blood and mud . . . Bottomless pits, bombardments, bombardments, bottomless pits opening over the plains, already ravaged and deserted centuries ago . . . millions of vanishing universes, millions of exploding stars . . . And then, infinite wastes of ice instead of incending fire, then the fire and the ice again . . . After that, there's nothing, nothing but abysmal space . . . abysmal space.[67]

As there is no up and down in space, Bérenger's ascension into the dreamworld of his inner space is simultaneous with his descent into the nightmarish reality of this netherworld. At the end of the Bérengers' journey through the countryside there is no innocence left, paradise has not been recovered, and except for Marthe's dimmed hope ("Perhaps . . . the gardens . . . the gardens . . .") there are only ashes of burned memories. The fallen clown and poet, his skeptical spouse and angel guardian, and the dreaming daughter stroll through a festive and peaceful landscape.[68] It could have been a paradise. But heaven is fiction; hell is reality. The visionary fool knows that. "Within me, there's hell. I know what hell is now."[69]

The vision of the end of the world, which coincides with the end of the world of an individual (King Bérenger I), is allegorically dramatized in *Exit the King*.[70] The apocalyptic landscape, instead of being presented at the end of the play as in *A Stroll in the Air*, is here metaphorized as the beginning of the end. A disintegrating world (the cosmic and the private, the outer and the inner) serves as a sort of introit to a modern version of liturgical drama in which ceremonial stage movements and verbal incantations, similar to responsories and antiphons in early medieval dramatisations of the Mass, accompany King Bérenger in his descent into or ascension to Death.

Written at a time when Ionesco was critically ill[71] and the fear of death, although a permanent feature in his dreams and plays, had become more than a metaphysical dread, *Exit the King* dramatizes a new version of the Art of Dying (*ars moriendi*). "I told myself that one could learn to die, that I could

---

[67] *A Stroll in the Air*, pp. 112–116.
[68] Jan Kott has described with humor the Ionesco family (*Preuves*, 1959): the anxious dreamer, the realist-pragmatic wife, the poetic and sensitive daughter. See also his characterization of our playwright: "Eugène is the most Ionescian among all of Ionesco's characters."
[69] *Fragments of a Journal*, p. 126.
[70] *Exit the King*, trans. Donald Watson (New York: Grove Press, 1963).
[71] *Entre la vie et le rêve*, pp. 77–78. "*Exit the King* is a play written in twenty days. I wrote first during ten days. I had just come out of an illness and I had been very scared. Then, after these ten days I had a relapse and was very ill again for two weeks. After that, I started writing again. And in another ten days I finished writing the play."

learn the art of dying, and that one could teach others how to die."[72] The fear of death is present in the earliest writings of Ionesco; in a text of 1934 ("No") he writes: "I'm afraid of death. I'm afraid of dying, probably because I desire, without knowing it, to die. I'm afraid, therefore, of my wish to die."[73] Ionesco was so obsessed with the idea of death that he planned, on his arrival in Paris, to write a doctoral dissertation on the theme of death in nineteenth century French literature. But even reading about death, or looking at death on a stage, was a cause for deep anguish. Shakespeare, with his terrifying death scenes, haunted his imagination. "When Richard II dies, I'm a spectator to the death of the one I most cherish. It is I who am dying with Richard II. He provides me with a strong awareness of the ternal truth which we tend to forget in the histories, that truth which we elude and which is so simple in its banality: I die, you die, he dies."[74] *Exit the King,* formerly called *The Ceremony,* is Ionesco's supreme attempt to exorcise his soul of this fear of dying by purgating Bérenger, his double and surrogate, of his physical and mental panic. Bérenger is literally Ionesco's scapegoat.[75]

Bérenger is Everyman: a King and a man, a god and a clown, a hero and a fool, Ionesco and a surrogate. The play is the last act in the history of humankind and of a human being. The catastrophic ending of the world is the vanishing world of the individual during the last hours of his life. The signs which announce the imminent apocalypse are taken from the traditional eschatological literature and used as metaphorical projections of an inner doomsday. It is also the last station for the journeying soul on earth, but the pilgrim Bérenger has not prepared himself for leaving this world without protesting. Time is running out very fast for him and he has yet to learn the difficult art of dying. Queen Marguerite, as his objective mirror, reflects without hypocrisy Bérenger's state of panic caused by his unpreparedness:

> He's been like one of those travelers who linger at every inn, forgetting each time that the inn is not the end of the journey . . .
>
> . . . He ought always to have been prepared for it. He ought to have thought about it every day! The time he's wasted![76]

Bérenger learns very slowly to accept his shortcomings, to admit his lack of

---

[72] *Entre la vie et le rêve,* p. 78.

[73] See Hélène Vianu, "Préludes Ionesciens," in *Revue des sciences humaines,* jan-mar, 1965.

[74] Eugène Ionesco, *Notes and Counter Notes,* trans. Donald Watson (New York: Grove Press, 1964.)

[75] One could cheer with the spectators: "The King is dead. Long live Ionesco!"

[76] *Exit the King,* p. 13.

preparation, but still lives with the illusion that time can be recuperated and that a new chance at life might be granted to him.

> I'm like a schoolboy who hasn't done his homework and sit for an exam without swatting up the papers . . .
>
> . . . like an actor on the first night who doesn't know his lines and who dries, dries, dries. Like an orator pushed onto a platform who's forgotten his speech . . .
>
> . . . I'd like to re-sit the exam.[77]

These thoughts lead him to wish a total regression in time, back into his mother's womb: "I can make a fresh start. I want to start again. (*To Mary:*) I want to be a baby and you can be my mother."[78] Step by step, guided by Queen Marguerite, Bérenger progresses in his apprenticeship; a great deal of his limited time is taken up by his reluctance to abandon his physical and emotional possessions and by Queen Marie's loving prayers for his salvation. At times, the stage situation of King Bérenger between the two Queens—one representing life and subjectivity, the other death consciousness and objectivity—resembles those late medieval woodcuts or paintings showing the dying person between an angel and a devil, between salvation and damnation. When Bérenger realizes that the love of Queen Marie cannot save him from death he is ready to start his real journey beyond his crumbling and disintegrating kingdom. "He'll start his journey with a picture of *me* in his mind," announces Marguerite, while all the other characters vanish one by one from Bérenger's presence. Their absence points to the shrinking of Bérenger's inner landscape and to his progressive loss of memory. Soon he becomes blind, deaf, and mute. Only the beatings of his heart still shake the house for a little while. Left without words, without sight, he sinks into a grey light (darkness? light?), slowly enough to enable Queen Marguerite to have the last words of the play: "It was a lot of fuss about nothing, wasn't it?"[79] This ambiguous statement leaves open the question whether this is the final end of Bérenger's journey on earth or the beginning of a new journey.[80]

---

[77] *Exit the King*, p. 39.
[78] *Exit the King*, p. 47.
[79] *Exit the King*, p. 95.
[80] Ionesco has mentioned on several occasions that he had in mind Rumanian religious incantations accompanying the dead on their last journey as well as initiative death rites to be found in *The Tibetan Book of the Dead*. We have no reason to doubt Ionesco's statements. But to deduce from them that the play is a kind of dramatization about death and resurrection or reincarnation is not warranted by the text. See Rosette Lamont, "The Double Apprenticeship: Life and the Process of Dying," in *The Phenomenon of Death: Faces of Mortality,* ed. Edith Wyschogrod (New

Ionesco is the living double of the dead Bérenger. Was not he this King's spokesman when he declared: "I ought to have embarked long ago on this stubborn quest for knowledge and self-knowledge. If I'd set about it in time, I might have achieved something. Instead of writing literature! What a waste of time; I thought I had all of life ahead of me. Now time is pressing, the end is near, and haste is not favourable to my quest . . . The tree of life and death is still here, bare and black. Nothing can mask the deepest, most incurable distress. I am face to face with truth."

University of Southern California

York, 1973), pp. 198–223. For an interesting and balanced approach to this question, see M. S. Barranger, "Death as Initiation in *Exit the King,*" *Educational Theatre Journal* (27, Dec. 1972), pp. 504–507.

CULTURE AND POLITICS*

Eugène Ionesco

In principle, culture cannot be disassociated from politics. In fact, the arts, philosophy and metaphysics, religion or other forms of spiritual life, and the sciences, constitute culture. Whereas politics, which have to be the science or the art of organizing our relationships to allow the development of life in society, an essentially cultural life, politics in our time have overtaken all other manifestations of the human spirit. They have become anarchy—organization for the sake of organization—in other words, disorganization of the cultural complex, to the detriment of metaphysics, of art, of spirituality and even of science. Developing as they did, therefore, by trampling on man's other activities, they have made men mad. Politics have become nothing more than a senseless struggle for power that mobilizes and monopolizes all the energies of modern man. Instead of being focused on a point of view that goes beyond politics, instead of allowing a liberation of man and spirit and the pursuit, in total freedom, of philosophical or scientific knowledge, of an inquiry into our ultimate ends, politics have become a fanatical and obtuse involvement, the rejection of all criticism and of all investigation.

Politics cannot exist without the support of a certain philosophy. And yet, they exist and prosper at the expense of all fundamental belief. We know very well that western humanism is bankrupt. We also know very well that the leaders of the eastern countries no longer believe in Marxism. Absolute cynicism and a great biological vitality are all that remain of their revolutionary faith and all that keeps them in power, active in the struggle for power and for the conquest of world supremacy: *imperium mundi*, to quote Spengler's prophetic definition.

*Address given by Ionesco at the conclusion of the Symposium. Translated by Silvie Drake.

It's a matter, then, of being the strongest for the sake of being the strongest, a deadly combat without scruple since all ideologies and moralities have vanished; a combat for the conquest of the planet and its material riches. The West's methods of response to this absurd war of domination, despite its enormous technical and economic capabilities, seem utterly insufficient, since the West, too, has no religion, no faith of any kind that will furnish it a reason to fight.

What would the West, our West, need in the absence of a philosophy? For the moment, simply the same cynicism and the same monstrous and amoral vitality retained by its adversaries in this struggle to the death. The strength and the weakness of Soviet Russia is its ability to fight without reason, like a wild beast chasing other wild beasts off the territory. The weakness and strength of the West is that it is unable to fight without compelling reasons to do so.

Obviously, Marxist cynics will talk to you of the utopian society they will realize, of the subjugation by man of all the forces of nature, of the freedom and fraternity that will finally reign over the world. But let us read the books of all the Soviet dissidents, of Sacharov and others; let us read the books of those who were able to escape and who find themselves among us to discover that, if our Western societies displease them, the societies they have left are a thousand times more hateful still. We all know there are injustices and social inequities in our countries. But there are also possibilities of protest and vindication. Whereas in the countries that call themselves socialist and where not only the same inequities and injustices are thriving, but also the enormity of privileges and the most rigorous social hierarchies, contestations, protestations and vindications are forbidden. Solzhenytsin and his friends are not the only ones who have testified and cried out for liberty. Many others have done it who paid for it with their lives—such as Kraventchenko—or with their honor, since they were showered with insults and calumnies by Western intellectuals such as Suarine, Koestler, Istrati and how many others. The most serious thing to have occurred, in fact, was the secret agreement that took place between the bourgeoisies of the West and the tyrannical bourgeoisies of the Eastern countries.

For we, too, were afraid of revolution. And ironically, we received the support of Soviet Russia, not only because she needed our raw material and our technical advances, but simply because she, too, feared an authentic revolution that would have threatened the comfortable conformity of her bureaucracy and her society. On the other hand, there appears to be a crisis today within the French communist party and some intellectuals are questioning the very foundations of the party and of its ideology. As a young thinker said recently, the communist party is a state within the state. The citizen of that most conformist of all states, is content with whatever advantages he can obtain from trade unions, and if he has no live philosophy to wake him up, the answers provided by his catechism still suffice. Thanks to some small arrangements, to the perfecting of techniques and to the mirage of a revolution he doesn't really want, his small bourgeois existence is enough. Then, too, he expends himself. He has two ways in which to expend himself: either through public demonstrations which are not at all forbidden to him as they are to workers in Czechoslovakia, Hungary, Soviet Russia or China—and through occasional elections; or through sports. We are all, in fact, like the occidental communist worker, infatuated with politics and sport. Burgers, artisans, workers, rich and poor alike, are completely absorbed for a month out of each year by the Tour Cycliste of France, and the rest of the time, on Sundays anyway, by French soccer and rugby matches. As for the Olympics, people become so carried away they do not even realize to what extent competitive sports play the game of all politics in turn. They do not even notice that athletes are false supermen, monsters of muscle and technique. These hypertrophied sports and politics constitute the new opium of the people.

All this, at the expense of what we call culture: science, knowledge, art, religion, philosophy. We are living in a fullfledged crisis of culture. And life and death having been equally sabotaged, we live from day to day. But lack of satisfaction, unhappiness, exist in the depths of the still buried soul, sleeping a deep, almost fatal sleep. There are complaints of a crisis of civilization. Young people readily admit they have no reason for living. To live without reason constitutes sufficient reason to live among the people of the East. But it is evident that, sooner or later, their conscience will wake up and the problem of why and what for will be reborn in their spirit. For to live and act, man cannot escape the problem of his ultimate ends: his individual destiny is not enough, he needs to believe that humanity has a future. The excess of politics has not sufficiently despirited man for him not to remain what he basically is, a biological being. And if biologists have chased away God and the preoccupation with ultimate ends, they have not been denied by the great physicists. Louis de Broglie, one of the founders of modern physics, is a practicing Catholic. Einstein was convinced that a superior, divine conscience governed the world. Only journalists, men of letters, ideologists, tenth-rate philosophers think that belief in God is a reprehensible failing. It is tragic that, for the moment, the majority of the world is composed of spiritually and metaphysically amputated individuals. I forcefully repeat that it is excess of politics that has caused the situation. There can be no cultural life without metaphysics and spirituality. Politics as they exist are no more than a dramatic and cruel pastime in which we indulge without any real conviction any more. People imagine politics are the only entertainment that, somehow, permits us to live. In reality, one dies of politics. In reality, politics are dead, since the ideologies and philosophies are dead from which politics pretend to originate. Politics may be the devil. They contribute powerfully to the reinforcement of Evil. They are Evil.

We have spoken of the death of man and the decadence of humanism. Between the two world wars, Jacques Maritain or Denis de Rougemont had rehabilitated humanism by raising it up, by giving it a sense of direction and a religious or spiritual dimension. Non-spiritual humanism, such as that of Albert Camus, based "on a morality without obligation or sanction," that is without transcendance, could not hold because it had no roots. But if atheistic humanism is in a state of decline, modern antihumanism isn't feeling too well either. The atheistic antihumanists that the new French philosophers such as Jean-Marie Benoist, Lardreau, Levi, and Gluchsmann have become, are haunted by morality. But how can morality be possible without a renewal of metaphysics? Morality is not, current beliefs to the countrary, the rules that each society invents and which self-destruct when that society disintegrates. If God does not exist, said one of Dostoevsky's characters, then all is permissible. Therefore, we are now in search of permanent foundations of behavior able to moralize politics and even able to point them towards metaphysics. The crisis is fundamental. We're walking a tightrope like ghosts threatened with a fall at every moment. It's simply a question of the problem of being, of the survival of the human being in the world. And humanity can only live through culture.

What is this culture? A crowd of special givens, learned more or less painfully, many of which disappear from memory of their own accord. But one must not believe them to be lost. The intellectual culture resulting from this apprenticeship endures. Didn't Edouard Heriot state that culture is what remains when one has forgotten everything else? And that this remainder was the essential thing? That's why Amiel said that a cultivated mind is that which has crossed a large number of realms of reflection and who can see from a large number of points of view. It is also why Alain asserted that culture is something quite different from instruction and Gaston Bachelard, in talking only about the individual, that culture can be found in direct proportion to the elimination of one's quota of knowledge. I will add that culture only really comes about when the mind stretches to a dimension of universality.

On the other hand, according to American formulations of ethnology and sociology, culture is the general configuration of learned behavior and its results insofar as those results are adopted and transmitted by the members of a given society. According to Margaret Mead, therefore, the word designates those acquired forms of behavior that one group of individuals, united by a common tradition, will transmit to its offspring: artistic, scientific, religious and philosophical traditions, political and technical customs, and the thousand mores that characterize daily living.

I will, however, add an amendment to this last definition. I will say that it is above all the artistic, scientific, religious and philosophical traditions that constitute the most essential and lofty expressions of the culture. For emerging from material conditions and structures, it is art and thought that make up man and define him royally, to the loftiest degree. And that is why, beyond the variety of different cultures, we find not only similarities but even identical forms and common aspirations that compete to express the unquestionable universal identity of all men. Culture then is the expression of our continuity and our multisecular identity across time and space. And it is essentially art that reveals that, beyond diversity lies this solidarity of spirit. Whether he feels integrated into or estranged from his cultural surroundings, the individual is bound to express his solidarity. It is he who is the carrier of values and who allows the renewal of society in this synthesis of collectivity and individuality. Thus Arthur Rimbaud, modern France's greatest revolutionary poet, the one who denied tradition and civilization, is retrieved by universal culture. And any poet wishing to disarticulate the language, rearticulates it in fact and enriches it. Thus, any writer seeking to express his alienation makes us feel freer within the prison of our terrestrial condition.

One should, on the other hand, distinguish one from the other, two types of writers and artists: those who become attached to the social world that surrounds them and those who are more attached to the world beyond. Balzac and Zola are, at first glance, political and social writers. So is Brecht. Shakespeare is a commentator on the history, on power and on politics, but isn't he also and above all a metaphysical writer? Are not Balzac and Zola haunted, one by metaphysical problems, the other by problems which dwell most particularly on man's mortal condition? All authors of any value or authenticity possess, either in the forefront of their minds and fully exposed, or in the background of their consciousness which suddenly reveals itself, an uneradicable quandary, a mystical calling. Artists therefore are inextricably mystical and social. In the concept of the committed writer such as was André Malraux, art is seen as the tragic cry, the anguished prayer of the man who reaches out for divinity or the empty sky. And it is the social aspect that a writer such as Eugenio d'Ors sheds light on when he considers that the most diverse societies constitute a single one. Culture is for him a vast parliament where Kant answers Plato, where Plotinus argues with Master Eckhart, where Freud interrogates Sophocles, where Hegel takes on and adopts Heraclitus, where Karl Marx responds to Proudhon, where Dostoevsky criticizes the grand inquisitors, where Heidegger questions Husserl and draws him out, etc.

In his book, "Utopia and Socialism," Martin Buber thought socialism might forge the way towards that culture. But it amounted to a waste, a more complete disintegration than ever occurred in capitalistic society or any other society for that matter. There is an excess of ills in the world at the present time and one of the aspects of those ills is the State. Because the liberal State, which was sometimes debonair and sometimes repressive, has been replaced, as we know, by another State full of horrendous violence and intolerance. The concentration of power to be found in the excessive State is the death of man, of the individual crushed by an immense machine. This excessive State, a true dictatorship, will not abdicate without constraint, without our revolt carried through to the end and successfully.

We therefore need a just order which is not possible in the absence of charity or love. I am well aware that these two words have been disparaged and I ask you not to smile because I've spoken them. Humanity must find again the necessary equilibrium between man and his society. In any case, the Utopian state has been demystified, the evil has been diagnosed, enlightened minds know it and say it. But it will still take a little time for these points to be understood by the multitudes who still constitute the masses, the crowds. Only then will we no longer have crowds, those crowds created by a monopolizing State. We ardently hope crowds will be replaced by multiple associations of free men, diverse, original, personal and united within the society.

Politics must therefore play their most important role, that of allowing the development of culture and more specifically that of art. Because since art is at once archaic and modern, very ancient and contemporary, it is what ensures our awareness of our continuity, of our identity.

As a reservoir of the collective unconscious, as spontaneous or calculated expression yet always inspired by the universal community, as prophetic language, art reveals man to himself. Artistic creation carries in its core man and the world, from prehistoric times to the present, and in so doing, also carries that which anticipates the future.

If politics often lie, art cannot lie. Even if he wanted to, the artist cannot lie because his creations are imaginary and imagination always unveils and points to meaning. Standing at the frontier between reality and unreality, art connects our world in its essentials to the world beyond.

Art takes us to the edge of mystery. If it does not give us the key—since no human effort can get it for us—it at least leaves the door ajar that opens on to the life beyond life, beyond nothingness. Better than philosophy lost in erudition, art poses the question of the insoluble problem, it confronts us with our own inquiry into our ultimate ends. And this inquiry is already the beginning of an answer.

Hence politics separate men since they bring them together only in an exterior sense, by a shoulder-to-shoulder of blind fanatics. Whereas art and culture reunite us in a common anguish that constitutes our only possible fraternity, that of our existential and metaphysical community.

Art is everything. Art is nothing if one does not commit oneself completely to its contemplation. If a masterpiece fails to lift you out of yourself it is because you did not look, you did not understand, you did not let it speak. Every apprehension of a piece of art is a struggle, a suffering. You must, along with it, put everything in doubt all over again.

DREAMS TO BE STAGED EVENTUALLY
(Three unpublished dream scenes)

by

EUGÈNE IONESCO

Translated by Pauline Baggio and J. Ramsay Bickers

November 4, 1980

A DREAM

A dislocated dream, almost impossible to describe, although I will try to do it anyway.

It concerns two families. These two families live in two apartments which are adjoining, or rather, sometimes adjoining, sometimes one on top of the other. These apartments belong to very rich people, one to a family of aristocrats, the other to a family of wealthy bourgeois. The family of aristocrats is even wealthier than the bourgeois family. I have forgotten the number of people which make up these two families. The aristocrats are in the military; the men wear uniforms and high kepis with plumes. In their apartment the aristocrats have a silk carpet. The women have silk panties also. How pleasant it is to touch the small but firm derrieres of the women in silk panties. The bourgeois have a carpet made of a less noble material, which gives off a certain odor. Is it possible to have olfactory dreams? In the house of the bourgeois, there is a certain unpleasant odor, which is that of the cheaper carpet. The men's clothes and the women's dresses and their underwear all have this unpleasant smell. Are they *nouveau riche*? Still used to choosing less noble material for economy's sake, or else is this the hereditary mark of their class?

At any rate, the military aristocrats look more haughty and more casual. The daughter of the bourgeois is annoyed by the unpleasant odor given off by the carpet and the clothes and complains to her father about it. She does not blame him for it. He considers it inherent to their race or their caste.

After having been one on top of the other, the apartments are now adjoining. The two families share the same balcony; but this balcony is divided by a railing. By simply passing the railing, you can smell both odors, the unpleasant one coming from the bourgeois home. The part occupied by the aristocrats does not give off a bad odor, an odor which, I repeat, comes from the clothes made of poor material and the carpet.

I have forgotten what happens later, except that there is no strong or apparent conflict between the two families. One can only sense the pride and scorn of the aristocrats. If I can make one scene out of this dream, it must be based on the lamentations and disappointment of the bourgeois daughter.

I have had that dream a few days before; it must have been longer at the time, I forget now. Then, three or four days after this dream, I am walking down the corridor of the apartment leading to the kitchen, itself leading to the servants' stairway. I can smell the odor that I had smelled in the dream. I ask my wife to walk a few steps down the corridor, she also notices this bad odor. This is due to the fact that some workers are repairing the broken window-panes on the landing and replacing the putty in the windows. It is this putty which smells (maybe it is made of fish). "How strange," my wife says to me, "to replace the window-panes in winter." It is also cold in the corridor, since for the time being the panes have not been replaced.

I think this is the first time I had an olfactory dream—which I thought was impossible—and one that was predictive in its olfactoriness.

It is my impression that this dream is accurate. At any rate, the odor was there. It was unpleasant and, in the context of the dream, humiliating for the bourgeois family, which was made up of at least four or five people and which I considered as my own.

One never knows if one is actually dreaming or if it is reality. Roger Caillois was telling me that only sociology can tell us if we have dreamt or not, if it was just a dream. In psychiatric hospitals they beat those who do not know whether they live in unreality or reality, if they dream or if they are awake. But to beat someone in order to know if he is dreaming does not prove anything. In fact, you can be hit in your dream by something other than a blow.

November 26, 1980

ANOTHER DREAM

SETTING: The curtain rises. No setting. Greyish light. Between two worlds. However, do not emphasize the mists and the haze as is often done when dreams are put on stage. In fact, the dreams seem real. The style of the dreams is properly "realistic." In the middle of the stage, a rather tall, old man, dressed in black, with a black armband. The character is grave, rather angry, with a bowler hat. Black overcoat, clean-shaven.
This character will be referred to as "The Father."

THE FATHER: *(looking at his watch and slightly shrugging his shoulders; he speaks)* It does not surprise me, *(putting his watch back in his fob)* he is always late.
(Another character comes in, in disarray, of the same age, maybe even a bit older. He will be "The Son.")

THE SON: Excuse me, Papa, I may be a little late.

THE FATHER: You still don't wear a hard collar or a tie. Even though you are getting older, that does not change, you are always the same, just like I have always known you.

THE SON: Forgive me for not having masses said for you anymore. I will though, one of these Sundays.

THE FATHER: There is that, too. But above all, you won't stop killing me.

THE SON: They are only theatrical games. They should not upset you anymore. However, I see that they do. I will change my writing and my subject. I no longer bear grudges to anyone; neither to you, nor to your wife, nor even to all my enemies, whether they are here or in your world.

THE FATHER: You say this, but yet you never forget anything. You should leave us alone for the time being. You take yourself for a judge, or an avenger. You don't know the laws; they are different from what you think. You remember, a few days after your mother's death, the large icon in the dining-room, the Baptism of St. John, fell down with a clatter. You had a priest come to exorcise, don't you recall that?

THE SON: It's you and your new family and your wife who caused all the trouble. However, I am the one who feels guilty.

THE FATHER: You have done just about what I did.

THE SON: Not quite. I have enjoyed life, as they say. I have been cruel, unconsciously or even consciously, I have lived between humility and pride, the quest for success and distraction. I have written many things, far too many things, I did not worry about the right thing, the right thing for me, the right thing for us. I was not mean, but I was not good enough either towards my fellow men, I was not on a quest for souls. But all your faults, your negligence, your cruelty. . . .

THE FATHER: You are guilty of having thought about my own guilt, my own faults and about judging them, when you don't know the criteria, the laws. You should have been much more innocent before setting yourself up as a judge. Besides, you know very well, or you should have known sooner, that morality, if such a thing exists, is quite different here from there, where you still are. Besides, who decides what morality is, in your world and even in mine, which is not so far from yours? We are not far apart. Just one step apart. One step.

THE SON: The more time passes, the more I feel that you dead people surround us. I am scared. I am afraid of retaliation. Will we have to go through that? And then, will there still be tortures, earthquakes, sarcasms, crimes? Do those killed keep killing each other? The other world, and then the third world, and the fourth world, are they all the same? Is the same war going on beyond the universe? Does it ever stop or does it just get worse? The circles of evil, are they more and more terrible? How to get out of this? We will never get out.

THE FATHER: Go *(he leaves the stage)*.

THE SON: He lets me go. Is it to give me time to redeem myself? To travel the path that I have not taken, do I still have time? The other path that I have not taken can be instantaneous, very short; it can also be long. Do I have time, does he leave me plenty of time or little time? And what should I do? I am going, unfortunately, I am going to continue writing. I would like, old adolescent that I am, very old adolescent, to break this habit, this vice. I knew however that I was not on the right road, I have always known it, what can I do and how, does he give me enough time to escape time? I roughly guess the meaning of my fault. I am trapped in there, I never learnt how to free myself from that. I could have done it, I could have done it. The weakness, the stupidity, the stupid seduction of the present. Having chosen what is mortal, I gave in to the Satanic ruse, the most vulgar ruse.

November 28, 1980

ANOTHER DREAM

THE SON: In fact, can one really kill somebody? One cannot annihilate anybody. Everything exists forever, that is for eternity. Eternity is an endless instant since it exists outside of time. It is time which scares us, but time is not a permanent situation. No, nobody is ever killed. It is absurd. You move in, you move out, you transfer, you are transferred in another time, in another space, or else you settle in the perpetuity of the moment. You can also be in several times and several spaces at once, unless you are all the time in all times. The danger is to have too many habits and to cling to one or the other of the manifestations. You both know it and don't know it, you are afraid. Everywhere, just with a few variations, we all speak the same language. Only the dialects differ.... *(A moment of silence)*

(In the background, a curtain rises, discovering an almost empty theater, since there is, in the middle of the hall, only one spectator in an armchair)

There is no one at my show. Only one spectator. Before, the theaters were full of young men, young men who would no longer come when they grew older. Other groups of young men would replace them. This does not happen anymore.

(Another character appears, who looks exactly like Jean-Paul Sartre)

JEAN-PAUL SARTRE: Not at all, look harder. Don't you see the balconies? They are full of young people.

THE SON: Hold on, that's right. Amazing.

JEAN-PAUL SARTRE: Young people, plenty of them. You should be happy.

THE SON: Yes, if what we do lasts for eternity, no matter how small or trivial it is. We are immortals among other immortals (too bad for the mutations), since they are of the same essence. Everything is made of the same essence.

JEAN-PAUL SARTRE: There is no essence, only existence. And after existence, the abyss.

THE SON: Yes, you told that to us quite often and quite loud, what is common, permanent, in all these successive generations is this eternal weapon of youth. But I am pleased to have been honored by your visit. It would even be an unexpected joy if the word "joy" was fashionable in our time, in our hell.

JEAN-PAUL SARTRE: I really wanted to see you.

THE SON: And me, too. How many times over the years haven't I wished to know you personally? Had I listened to my wife, I would have done it a long time ago. I was reproaching you your politics and your excess of politics. You were mistaken, we were all mistaken. You say it and I said it. I also suspected you of knowing that you were mistaken; therefore, you were not mistaken, you knew it, but you were pretending.

JEAN-PAUL SARTRE: You should have come and talked to me. Maybe *I* should have come to you. But I was Sartre. Maybe we could talk now.

THE SON: When you happened to write a line about me to quote me, you always did it in a very courteous fashion. You always accepted that my plays *The Chairs* or *The Bald Soprano* be played at the same time as your work *No Exit* in a double bill.

I was very struck by *Being and Nothingness* and its rejection of humanism. *Being and Nothingness* was the the last great philosophical work that I have really read. I resented you for thinking that the behavior of individuals among themselves is ruled by force only. Theoretically, you did not believe in friendship, but in practice, you lived it. Maybe. Or maybe not. Or perhaps yes, since you come to see me now, as a ghost. Is it the last good-by or the last farewell that all the dead say to the living? We could not talk to each other. However, we should have.